Suddenly
Alone

To Jane
with much love

Phil Jacobs

Philomene Gates

Suddenly Alone

A Woman's Guide to Widowhood, Divorce and Loneliness

GRIDIRON PUBLISHERS
P.O. Box 724201
ATLANTA, GA 31139
(770) 431-0962

A hardcover edition of this book was published in 1990 by Harper & Row Publishers.

SUDDENLY ALONE: A WOMAN'S GUIDE TO WIDOWHOOD.

ISBN 0-932520-59-6
Library of Congress Catalog Number — 97-074906

First HarperPerennial edition published 1991.

Cover design by *Zoom Design*, Atlanta, GA.

The Library of Congress has catalogued the hard cover edition as follows:
Gates, Philomene A., 1918 —
SUDDENLY ALONE: A Woman's Guide To Widowhood / Philomene A. Gates — 1st edition.
p. cm.

Includes index.

ISBN 0-06-016352-6
1. Widows — United States — Life skills guides. I. Title
HQ1058.5.U5G38   1990
306.88 — dc20   89—46092

This book is dedicated to my three daughters, Gilda Gates Wray, Sharon Gates Stearns, and Kathe Gates Williamson, with admiration for the wonderful daughters, wives, and mothers they are, and with gratitude to them for their continued encouragement during the preparation of this book.

If I should die and leave you here awhile,
Be not like others, soon undone, who keep
Long vigil by the silent dust and weep.

For my sake turn again to life and smile,
Nerving thy heart and trembling hand to do
Something to comfort weaker hearts than thine.
Complete those dear unfinished tasks of mine,
And I, perchance, may therein comfort you.

— Mary Lee Hall, "Turn Again to Life"

ACKNOWLEDGMENTS

Sam Gates died more than eighteen years ago. We were married thirty-eight years.

Ever since his memorial service I have wanted to share my adjustments to a widowed existence, who are similarly situated, with the hope that it can help them. Not being a professional writer, I found it difficult to get this book together. I cannot list separately all of whose opinions I sought, who gave freely of their advice, but my gratitude to them is immense.

My thanks to my agent, Jane Gelfman, who believed in the book and gave me support, unfailing patience, and guidance. An appreciation also goes out to Barbara Robinson of Debevoise & Plimpton, my distinguished colleague in the law, who combed the script for possible errors. Dr. Fred Plum, Head, Neurological Institute of New York Hospital, was most helpful in giving me a number of insights on stress and sleeplessness.

The late Maggie Cousins of San Antonio, Texas, one of the wisest editorial talents in New York, as well as a fine writer herself, read the first draft and made invaluable suggestions.

I acknowledge with particular appreciation the poems supplied me in my own hours of grief by my two friends of many years, Mrs. W.A.M. Burden and Mrs. Livingston Ireland. I hope they will comfort others as they did me.

Thanks to Ivy Wright, Deborah Cali, Mary Fritchi, and Mary Emeich, for their secretarial help and for the deciphering of my poor script.

And a heartfelt gratitude to my Harper & Row editor, Terry Karten, who believed.

Also very special thanks and appreciation to writer Margot Joan Fromer, who helped make this book a reality. A particular thanks also goes to Michael Meatheringham and Bill Cromartie for their time and effort.

CONTENTS

PREFACE

One March evening in 1979 my husband Sam and I danced the night away at a seventieth birthday party for a friend. Eleven days later Sam was dead.

Six hours after I waved good-bye to him as he drove off to New York, he collapsed at a gas station near Philadelphia. He had a ruptured aneurysm and needed immediate cardiac bypass surgery.

Thus began the premonitions of widowhood, although I didn't know it during those eleven days that Sam lay in the hospital, first in the intensive care unit, hooked up to machinery, then in a private room as he began to recover.

I didn't know it because I didn't want to believe that this was the beginning of the end of my thirty-eight-year marriage. I didn't know it because I was scared and lonely, even with my three daughters and their husbands holding my hand. I didn't know it because I didn't *want* to know it.

For eleven days my daughters—Gilda, Sharon, and Kathe—and I sat by Sam's bedside. We were convinced that the strength of our faith and love would help pull him through. And it almost did. At one point Sam's doctors, after originally giving him only a 20 percent chance of survival, said that he had made much better progress than they had expected. We were heartened and began to plan for his recuperation.

Sam was about to become president of the American College of Trial Lawyers, and on the afternoon of the eleventh day, his old friend Leon Jaworski, who had held that post, called. "Sammy," Leon said, "you've had a big operation and you're not going to be dancing around the ballroom or beating your colleagues on the golf course as soon as you think. I know because I had that operation last year."

Sam laughed and said, "Leon, anything you can do, I can do better."

He died that night.

I wanted to die too. I felt as if my future had been wiped out along with his.

Of course I knew I would be a widow someday. Sam was eleven years my senior, and I know the numbers. American women outlive men by about seven years, so why should I be different? There, staring me in the face, were the statistics and a considerably older husband. But knowing is not the same thing as believing that it will happen to *you.* Knowing it *might* happen doesn't prepare you for the reality.

Nothing can prepare you for the shock and grief of widowhood. There are few things as devastating.

Surviving the death of a husband is the loneliest challenge a woman will ever face. Whether he dies suddenly or after a long illness, whether the marriage was a forty-year-long romance or fraught with conflict from the beginning, the newly widowed woman is left behind to cope with and make sense of financial, legal, and emotional issues as frightening as any she has ever experienced.

Like most wives, I had become accustomed to Sam's companionship and the intimacy of living with someone and sharing a life, the comfort of being half a couple in a couples society—even in today's world of a 50 percent divorce rate and 12 million widowed people.

For the first time in thirty-eight years, I had to face the world as a single woman. I felt vulnerable, unattractive, unloved and hideously alone. What I needed and craved was familiarity and moral support; what I often got was rejection because as a widow I threatened the security of my married friends.

• • •

For thirty-eight years Sam had been my dearest friend, my lover, my confidant, and my personal and professional advisor. We had mutual interests in politics, public affairs, current events, performing arts, and most especially the law, a profession we shared. Sam was a partner in a large New York firm, and I had practiced law until Kathe, my youngest, was a year and a half and we moved to New York from Washington.

The shock of Sam's death left me feeling physically and emotionally paralyzed. I had heard of this phenomenon, but I didn't really believe it happened. I had always considered myself a strong, competent woman. I *am* a strong, competent woman, but the first few months of widowhood almost flattened me, and I felt incapable of pulling myself together. Things that had always been automatic—dressing and eating and getting the groceries—left me exhausted. Even getting out of bed was sometimes more than I could manage. Putting on my makeup, deciding what to wear, thinking of what I had to do—it all took as much energy as climbing Mount Everest.

I was angry, too, and I wasn't prepared for that. And it was Sam— poor, dead Sam—who bore the brunt of my anger. I was angry at him for going off and leaving me alone. I was furious that he hadn't stopped smoking, even after I begged him to. "If you don't quit smoking, you're going to make a widow of me," I used to rage at him. What *right* did he have to do this to me? How *could* he?

The anger exhausted me, and it made me guilty. If it wasn't Sam's fault that he died, why was I blaming him? Why did I resent him?

In those early days I had no idea that anger, often escalating to rage, is a natural part of intense grief. I shared my feelings with no one because I had always believed in keeping a stiff upper lip, crying in private, and putting on my best face for family and friends.

How wrong I was. If I had only known how much help and support there is for widows. If I had only known how much we can offer each other.

But back then I didn't know that every widow goes through the same reactions. Naturally there are variations on the theme, but everyone feels thrown by even the simplest decisions. Even armed with degrees in law and accounting, I felt unable to think about essential financial and legal matters. At a time when I had to make important decisions that would affect me for the rest of my life, my brain turned to sludge. I couldn't understand the basic information I needed in order to make those decisions.

But I put on a good face for everyone. I managed, better than I thought at the time, to be my usual self. "She's doing so well," I'm sure my friends said to each other.

I needed help, but I didn't know it. I'm not sure I would have taken advantage of the many opportunities for widows to obtain advice and support (not everyone wants or needs to reach out to others), but it's important to know what's offered. It's crucial to know that you're not alone, that thousands of women before you have plunged into that seemingly bottomless pit of grief and despair, and they have climbed up again, often to better, more fulfilling lives than they had ever imagined possible.

That's what this book is about. It offers the companionship of shared experiences—my own and that of other women—and suggestions about how to get through widowhood: the first shocking months, the period of black depression, and the slow, steady time of healing and renewal.

Today I live a very different life from the one I shared with Sam. I still miss him and always will, but I'm able to be happy because I've found positive solutions to the problems imposed on me by widowhood. Some of them came out of what I know about the practice of family law, some came from discussions with other widows with similar concerns, and some arrived through trial and error.

•   •   •

The death of a spouse is incredibly stressful, and the symptoms are physical as well as emotional. Despite my outward control, inside I was trembling so badly that I worried about falling down the stairs or tripping over a nonexistent crack in the sidewalk. My coordination was shot, and my memory seemed to have deserted me; suddenly I couldn't remember why I had just walked into a room, and I would pick up a book, a plate, an ashtray, and wonder what I had meant to do with it. I forgot the names of people I had known for years.

I lost my appetite. I—always renowned for my sociability—had no will to make phone calls or see people. My friends urged me to go out, but all I wanted to do was squirrel myself away and wallow in misery.

I was certain I was on the brink of poverty ("going to the poorhouse," my mother used to say) and that added to my sense of fear and helplessness. One afternoon my daughter Sharon pronounced me "definitely flaky."

It was true. I was suffering from all the symptoms of acute grief and depression, but I didn't know then that what was happening to me happens to everyone who suffers the loss of a spouse. And suffering it was. The pain was so intense that at times I thought I would never escape its oppressive weight.

And I made some decisions that probably weren't appropriate. For example, about three weeks after Sam died I went to a black-tie dinner to which we had both been invited. I dressed up in a cerise beaded gown that I had been so anxious to wear, and I had a horrible evening. So did the other guests because it was obvious that I was still in the first throes of grief and should not have been there.

My anger at Sam spread to my friends and family. I was convinced that I was being ignored and forgotten—despite the reality of more than three thousand notes of condolence and sympathy sitting on my desk waiting to be answered. I felt lonely and unattractive, and of course my anger turned inward too and I began to cave in to the overwhelming temptation of self-pity.

I sulked. "No one wants to be with me," I thought and reached for the phone to call my daughters one more time—too many times. I remembered how I felt when my father died. I was only twenty-three, and I watched from an upstairs window as the people who had come to comfort my mother and my sister and me got into their cars. They were laughing and joking as though nothing had happened. How callous of them, I had thought, to go so blithely about their lives when we were so crushed with loss. I felt that way now.

•　•　•

But there comes a time when a little window of hope and joy opens into the grief. At first you're surprised, and perhaps a bit guilty, to feel that small gust of pleasure. Mine came less than a month after Sam died. I had invited an English woman to tea to thank her for being so kind to my daughter when she visited London. We had a delightful two hours, and when she had left I realized that after Lillie had made her initial expressions of sympathy, we didn't speak at all of Sam. And I hadn't thought about him—and about the fact that he was dead—for the remainder of Lillie's visit. We had talked of other things and had even giggled like schoolgirls.

Later, sitting at my dressing table, I was shocked at having had such a good time. I felt that I oughtn't to have had pleasure in the midst of grief and pain, that I didn't deserve it. I felt as though I had been unfaithful to Sam.

But it kept happening. The window was open, and I had to acknowledge it. I had to let the breezes of life wash over me. It was time to decide whether to continue with my law practice, to restructure my friendships and professional associations so that my anger and sorrow over Sam's death did not become compounded by the permanent loss of all emotional and intellectual nourishment.

The beginning was difficult, as beginnings so often are. "Hold yourself together and smile through your tears," I told myself. A glib cliché, I thought, even as I gritted my teeth at the banality of the expression. But the age-old advice started to work.

All right, I decided, if getting out of bed in the morning is such agony, stay there until eleven, but use the time constructively. "Don't just lie there and feel sorry for yourself."

It was a good compromise. I treated myself to breakfast in bed and then returned phone calls and began making a dent in the mountain of condolence letters. As I read them over in preparation for writing thank-you letters, the grief stabbed me afresh and I often dissolved into tears and got nothing accomplished. Then I would feel stupid and paralyzed and weak again (and guilty because I wasn't getting the thank-you notes written), as if I would never pull my life together.

But again I compromised: If I could write four or five notes each morning, I would allow myself the luxury of a cry. I treated myself like a child—and it worked. Some mornings I was able to write six or seven letters and the bouts of tears grew less frenzied. Sometimes I didn't cry at all.

I felt encouraged by this progress and decided to arrange my entire widowhood this way: proceeding from goal to goal until I had everything the way I wanted it. That's the way I had always lived, and, despite that one gaping hole that would never be filled, that's the way I would continue.

But I didn't know then about the emotional vagaries of grief, how I would be fine one minute and dissolved in hysterical crying the next. I hadn't realized how the thought of eating dinner alone every night would throw me into a near-panic, so much so that I practically stopped eating because I couldn't face the empty place across the table. I hadn't realized how quickly the social invitations would drop off because I was no longer part of a couple. (In fact, to this day many of the couples with whom Sam and I had spent many happy hours have not invited me to their homes since his death. It's an unpleasant fact of widowhood that I had not expected—and that still hurts.)

I knew intellectually but didn't *understand* the value of time, of sharing feelings with close friends and family, of sometimes forcing myself to do what I believed I had no energy or inclination for, and the value, too, of allowing myself to give in to inertia or the spasms of grief that would appear suddenly when I thought I had things under control.

I learned the value of getting to know myself, and slowly—with many episodes of backsliding—I have learned how to be a widow: how to eat and sleep alone, make decisions alone, how to travel alone, fight with car mechanics, how to open jars and bottles and stuck windows, and carry heavy packages. I have learned how to get through holidays, anniversaries, and birthdays, how to be sick alone, and how to grow old alone.

In this book I shall take a hard, honest look at widowhood and what must be done to move successfully beyond depression and heartache to recovery and a full, happy life. The book offers reassurance and comfort, and it also answers questions.

- How will I ever accept my husband's death and survive this grief?
- How can I rebuild my life without my husband?
- How am I going to accept the changes in relationships with friends and family, especially my children?
- What am I going to do about needing or wanting a man in my life?

- Who's going to do all the things for me that my husband always took care of?
- How will I ever manage to survive alone?

After all these years I still say "we" when I mean "I." I still turn over in bed, expecting to share the day's events and gossip with Sam. I still want to hand over ominous-looking letters from the bank or the IRS, and I still want him to deal with the apartment building superintendent when something mechanical goes wrong.

But I *can* deal with the letters and the garbage disposal. I can keep the car running. I'm often lonely at night, but I don't feel devastated anymore. In fact, I've learned to be happy with my new life. It took a long time and came as a shock when one day I found myself actually looking forward to an evening at home alone. I didn't feel deprived or sorry for myself, and I enjoyed the solitude.

Another surprise was learning to enjoy the company of my women friends for themselves and not as "poor substitutes" for men. I remember with pleasure the day I called a woman friend, also a widow, to suggest dinner because I preferred her company to that of a man who didn't interest me. Two years earlier, I couldn't have done that, and I knew I was feeling better about myself.

I've also learned to let go of the bitterness and resentment toward people who should have reached out to me and didn't, who should have invited me to their dinner parties and didn't, who took advantage of me when I was most vulnerable. I've learned to restructure my friendships, to separate those that are real from those that were based on Sam's business interests or pure expedience.

• • •

As I mentioned earlier, there are about 12 million widowed people in the United States, 10 million of whom are women. Each year more than 175,000 women are widowed. All but a handful are more than fifty-five years old. Eighty percent of them live alone in their own homes and 13 percent live with relatives. And there are no books to help them cope with the emotional and practical problems that accompany widowhood.

This means that there are more than 9 million widows living independent lives, adjusting to various stages of grief, making progress, finding their own way in the world. And they're doing it, for the most part, without much likelihood of finding a husband (2 million widowers are spread pretty thin among their 10 million female counterparts). Many of them are resigned to spending the rest of their life unmarried and many *want* to stay as they are once they learn to be happy and find fulfillment.

This book is for all widows: the newly bereaved, and the "veterans" like me. Make no mistake about it: Your life will change drastically, and it will *never* be the same again. Most of you will go through more emotional pain than you have ever endured.

Some days you'll think you're losing your mind. One of the many purposes of this book is to reassure you that you're not. You're in good company. Every widow before you has gone through the anxiety, depression, fear, panic, and emotional paralysis that accompany the death of a husband.

In the pages that follow, you will find strategies for coping with all the disasters you can imagine (and some you haven't thought of yet), and how to prevent most of them. You'll learn how to make it through the shock of grief and how to get your life back in order when recovery begins. You may even learn to make a better life.

We'll talk about looking good and feeling good, how to travel alone or find compatible people to vacation with, how to get back into the swing of dating and how to develop close platonic male friendships, which often turn out to be more lasting and valuable than romantic liaisons. You'll go out alone in the evening to community and church or synagogue groups, and you will find pleasure in giving yourself to others. You will learn to seek activities that will provide companionship and transform empty blocks of time into life-enriching experiences. You'll learn to be *happy*.

●   ●   ●

I had thought of calling this book *Last Clear Chance,* a phrase used in the law; it refers to the efforts that a defendant in a negligence case might have made to lessen or avoid the injury suffered by the plaintiff.

When Sam died, I felt I had one last clear chance to prevent myself from withdrawing into grief and depression, to avoid being ignored and forgotten by friends and colleagues. I knew that if *I* didn't move out into the world of life and reach out to whoever was willing to help me, I would be compounding the injury—the wound caused by Sam's death. I have taken advantage of this chance for happiness. I am now a happy woman and am writing this book to help others, to tell you what I have learned about living again after that most devastating of all hurts.

1

▪ WIDOWHOOD ▪

THE SHOCK AND ITS AFTERMATH

ON SORROW

Grief, being private, must be borne alone,
And though I cannot share your sorrow, still
Your anguished tears are mingled with my own;
I walk unseen beside you—up the hill.
I can but hope that the pain within your breast,
Will lose its sting, your loneliness will melt
When spring returns to meet the yearly test,
When on the pear the first white blow is dealt.
I shall not surfeit you with vapor words,
Claiming to know the answers to it all;
I only ask, so long as darkness girds
Your world, to let these shoulders ease the fall.

My first reaction to Sam's death was disbelief. During those eleven days in the hospital, I *knew* he could die, but I didn't *believe* it. No woman believes it, especially if her husband dies suddenly.

I suppose a sudden death may seem "appealing" to those who have suffered through a husband's long terminal illness, but losing him unexpectedly is like a punch in the solar plexus: There's no warning, none of the anticipatory grief said to be so beneficial. And there's no time to say good-bye.

1

Although Sam and I had been close and had expressed our loving feelings, there are things I wish I had said (and of course some I wish I hadn't), and I'll always regret that. But now as I look back over those first weeks, the primary emotion was shock and disbelief. I couldn't take in that my darling Sam was no more.

· · ·

We met at a dinner party in March 1940, in Washington, D.C. I hadn't wanted to go, but a law school classmate persuaded me to attend a party he was giving to impress a prospective employer. I couldn't refuse a plea like that from a friend.

It's a good thing I didn't, because the man my classmate was trying to influence turned out to be bright, engaging, charming—and eventually my husband!

As it turned out, Sam hadn't wanted to go to the party either. He had a friend in town, a beautiful Canadian model, and wanted to be with her, but his secretary wouldn't let him cancel the dinner obligation he had made weeks before. And so we made our separate ways to the little basement apartment to enjoy the meal that Sigmund Sichel had spent three days preparing. He had even hand-lettered menus for the guests, and ours still hangs framed in the kitchen of our summer home.

We lived in Washington until 1948, when we moved to New York where Sam had been spending much of his time—so much that I was beginning to be a weekend wife, and neither of us liked that. Once at a party in suburban Virginia, I heard myself introduced as Mrs. Gates. "Mr. Gates is a myth," joked the host.

I remember crying all the way up on the train clutching my three little girls, but Sam began to win important cases for his firm and grew to love his work. For the first five or six years we both felt very out of place in New York. I had quit my law practice to raise Gilda, Sharon, and Kathe (never for a moment do I regret spending the best years of my young adulthood as a full-time mother), but gradually we made friends and developed a social life.

We bought a summer house in Westhampton where Sam could

indulge his passion for gardening. He adored trading dahlia bulbs with the neighbors and was always winning blue ribbons for his flowers. He planted a vegetable garden to please the girls and to help ease the budget in those early days, but flowers were his real passion.

I still smile now as I see Sam in my mind's eye, walking Kathe to nursery school in the morning, the two of them holding hands as they skipped down the street, Kathe in her little skirt and Sam in his homburg or derby, so dignified and so carefree in the company of his little girl. And I still have to laugh as I hear in my mind's ear his off-key voice soaring above the rest in the Fathers' Chorus of Brearley School.

As I sat with him in the hospital I remembered how he loved to dance. He especially enjoyed the old-fashioned dances: the fox trot, the waltz, and the Latin steps. One summer night when we came home from a party, we weren't tired yet and put the radio on the back porch and danced for an hour—just the two of us under the stars.

Images like that—and like the time I watched him in the garden when he thought he was alone, stroking a particularly beautiful flower as though it had bloomed just for him—were the ones that floated crazily through my mind as I sat numbed at the funeral.

Numb is truly the word. I felt as though I had been given a massive dose of emotional Novocaine right after the doctor phoned to tell me that Sam had died. My mind simply shut down as I dressed mechanically, phoned his office, and notified close relatives and the children. The shock acts as a protective shell for a while, but all the time you know the pain will set in. You're grateful for the reprieve even as you wait for the agony to begin. It's like stubbing your toe hard; there's that second or two of nothingness before the pain races up your leg.

But even though you're convinced you can barely function, there are things you must do in those first few days. Family and close friends can help, but some women are alone or want to perform these tasks for themselves: Many think that doing them yourself serves as a cathartic, that although it's difficult now, in future years when you relive the pain of those first few days, you might regret abdicating some or all of the responsibility.

• You must make funeral arrangements. This involves choosing a

3

funeral home, selecting a coffin, picking a place for the funeral and a gravesite if you haven't already done so, deciding what your husband should wear for burial, and whether the coffin should be open or closed. Religious requirements relieve you of only some of these choices, and this is the time when widows can be exploited mercilessly. Although *you* should make the final decision about funeral arrangements, do not go alone to the funeral home. You should be accompanied by someone who will offer practical help as well as emotional support.

• If there is to be a public memorial service or if the funeral is private or out of town (the difference between a funeral and a memorial service is the presence of the deceased), you will have more time to arrange it.

• You must write a death notice for the newspaper. (The difference between a death notice and an obituary is that the former is a paid notice, looks like a classified ad, and contains information of your choice. The latter is a news story, the existence and content of which is solely the prerogative of the newspaper.) The form of a death notice is fairly standard, and most newspapers have sympathetic clerks who will help you with the wording.

• If you want to say that the family prefers contributions instead of flowers, you must decide on a charity. Because Sam was a passionate horticulturist, we said, "Instead of flowers, send contributions to the Samuel E. Gates Garden Fund" for the beautification of our country village, which he loved. It stands today as a memorial in front of a church in Westhampton, New York.

• It is customary for the mourners to return to the house for a meal and/or drinks after the funeral and burial. Someone must arrange for food to be brought in (or engage a caterer), served, and the aftermath cleaned up.

Although one would hope and expect one's friends and family to offer help, sometimes they don't. Try not to condemn those close to you for insensitivity or callousness. People are uncomfortable around grief and bereavement. It reminds them of their own mortality, it reopens painful memories, and sometimes people's discomfort overrides their obligations to friends. It's not nice and it's not helpful to you at a time when you need them, but that's the way it is.

But of those friends who extend sincere offers, ask them to

- sit by the telephone to field condolence calls and provide information about funeral and burial details;

- arrange for hotel or other housing accommodations for out-of-town guests;

- call those people whom you have forgotten and inform them of your husband's death and invite them to the funeral;

- arrange cars and logistics for the procession from the funeral home or church to the cemetery and back to the house;

- find someone to play hostess at the house after the service;

- make sure there's enough food and drink in the house for the days immediately after the death and before the funeral—or deal with the overflow of food, which is usually more of a problem;

- deal with flowers that arrive at the house (some people are bothered by an abundance of overarranged flowers and want them donated to a hospital or nursing home);

- make sure the cards from the flowers are labeled with the name of the sender and the type of bouquet so you can write the appropriate thank-you note later; and

- keep all condolence cards and letters in a pile that won't get lost.

When the funeral is over, when the out-of-town guests have left, when the flowers begin to wither, the *real* pain sets in. You're alone in an empty house and the reality of your loss hits you. There is nothing you can do about the magnitude of the grief; it just *is* and you have to accommodate it. It will become a part of your every waking and sleeping moment, a physical presence like your very shadow; at times you think it will defeat you.

Having managed to survive the funeral and the solicitous attention of family and friends, we long to be left alone so we can stop being brave and give in to the grief. In this chapter, I will talk about how I and other women have managed to grope our way through the initial mourning period. There is no "right" way, but most women eventually find that it's important to accept what they're feeling and learn to express the anguish and loneliness, the anger and bitterness.

A friend, whose husband died only a month after Sam, said about the grief, "It won't go away. It's always there. Sometimes you can get *around* it for a little while, but it's always there, like a snake waiting to strike at you with its nasty little fangs."

Lenore is absolutely right. It *is* always there, and you might as well get used to it. The only thing you can control is the number of ways you use to get around the grief, to go outside yourself for an hour or an afternoon, to take a vacation from misery for a while. And you *can* do that. Some of the things that helped me so much in the weeks that followed Sam's death were creative acts of friendship. For instance, one of Sam's partners sent over a really fine bottle of wine about a month later with a sweet note about how he and Sam had spent many hours together drinking that wine. That bottle saved me from three sleepless nights.

Another friend sent me two tickets to an exhibit at the Metropolitan Museum of Art. The accompanying note said, "I'll pick you up at 10:00 A.M. No excuses." The beauty of the pictures and the pleasure of her company took me out of myself for the morning, and I felt nothing but gratitude.

You will have moments of pleasure, perhaps even happiness, during those first few weeks, and you'll probably feel guilty about it. Don't. Your husband wouldn't want you to, and it doesn't mitigate the pain of your loss to derive pleasure from being alive. Don't worry, the suffering will be there for a long time.

After the funeral or memorial service is over, so many people say,

"Let me know if you need anything." But very few of them call you regularly afterward. It's disappointing, but again, it's the way people are. The best thing that loving friends did for me was to keep calling me two or three times a week after my children had gone home and I was alone. They invited me to dinner (and *made* me come when I didn't want to); they offered to take me to church with them or give me a ride to a gathering to which we were both invited. Sometimes they called just to let me know they were thinking about me. My best friend called daily, offering to have me for a simple drink and supper with her and her husband.

Many who knew me well realized that my wedding anniversary, my husband's birthday, Valentine's Day, and other special days would be difficult, and they made arrangements to be with me on those days.

The first time we venture forth alone in public without our husbands, most of us feel shaky and vulnerable—and we're sure we look as though we've aged twenty-five years overnight. Even the most independent, fulfilled women I know have talked about feeling "identity-less" after the death of their husband. Some situations may indeed be too difficult to handle, and you must accept the fact that you don't have infinite strength. For instance, one woman began to cry when she described the pain she felt when she attended a surprise party in honor of friends' thirtieth wedding anniversary four months after her husband had died.

•   •   •

Sooner or later you will be forced to attend to details that didn't have to be dealt with immediately after your husband's death, but neither can they wait forever.

• You'll have to go over your financial situation to see if you have enough money to live. I discuss this in detail in Chapter 2, but you must, within the first week or so after the funeral, examine your checking and savings accounts to see if you have enough for immediate needs, and you must make sure that your health, homeowner's, and automobile insurance policies and taxes are paid. You can attend to the rest of the financial details in a few weeks.

• If there is to be a reading of your husband's will (a practice that occurs more often in British murder mysteries than in real American life), your attorney will contact you about time and place. Even if there is no reading, you and your lawyer must meet to discuss the actions to be taken based on the provisions of the will.

• If your safe deposit box was jointly owned and you have a key, open it and go over the documents to see what requires your immediate attention. Put aside things you want to save for your children or grandchildren, or things that you don't need to deal with now.

• Go through your husband's desk or other files for the same purpose. Make sure there are no unpaid bills.

• Answer all condolences with a letter or short note. All flowers, gifts, donations to charity (each organization will notify you of the contribution), and personal visits must be acknowledged. I had more than three thousand letters to write, and my daughters helped with some. It was a monumental task that I thought would absolutely flatten me, but the opposite happened. I felt immensely cheered by the outpouring of affection from people I hardly knew, and from close friends of course, and some whom I didn't know at all. It made me realize how much everyone loved Sam and how deeply he would be missed.

Between these tasks, which didn't turn out to be as onerous as I had thought, I still felt devastated. Many times every day I wanted to beat at the walls with my fists and scream out my heartache. But that type of release doesn't come easily to me. I could sob over a movie or a television program, but when my own heart was breaking, tears wouldn't come. I prayed to cry, but I hardly ever did.

I was angry, though, at Sam and continue to be furious at him. What right did he have to abandon me by dying because of his incessant smoking when I begged him for twenty years to stop?

I was afraid, too. I was afraid of being poor even though I knew I wouldn't be. I was afraid of growing old, I was afraid of becoming sickly, of losing my health and energy, and I'm not sure I would have minded too much, back then, if I had joined Sam in death.

I know now that most of these fears, common to all widows, come from exhaustion and too much introspection. Of course, they're realistic: We *will* age and become tottery and frail, and many of us will fall ill, and thousands of American widows are destitute. But it's the paralysis these fears create that I want to help you overcome.

My heart was warmed by friends who kept urging me to emphasize the positive and to think about the wonderful life Sam and I had together. But I wanted only to wallow in my own grief. I remembered what Sylvia Plath once wrote to her mother in response to the latter's advice to write more "cheerful stuff": "What a person out of Belsen—physically or psychologically—wants is nobody saying the birdies still go 'tweet-tweet,' but the full knowledge that somebody else had been there and knows the worst, just what it is like"(from *Letters Home*, Harper & Row, 1975).

Fresh grief is a blow to your soul. It feels like emotional anarchy, like a predicament that saps your strength and will to go on. But you *will* go on because you have no choice. You'll learn to recognize and accommodate the times when you're at your lowest ebb, and not to panic when faced with the finality of solitude and living alone. You will learn to develop the skills necessary for independence, and you'll learn to establish a life style that offers friends and family the opportunity to help you. You'll learn to get advice and help from someone other than your husband, and eventually you'll learn to look forward to hope, not backward only for the sustenance of memories. You'll learn how to get your body and soul into shape for the task of mourning—because it takes strength to grieve well. And you'll learn to avoid self-pity and resentment, which are more toxic than any drug.

If you have faith in God or some other higher power, now is the time to call on it for strength. If religion has been important in your life, it should surely help now. Life is full of so much noise, confusion, tension, cruelty, and pain—especially now in the midst of your unhappiness—that it's difficult to remember that it's also very beautiful and precious. You must go out of your way to look for aspects of life that have always provided you with a sense of peace and beauty. I've always loved the ocean, and I found that the ceaseless and timeless wash of waves on the shore calmed me. I found pleasure in flowers because Sam had loved them so much and they were such an important part of his life. I went often to the museum because art has always been uplifting to me—and I made no effort to try to like the paintings I didn't know or understand. I went again and again to sit before my favorites and drink in their beauty.

Go slowly with yourself. Be patient. Hang on to your faith, and you will pass through this time of bereavement.

2

DIVORCE AND HOW TO COPE

Another agonizing grief can occur which will force you deal with life of "Suddenly Alone."

Between the sorbet and the entree, your husband of a number of years has just told you over dinner at an exclusive, charming restaurant, that he has fallen in love with someone else. Their affair has been going on for some time — in fact, enough time for him to feel personal agony at what it would do to you and the children; but, for a sufficient period of time to know that he had to level with you and tell you of his desire for a divorce. He would be fair, you could stay where you live. He would have his attorney call you tomorrow to work out the details. Some seeking divorce aren't even sure when they become so unhappy that they simply did not want to try anymore. This throws them both, especially the partner who does not want the divorce, into an emotional abyss.

What does an intelligent woman, who thinks she has been a supportive partner, who has grown intellectually with her spouse and has maintained her looks do? Some wives have not kept their minds alive nor their bodies beautiful. They too need guidance. But the answers to an announcement like the above result in a variety of scenarios. An explosion of anger; a quiet sob-repressive reply, "If that is the way you want it, what choice do I have?" A poised attractive riposte, because she has been expecting something like this: "Perhaps, darling, I have not been as understanding, as good a listener, as sexy a bedmate, after all of our years together, as you need. But can't we try it for six more months, and, with or without therapy, give it another chance?" If you don't want him to leave, that's a good answer.

11

Suppose nothing works. As a sometime matrimonial lawyer, I know from experience that it often does not; especially when there is another woman involved. You're left to cope with "ONE HELLUVA MESS." Some throw themselves into another love affair. Some try to figure out what "love is." They thought they had it and now they don't. It results in pain for both parties. Had they just not tried hard enough?

Suppose you are the one walking out. You fix your spouse of a number of years a nice dinner and break it to him gently. There is no one else (there often isn't). "Dear, I cannot bear another month of your silence, lack of communication, your mental or physical abuse. My own unwillingness to live another minute in a relationship in which I cannot have a chance to fulfill myself has made me leave you." Or, "I am just plain tired or bored, and my own androgynous qualities have given me a yearning to pursue an alternative to our marriage. I would very much appreciate it if you would give me a divorce."

Whatever the reason for one partner in a marriage deciding to call it quits, it is a heart-wrenching crisis for both spouses. It is useless, at that point, to blame yourself or him (if you are the wife) for omissions and commissions of sins of incompatibility — of whatever form it has taken. If you ever get another chance to build a marriage, you and he will not make the same mistakes again, if you can avoid them. Sometime a wandering eye for the opposite sex, and a paranoic temper, will plague successive relationships forever. For the purpose of this chapter, we should address ourselves to fairly normal, reasonable people whose marriage is falling apart.

If reconciliation becomes an impossibility, then the sooner the details are settled, the spouse who does not want the divorce will have to re-structure a life alone, budget what your assets will be and your whole orientation to life.

All of the advice outlined in this book about finding and choosing a professional — banker, stockbroker/investment advisor, insurance agent, realtor — is just as valid for a recently separated and about-to-be divorced spouse as it is for a widow.

Often, I must recommend an attorney to a friend or a stranger. I always suggest at least two, or perhaps, four fellow practitioners with whom I have been involved in matters, or whose reputation is without blemish. That being said and done, I very often hear that the person I advised, who was looking for representation, has engaged someone of whom I have never heard, certainly not on my "approved list." That is fine, because the first requisite of an attorney-client relationship is that the parties LIKE and TRUST one another. What will transpire between you will be exhausting, agonizing, and sometimes extremely demanding of patience.

I have often heard from the lawyer to whom I have referred a client, "Phil, she is driving me crazy, calling me just as I am sitting down to dinner, and so forth." When I caution the client to cease and desist of this conduct, she will say, "Well, he cannot be reached at his office as he is always in court or in conference!" That happens frequently. When you hire counsel you are buying legal service, you must know, before you engage a lawyer, how much the hourly charge will be and just when just when can you expect your phone calls to be returned. Also ask about how often you'll be billed.

Your life is falling apart. You absolutely HAVE to know the answer that day in order to make summer plans, school enrollments, job decisions (if you are lucky enough to have one — many women with children are not so fortunate). All of the other guidelines pointed out in Chapter 4, dealing with hiring professionals, are important. The decision of who will represent you in your divorce proceeding is one of the most important decisions you will ever make.

All of this can happen. Today's statistics are frightening as they indicate that about one-half of marriages end up in divorce. That is a misleading statistic because some of the divorces are happening to two or three-time losers. No one goes into marriage thinking it won't last. Divorce is surely not contemplated. Even though it doesn't cause a social stigma as it did at the turn of this century, it still creates just as much hurt and pain for the children. It's about loss and no one ever really forgets the blow dealt by one party or the other. After a sleepless night, you tell yourself to stop self-pity and start to get "your ducks in a row." One of the most important stages of a matrimonial case is the first interview. I feel that the purpose of that first session is to establish a feeling of trust and confidence. Both you and your lawyer must trust one another, and "Really Like One Another."

As the lawyer must decide that I do not have a conflict of interest, I do not represent anyone if I have been a friend of them both before the problems arose, as that may affect my judgement and damage my effectiveness with the other spouse. In the first interview, I always say that I am asking only for the most basic facts. The venue (or where the action will take place) is to be settled immediately. The client must be

13

certain that the lawyer is licensed to practice in the state where the suit will be filed and you live. It is not satisfactory to have to call long-distance in your future conversations.

How much will it cost? A charge for the initial session with the lawyer must be agreed upon. You, as the person seeking help must know WHERE YOU STAND, and WHAT YOUR RIGHTS ARE. In order that an attorney can properly advise you, you must gather and make available all the basic records which will form a basis for your claims. These are listed below. Remember that college and post-graduate tuitions must be provided for in the divorce settlement, even after children are no longer minors (in some states 18 years of age). Many states hold divorced parents responsible for tuition and post-minority children but they do this by weighing many factors. It's better to provide for your children's college support at divorce time than many years later. Statistics tend to show that children are much more likely to ask their divorced mother for their college tuition than their *father,* even though she has less money. They also consider their mother's home "their home."

Make it clear to your lawyer if you do not wish to be called by your lawyer at home, or at your place of business. You must be clear as to HOW you wish to be called; particularly if business secrecy is involved. If your attorney is not giving you individual attention or is not supportive or understanding, cut the initial interview short and begin again.

You will get help if you are not too emotionally distraught or vengeful, or if the facts of your relationship with your spouse are not misrepresented or inconsistent. Nothing ruins a professional relationship as much as a lawyer finding out later that a client has not leveled with him/her. Try to stick to the important facts — don't wander off the subject. Never suggest any unethical conduct be followed by you or your lawyer. Do not expect unrealistic results, but always emphasize that this is your ONLY chance to settle your case fairly and you do intend to see that your rights are fully protected.

You deserve, after you have spilled out your own grievances, to have the lawyer explain VERY clearly what the law is as it applied to your set of facts; what are the realistic projections of the results as he sees them; what are the timeframes practically viewed; what will be the initial, but tentative, strategies and approaches he will make to the opposing counsel. Will he suggest marriage counseling? Will he feel that either party needs therapy before proceeding with the final motions? Remember you are contracting for a service and insist on getting what you paid for.

The fees you will be responsible for must be clearly WRITTEN DOWN for you and initialed by you both. Your spouse should pay your attorney if he wants the divorce. Ask your lawyer about "equitable distribution" for you. I live in a state which has such a statute. *The New York Law Journal* revealed that courts award an average of 70% to husbands and 30% to wives. Some form of equitable distribution operates in 42 states, treating marriage as an economic partnership.

Courts distribute according to each member's contribution as a wage earner, spouse and parent. Mothers have not been ever awarded an amount commensurate with the value of their giving 80% of the parenting. In most cases there are many inequities in "equitable distribution."

You will be asked to assemble copies of whatever critical documents you have not brought with you; to inventory your safe deposit box, if you have one, photograph valuable household goods, maybe even for you to write a letter to your lawyer (I often suggest this) summarizing your marital history. You will be cautioned not to confide in relatives and friends; not to keep a diary; not to negotiate in any way, with the estranged spouse; and, whatever you do, not to put your children in the middle of the conflict.

The following is a check list of information a lawyer usually seeks before agreeing to "take on" a case: you will save him many hours — and save yourself lots of money — by assembling the following for your visit:

- Name, resident address and telephone number (including maiden and former names, if previously married.
- Mailing address (may need to suggest opening post office box to preserve confidentiality).
- Business address and telephone number(s), including telecopier.
- Name, resident address, and telephone number of other party.
- Dates and places of birth and religion of each party.
- Status of each party's health (physical and emotional).
- Prior marriages of each party and details of termination.
- Children of prior marriages and custodial arrangements.
- Financial obligations (or rights) such as mortgages and personal

loans, taxes owed from prior marriages.

- Length of residence in the state.
- Name and address of lawyer representing other party if you know it.
- Date and place of marriage.
- Existence of pre-nuptial or post-nuptial agreement.
- Whether the wife is pregnant.
- Names, dates of birth, and educational status of children.
- Physical or emotional problems of children.
- Party with whom the children are residing.
- Date of separation and which party left the family residence.
- Counseling and therapy history, if any, and any prior separations or court action.
- Past two or three years of tax returns.
- List of investments and their current value.
- Future cost estimates of children's education-activities.
- Any non-routine medical expenses which you foresee.
- Grounds for divorce or any relief.
- Client's objectives (divorce, legal separation and reconciliation).
- Behavioral patterns of the parties toward each other.
- Employment and income history and income potential of each party.
- Contributions of each party as homemaker or to the career enhancement of the other.
- Income of each party from sources other than employment and expectancies.
- Life insurance of each party (whether term, whole life, and the cash surrender value, if applicable.
- Each party's assets, including marital, nonmarital, separate, community, and quasi-community property (without overlooking less obvious items such as pension plans from previous employers, collectibles, receivables, life insurance cash values, and income tax refunds).
- Assets of the parties jointly owned.
- Identification and tracing of nonmarital or separate property of each party.
- Income and other assets of the children, with identities of custodians and trustees.
- If either party is self-employed or in business: identity of business

or profession, product or service, stock ownership, number and identity of shareholders, partners, directors and/or officers, identity of CPA and interest of the other party.

- Safe-deposit boxes, location, contents, and party having access.
- Manner of handling family finances — who has decided what.
- Manner in which household and family bills are paid and whether spouse and children receive adequate support.
- Where are financial records located.
- Existence of domestic abuse, threats to transfer assets, or other facts warranting injunctions, order of protection, and other interim relief.

You must, after you have decided you have chosen the right person to represent you, INSIST THAT HE CONSULT YOU BEFORE ANY IMPORTANT STEPS ARE TAKEN IN THE CASE. You must graciously ask if nothing is happening in the case, that you be notified on the lack of progress. You want him to be perfectly candid with you, even if the news is bad. It doesn't hurt to inform him that you do not want him to make any public statements to the press at any time. Not only the latter is unethical, but it could prejudice you before judge or jury, if the case goes to trial and is not settled without a trial. Under NO circumstances should you have romantic relations with your counsel. After all is finished, you will be free to act independently, but not until the final decree is delivered, signed and sealed, by the parties.

An additional worry on the part of wives who have no independent source of revenue is, "How am I going to live and support the children until this is all settled?"

By all means ask your lawyer what he will do about your maintenance during that period, and about a division of your properties; about your request for alimony or spousal support pendente lite (until the divorce is granted); your request for temporary award of counsel fees, appraisal fees, cost and actuarial fees; your request for exclusive possession of the marital home pending the outcome of the litigation; your request for child support; your request for custody; INJUNCTIVE RELIEF TO PRESERVE THE ASSETS PENDING DISTRIBUTION (very important); and a request to prevent the spouse or assets belonging to both of you from leaving the jurisdiction.

In addition to the above checklist, certain actual expenses occur and you have to meet them, often by yourself (keep in mind divorces take twice as long as you think).

Utilities
Rent or mortgage and realty taxes
Property and car expenses
Car payments
Personal property taxes
Insurance: medical, property, life, disability
Food: household
Clothing
Medical (uninsured)
Vacation and entertainment
Auto repairs
Projected expenses
Repairing gutters, major appliances and windows
Replacing automobile
Painting home
New roof
New driveway
Major dentistry: periodontal and orthodontia

All of this will seem inordinately tedious, detailed, and, perhaps, too onerous for you to deal with when you are so wiped out. It is important to remember that YOU WILL NOT HAVE ANOTHER OPPORTUNITY. You must protect yourself and family as NO ONE ELSE is going to do it for you.

Do not believe that yours will be a SIMPLE divorce. In my many years at it, I have never known one. Divorce practice is highly emotional and adversarial. Sometimes the parties direct their frustrations, anger and bitterness towards their counsel. Do not do it! Your lawyer will be, for a long time, your best friend, and you do not want to endanger your relationship, surely not his caring for you to emerge whole both financially and emotionally.

By all means, ask counsel about settling your problems through mediation or arbitration. The American Arbitration Association makes this possible if both parties are agreeable. It is much cheaper, provides fewer delays, and often is all settled within one hearing day. Some courts maintain their own staff mediators or panels of course-approved mediators, which often are provided with no cost. If spouse abuse is an issue, or if one spouse is especially naive about financial matters, special precautions are in order so that the vulnerable party is not taken advantage of. Many are using arbitration to reach compromise.

Lower cost and fewer fireworks lure them to take this route. Both spouses must be willing to be divorced, or it won't work.

There can be no binding arbitration when it comes to visitation and custody matters. The court cannot delegate its Parens Patriae responsibility to the children; therefore, all orders making custody arrangements are modifiable in the future if the circumstances of the parties change.

There is no facet of modern life not governed by taxes and their consequences. Be sure to find out if your lawyer feels competent to advise you of your exposure toward income, gift and other taxes. Some lawyers suggest that a tax expert approve any settlement. Even if all other aspects of your case seem to be falling in line, be sure to examine the tax problems incident to each part of the proposed settlement.

A bereaved, half-sensitive person certainly shows it. Some divorcees, like widows, are a sort of walking symbol of their own mortality. Women alone, I suddenly realized, are often made to feel like some outer space alien or E.T. People smile rather weakly at you, say you are looking very well, and move on to the next cluster of conversationalists. Try to counteract that. I often forced myself at cocktail parties to join a third group of guests, usually by saying, "I don't want to talk to the people I already know here, my name is Phil Gates, what's yours?" Perhaps it was too pushy and occasionally it immediately felt like a mistake. If I joined in their laughter at a joke and said, "Sam would've loved that story," the silence was deafening. I probably talk about Sam too much, even now, seventeen years after his death. But the feeling of incompleteness never leaves me — walking along the enchanting boulevards of New York, Paris or Orlando, Florida, one sees couples, old and young, COUPLES, COUPLES, COUPLES. It is a "couples world" and when you are without a companion it is abundantly clear. You are incomplete. One widow wrote *The New York Times* and said people looked at her as if she were handicapped, as though society was still built like those creatures boarding Noah's Ark.

Recently divorced women sometimes tell me the same things. My clients, who are women, as I have also represented a number of men (who don't experience the same thing) tell me that they begin to look at themselves to be sure they still have their clothes on. Somehow, THEY feel that even today, when divorced people are 30% of our population, there is an opprobrium to their alone status.

The same procedures for building a new life for oneself apply to all states of "aloneness." Begin as though you are a senior in college and need some counseling as to your future. Seek a mentor in whom you have great confidence as well as empathy. Ask him/her what you should be doing that you are not, what skills you need to learn that you do not have, what cosmetic changes in your looks, your walk (yes) you must make. The way you hold your shoulders and your head can immediately give a message — they now call it body language. If you know no one who can fill a "mentor's bill," there are innumerable counselors you can hire. Churches and social work institutions can help you find them, if they don't provide such services themselves.

Activities which only involve YOU, such as writing, painting, gardening (unless done with others, sharing a part of the interests) just WON'T DO. They are wonderful paths of self-expression and creativity, but they will not get you "out" into the real world of give-and-take. None of us is made alike and there are many who need much less of other's company and can survive, happily, by seeing other people occasionally. If you really need friends and family contact, then only YOU can make that happen.

Being divorced is more painful than widowhood. Women have a worse time in all arenas than do men. I recently sat next to a man at a luncheon club I belong to (which after seventy years, just admitted women to membership!) who said, "When a man dies, he leaves a widow — when a woman dies, a star is born!" He cited several WOMEN we both knew who HAD emerged into their own stardom, after their husbands' death. But these were only a few.

This says it pretty hurtfully to us women. A single man in my New York world, and in most places in the world, is a star so sought after that, if they are half-way attractive, they "fight" for an evening alone. More than a dozen of my single men friends have admitted to me that no matter how enticing a woman they have recently met is to them, they never pick up the telephone to invite her out. Obviously, there are some exceptions, but, generally, the extra single woman is a dime-a-dozen in most circles. If divorced, one has to fight silently to keep one's own friends, who begin to take sides. One faces the awkward situation of "dating." There is real trouble trusting your own instinct sorely damaged by the divorce process.

References to life alone after divorce have been made on other pages of this book (see Index). In many cases, it is much worse to face life alone after divorce than after the loss of a loving husband who has also been your best friend. As a divorced friend of mine told me when she had been alone for only about two weeks, "I miss someone who cares whether I have a bad cold!" Even during the hostile and bitter several years before they parted, they had, as civilized decent people, lived together and CARED whether each other felt well. Now you face alienated children — you are in doubt and despair. Some have likened it to a long root canal operation. One's heart cries for help and understanding.

I was persuaded to represent two extremely gifted children, ages five and ten, multilingual students at the Lycee Francais. Their parents had been divorced and the provision in the divorce decree provided that they should visit their father on alternate spring and Christmas holidays, as well as a month in the summer. Their father was, as well as their mother, a gifted musician. In fact, he is still one of the most famous symphony conductors in this country. He had remarried, there was a new baby and his work demanded that he travel all over the world. Therefore, the two children had to be delivered by the mother wherever he happened to be performing. Each time this happened, the children came back from a visit traumatized and subject to nightmares. They were, also, suffering from "daymares," if I might coin a word. Following a visit with their father and stepmother, their grades at school plummeted.

A fellow counselor had sat by the mother on a trans-Atlantic flight and she was so visibly upset by the children's latest visit that she confided in him. He was a fine lawyer and listened. The children were on the same plane as she was taking them back to the United States from one of these disastrous visits. I received a call from my friend asking me to see the mother and take on the "Modification of Visitation Rights" in the Family Court. I said, "Why don't you do this yourself?" He said, "Because I am being remarried after our divorce and want to have a honeymoon, and you are better at this kind of thing, anyway, Phil."

This began a several-year litigation, in which I asked another, more famous, matrimonial firm to join me. I was busy in my office, traveling with Sam, so that I could not give it my undivided attention. I did attend, and participate, in the endless trial to "modify" these visitations so that the children, as suggested by the psychiatrists, those appointed by the Court and those appearing for the children, could become older and more able to cope. In order not to be so upset by these protracted visits, the doctors advised, "Only allow the children to see their father during the day," returning at home to sleep well and be comforted by their mother.

The cases in these matters do indicate that children are often permanently damaged and often USED by estranged parents as pawns to exact revenge between them. Judges are extremely aware of this. It had been a bitter divorce (the father had married his second wife BEFORE being divorced from the mother and had cut off the alimony she was due under their divorce decree when she brought this suit to protect her children). Of course, she must have said mean things about their father to them. I am sure she did not do anything to make their visits with him easier. It was, however, clear to the doctors and teachers observing the children that these visits were inimicable to their best interests. Unfortunately, the Judge, a woman who should have known better, ruled that the visits, as set up in the divorce decree, should be maintained and, if the children refused to go to their father's home (they had said they would refuse to go), she would appoint a psychiatrist to go with them and make them like it! Her decision shook my faith in the Family Court. My client, having been impoverished by this suit by the time it was decided, could not afford to appeal this ruling, to her an arbitrary and capricious decision, and she and the children had to live with it.

I mention this case as the divorce was already final. Many other things can happen after the final decree, which can upset you as well as keep you from beginning to live a new life again. It is all very well to suggest that, if the advice contained in this book is followed, you can have a second chance at life. So much has to be "right" in your new life alone before you can plunge in and tackle it as a single. One has to be prepared for the unexpected.

If you are in the middle of a separation, looking toward finalizing it, in divorce, many considerations must be given your careful attention:

(1) How, if there are children, will the custody be handled and ENFORCED.

(2) Custodial fitness, on the father's or mother's side, must be examined.

(3) Provisions for promptness in delivering the children to and from visitations can be often abrogated, and constitutes one of the peskiest realities of living up to one's agreement.

(4) How have you made definite the waiver of one another's claims on each other's estates?

(5) Have you access to each other's annual income statements?

(6) How have you dealt with the occupancy and ownership of the marital home?

(7) Are the provisions definite and easy to obey so far as support and maintenance payments?

(8) Has the division of marital properties, especially those acquired since the marriage in community property states, been fully agreed to by both parties?

(9) Have any extant debts been paid and who is responsible for any which are still outstanding?

(10) Has an arbitration clause been made a part of the arrangements in case either party defaults?

(11) Who is to pay for the attorney's retainer and subsequent bills?

(12) Has any provision been made in case of remarriage of either spouse or modification of custody arrangements?

(13) Has any thought been given to the establishment of a security trust to produce income for a dependent spouse and child to satisfy the goals of the separation agreement? (This provides a steady source of income free of the whims or economic fluctuations in the life of the payor spouse.)

(14) What provisions have been made in case the alimony, or lump sum payment, cannot be met because of sufficient change in the economic circumstances of either party?

All too often, after alimony or lump sum payments have been decided upon, there occurs a default in payment, and an attorney has to be hired all over again to try to collect these monies owed the dependent spouse.

When figuring out how much financial support the spouse, with whom the children live, must have to maintain the child, so many elements of education and maintenance are overlooked: long-distance calls home from school, sports equipment, fees and club dues and travel back and forth to home or to visit classmates. Summer "meaningful" programs, camps and additional schooling are expensive, even though often a very good idea for children of divorce, and are not "figured" into financial arrangements.

A divorcee has two strikes against him/her, while the one who has been widowed does not. The friends they shared as a couple very often will feel that they have to "choose" between the parties. Even though they really do not want to do so, the man of the couple is so much easier to "include" than is the woman. A newly divorced wife is a rather indigestible addition to an evening, even if she is the more attractive and interesting of the two. Unfair, yes, but so is life.

A divorcee faces an additional trauma — the likelihood of seeing her former mate walk into a public gathering or a private party on the arm of another, perhaps a younger and more beautiful version of herself. An announcement of his remarriage. That hurts! An additional blow is the knowledge that one's former spouse has just had a new baby by your replacement; especially if one has remained single. This is painful, as well, to any children who are still at home and breaking the news that their father, for example, has a new baby has to be carefully handled, usually by an embittered, broken-hearted mother. If that person is you, fight like a tiger not to transmit your sadness and disappointment to your children. They will have a hard enough time adjusting to this new piece of news without your making it even more difficult. This takes an enormous amount of magnanimity. TRY!

Re-making one's life in the new single MODE takes all the doing you can muster. Do not fall for the unvoiced presumption that single women of middle years, who are enjoying an active romance, are doing it with someone else's husband. It is not to ignore the fact that affairs with married men are probably thriving, as they always have. I heard about such things when I was a little girl. Most men cannot afford divorce. As someone said, serial monogamy is a luxury reserved for billionaires. Many, long-married and reasonably comfortable husbands, long to revive a "moribund erotic life," to quote Erica Abeel in *The New York Times*. It can be their last chance for a little variety in their sex life, long-since become routine — such yearnings are innate characteristics of a human male, we are taught. Today's divorcees are usually in the marketplace, in some form or another, and often meet such men at lunch or at a business conference. Perfectly proper subsequent meetings follow and, sooner or later, they find themselves over their heads and they do not want it to be a tawdry "one night stand." Platonic friendships are on the wane. Women, who were the traditional "glue" holding a family together, are fighting for a place in the corporate sun and are too much emulating their male counterparts' workaholism. Ethical and moral considerations of old are ignored.

Rest assured that most of the philandering husbands I know do not leave their wives to remake their life with their new love. His fidelity to his wife and family is not an issue on the table, nor is he riddled with guilt. He is just succumbing to undisciplined, physical desire.

A divorcee is at her most vulnerable after she is "suddenly alone." She must be aware of the womanizer, of the husband with the wandering eye. He will take her to lovely restaurants and, perhaps, ply her with expensive jewelry or other gifts, while urging her to see that their time together will result in mutual satisfactions of all sorts. He will usually hold out the bait that he wants to "take care of her permanently." By that time, our heroine, who feels that she is someone no one wants anymore, has swallowed his line. This otherwise sensible, well-organized, realistic woman is "overboard" and the outcome is not amusing. Pre-World War II Europe had its code of conduct for mistresses of married men, as we know from the biographies of philanderers in the time. In the good old USA today a woman *abandoned* by her former spouse for another has, or better have, her feet on the ground. The lovely apartment for her lifetime is usually not a part of these extra marital romances.

She will begin to look into the mirror and begin to "know herself." She will not keep repeating, "Boy, did I blow it!" Rather, she will say, "Okay, what I did in my marriage did not work, and NOW I know it. I did the best I knew how at the time. If I ever get another crack at a marriage relationship, I'll do it better."

We all err, it's human, right? Missteps, or mistakes, are experiences which lead one onto the road of progress. If we cannot make mistakes, how are we supposed to be wise about our future actions? Just remember, we must try to be complimentary to ourselves by saying that we are doing the best we can. That kind of attitude will surely make you feel better.

After turning your back on mistakes, and we all make them, look into the future. Marriage counselors learned a long time ago to recognize a marriage which is falling apart. So if it is not too late, seek such advice. Realize that men's and women's priorities differ when it comes to what to expect of a marriage relationship. For a man, often the Number One priority is a good, steady sexual relationship. For a woman, that is usually, according to the studies, Number Three. Rather, women seek shared thoughts and feelings, or COMPANIONSHIP and COMMUNICATION. Those are way down the list for her husband. All couples having difficulties say that their communication has broken down, no matter what place on the list it occupies.

When a couple disagrees, it is important for both of them to try their level best to be fair to one another, no matter how strongly they nurse their carefully built-up grievances. The shorter the temper tantrum or the disagreement the better for a long-lasting entente. A research project on thirty couples lately, who had lasting marriages, stated that loyalty to one another was a prime importance. In other words, the best marriage is that in which one's spouse is one's best friend. SEXUAL FIDELITY DOESN'T HURT. Religious backgrounds more or less the same is a plus. Agreement of one's priorities above described if faithfully obeyed helps enormously. A good marriage always contemplates that, as we get older, our needs and commitments could ever be renegotiated. Our physical conditions change — some have suggested couples make a social portfolio to plan for seeing one's friends more often after the children have left the nest, to involve yourselves in more intellectual pursuits, perhaps going back to take courses in something you neglected to learn about when you were busy making a living, or a family, or a home.

This social portfolio can be a useful tool; especially to a divorcee. List what you have to offer in a social context. Build on your assets — reach out to friends you know who are like you and would enjoy a simple supper with you and a few interesting friends. This does not require that you, whatever your sex, have a "date." It does mean that you recognize that if you want to stay in a couples world you have to invite couples almost twice as often as you did when you had a mate.

If you ever become interested in another person, after a divorce, keep all of the above in mind as to what goes into making a lasting marriage. The difference in what each spouse thinks is important in your marriage; abide by it. Don't, for goodness sakes, try to overburden your marriage. Give each other a lot of space to continue to grow as individuals and to learn new things all of the time.

Child-rearing years place the most stress on a marriage. If you can survive those harrowing, sleepless nights, almost anything is possible if there is a will to Make It Work. If there is not, especially if one of the couple has fallen in love with another — which so often happens — then try to be as calm and accepting of the new situation as you can when divorce happens. A bitter face, which reflects a bitter attitude, will never win friends nor keep your old friends around you.

3

GETTING YOUR LIFE IN ORDER

*O*ne day, in two months or six months or more, you accept the fact that life will never be the same. You take a deep breath and say good-bye to your husband.

You were right to grieve for as long as you did, and you know that occasional sadness will wash over you, but you know it's time to get on with things. There's nothing you can do about the death, and you might as well take the step back into life. Once you can see that, you're on your way.

Some women find that the grief is worse now than it was when their husband first died, but the initial shock has worn off and you begin to face different sorts of problems.

Difficulties arise. Problems crop up. You have to make decisions about things you may not have even thought about before. Things seem impossible without the support and guidance of the absent one. Only now do you begin to realize how often your husband

- tended to the structural and mechanical functioning of the household;
- paid the bills and balanced the checkbook;
- took care of all insurance, financial, and legal matters;

- handled your investments and bank accounts; and
- kept the car gassed and oiled and on the road.

Now it's all in your lap, and many women have a tendency to panic when the roof leaks or the car makes a funny noise or the checkbook and the bank's statement don't agree.

Don't panic. You can do it. You can handle anything if you think it through clearly and logically. Unless your house is on fire or you smell a gas leak, don't do anything in a rush. That's the first thing.

The second is to look around at your women friends and find one or two who have been alone for years (perhaps a single woman who has never married) and who are organized and competent. Have lunch or dinner with her and say frankly, "I want you to be my mentor and teach me how to live alone. I don't want to fall apart every time the lawnmower won't start or I need someone to replace a broken window pane."

Tell her you'll try not to make a nuisance of yourself but that you *will* seek her advice often and ask her to teach you things. She'll be delighted and flattered (everyone likes to think of herself as competent and admired) and will probably give you much more than you had hoped.

The third thing is to get yourself organized, and that's what this chapter is about. You'll need to learn to do a great many things yourself and find reliable, honest assistance for the things you want someone else to take care of.

You also must get your personal life in order. You have to get out of the house and begin to socialize again. You may want to become involved in community work or take courses at an adult education center or college. You need to invite people in. It's time to assess the quality of your friendships and make new friends and acquaintances. You need to identify and plan for a realistic life style. Perhaps what you did with your time before your husband died has not or will not provide a fulfilling future. In fact, you probably have skills and talents you have never used (or never realized you had) that now can be a source of satisfaction, new friendships, a commitment to the community, a sense of being needed—and may even provide income.

And you may need to find a job—either quickly because you need money to live, or eventually, because you want to work.

MONEY

The subject of money is crucial to you now. If you have plenty of it, you need to protect and manage it so the supply lasts until your death. If money is in short supply you'll have to get some, because until you are financially secure (or at least until you're sure where the next mortgage payment is coming from), everything else is secondary.

Every widow, no matter what her assets, falls into a panic over her financial future, and you're not going to sleep well until you've done some financial planning and know where you stand.

It may be that you'll have to modify your life style somewhat, but the sooner you realize that, the better. You may have to move to a smaller house or rearrange your spending priorities so you can live well on the money you have. When my father died, my mother turned our house into four apartments, and she lived on the income they produced. I remember how humiliating that felt at the time.

Drawing up a Budget

If you have not done so, add up your assets and liabilities and then develop a budget so you'll know not only if you have enough money to live on but whether you have extra to invest. If you need a banker or stockbroker to help you do this, hire one or use the one your husband employed (see the section later in the chapter about hiring professional help), but get everything on paper.

The first thing to do is collect data about all sources of income:

- your own salary if you have one;
- pensions you're entitled to on your husband's death (don't forget Social Security and veterans benefits);
- death benefits from your husband's insurance;
- stocks, bonds, and other securities and investments; and
- income on real property.

Next, you need to know what your liabilities are, that is, how much it costs to live and what debts you must pay. The easiest way to figure this out is to go back over your canceled checks for the past two or three years and write the amounts you paid out into categories on a multicolumned ledger (you can just as easily use plain paper onto which you've drawn lines)—so much for groceries, so much for rent/mortgage, what you've been spending for clothes, vacations, charitable contributions, entertainment, utilities, state, federal, and local taxes—everything you spend money on. If you go back at least two years, you're more likely to have an accurate picture of how much it costs to live.

Now add up the money you have coming in and what you pay out, and you'll have a pretty good idea of what your financial situation is. If your expenses are greater than your income, you'll need to find sources of income, perhaps from

- a job, although finding one is not easy;
- the sale of property;
- liquidating paper assets;
- help from your children;
- government and private pensions to which you didn't know you are entitled; or
- loans.

If your income is greater than your expenses, count yourself lucky—and don't let it slip through your fingers! Hire a good investment counselor and keep your money safe. There are few things more frightening to widows than facing old age alone and poor.

I had tried for years to get Sam to cooperate in establishing a budget for our professional and household expenses. He always laughed and said, "Budgets are for Cro-Magnon man. The only thing that's really important is nonrecurring items that seem to recur each year in ever-larger amounts, which means you do the best you can. I'll do the best I can and we'll manage."

That satisfied me at the time and I suppose it's all right if you have a husband who has a steady and generous income. But it's not all right now. Even though Sam was the "provider," I had paid most of the bills and thought I understood our situation. But I hadn't figured on travel expenses, taxes, insurance, and a number of other "big-ticket" items that took a sizable chunk out of our income. So I really didn't have an accurate idea of my financial picture until I sat down with my canceled checks and ledger.

You'll also need to decide what financial services you require, and here you can use your mentor (don't forget to choose one who lives in basically the same financial neighborhood you do). Perhaps she has a banker she trusts. Does she need a banker at all, or does her lawyer take care of all that for her? Does she recommend an investment advisor? What does she think is right for you? How much control do you want over your money affairs?

The important thing is that once you've determined that you have enough money to live on (or if you don't, to find at least some temporary sources of income) and that it's *safely* tucked away, *don't* rush into decisions about financial management. Investigate the wide variety of services.

Commercial banks are so competitive now that they all vie for business by offering many services. If you have need for a custodian for securities, a lender for short- or long-term loans, a money fund (sometimes called money market account) to invest cash for its maximum income, an IRA (individual retirement account) to defer taxes on its income until you retire, as well as a checking account, you ought to have *one* person at the bank to whom you have immediate access for everything.

Avoid all the many inefficient and unaccommodating tellers and find a senior officer who is willing to treat you like an adult, who talks to you in language you understand, and is willing to take the time to explain whatever you need to have explained. If you're shy about walking cold into a bank, ask your mentor for her banker and call him to recommend one at your bank—or switch to her bank if it's convenient. This may seem elementary, but I have become almost hysterical over inefficient banking practices and rude employees who refused to take responsibility for their actions.

Take your balance sheet and sketched-in budget to this officer, and you and he or she will decide what services you need and how best the bank can serve you. Don't worry about taking this person's time; that's what banks are there for and they'll do almost anything to keep your business—especially if they think you will refer other customers.

Stockbroker and/or Investment Advisor

Because we traveled so much and had no enormous stockpile of savings and no investment advisor, Sam and I asked a broker to act on our behalf. Whenever we saved enough to make an investment, we gave our funds to him to invest. Then when his management showed a poorer performance than the Standard and Poor, Dow Jones, and T. Rowe Price indexes, we dispensed with his services, which simply means that no matter how completely you trust your investment advisor, or how trustworthy he or she is, you must keep track of things yourself.

I finally took over the handling of our funds. I had the time and inclination and read more investment advice than Sam did. In addition, I served on three investment/pension committees of charitable organizations and learned much from that experience.

I'm old enough to remember the Crash of 1929 and the awful Depression that followed. My father was well off one day and practically broke the next. He was forced to sell all his real estate holdings because he couldn't pay the taxes on them, and the mortgage on our house was foreclosed. Those memories don't fade easily, and I vowed not to let it happen to me. Many of you probably feel the same way.

Unless you have a good deal of expertise in financial matters, you must find a business manager as soon as possible. It can be a close friend or relative (but there are problems inherent in doing business with friends) whom you trust to have your best interest at heart, or you can hire a professional.

One of the things you want your money manager to do is be familiar with the laws dealing with estate planning and taxation—many of which change frequently. Therefore you need someone who's an expert in trusts and estates. Most states allow the surviving spouse to inherit one third or one half of the deceased spouse's assets if he or she did not specify in a will or if the spouse died intestate. As a woman alone now, you should be aware of what you need to know to plan *your* estate.

Your financial advisor may be a stockbroker if you have need of one. A stockbroker is a person who makes money on the commissions earned buying and selling securities. If he or she is wise and privy to good financial market research and trustworthy to watch over and increase your nest egg (keeping in mind that no one is correct all the time), hiring a such a person for brokerage and advice is an inexpensive way to handle investments because brokers are not investment advisors and thus don't charge for advice. But remember, they earn a fee on every sale and purchase, so frequent turnovers benefit them but perhaps not you. You are not obligated to accept all your broker's recommendations, but if you don't accept a major portion of the advice, you're not giving him or her a chance to prove his worth; it might be advisable to look at why you're not and perhaps change brokers.

An investment advisor charges a fee based on a percentage of the money you have to invest, but he or she is not licensed to buy and sell securities. If you have a complicated balance sheet with income from a variety of sources, trust money coming in and going out, and a complex portfolio of stocks, bonds, and other securities, the amount you pay an investment advisor may be worth the fee charged *as long as* he or she does well by you.

In addition to handling your portfolio, an investment advisor/manager can give you advice about

- whether you're in the correct tax bracket and how you can decrease your tax liability;
- owning vs. leasing a car;
- whether you are over- or underinsured;
- refinancing mortgages or outstanding loans; and
- your ratio of stocks to bonds and the amount of liquid assets you require.

Do beware of stock tips from taxi drivers, hairdressers, or even dinner companions *unless* you're a gambling lady and can afford to lose what you invest on an amateur's hunch.

You might want to consider enrolling in an investment class (most community colleges and university extension programs have them), not to learn how to speculate but to become a more sophisticated investor and to become familiar with the vocabulary of the financial world so you can ask more intelligent questions: The one who asks the best questions get the best advice — from stockbrokers, lawyers, physicians and auto mechanics.

Some major investment firms — Shearson Lehman for example — use women on their TV commercials portraying female investment advisors.

Their market, obviously, is women and more than a few of these ads are run in the afternoon when demographics suggest that their viewership is predominately women.

Most of the ads have their basis in the fact that most women have special financial needs and their education regarding financial matters needs to be improved.

Further, Marilyn Crockett, a Paine Webber V.P. and frequent guest on CNN's "Moneyline," offers seminars for women through Long Island University's National Center for Women and Retirement Research. These seminars offer such titles as, "Good News for Women," "Divorce" and "How to Outlive Your Assets."

Most women feel, or would like to feel, that they will have someone to take care of them. However, women *must* realize that not only can they take charge of their finances, but they *must* be able to do so. This, in spite of the fact that many women have been left in jeopardy when widowed or divorced. I personally feel that most women are more comfortable working with a female financial advisor. As I pointed out earlier, more and more women are being promoted to "positions of authority" — reach management — today and this makes them more readily available to the female client. In contrast to their male counterparts, women go to considerable research in regard to their investment decisions. The process is both slow and deliberate and most women only act when they feel "comfortably safe" about their final decision. To this end, many female advisors establish in advance parameters in which the account will be managed. They will first get you to come to grips as to how your assets will be allocated. My advisor asked me how I would feel if my stocks went down more than five points in one day, or if I would sleep better if I were in "low risk" treasury bills, or AAA municipals which are designed to provide a steady income, but little in the way of capital accumulation. She found that most of her clients, myself included, were primarily interested in income, but also wanted the value of their assets under management to increase at least as much as actual inflation.

Once assets are allocated, individual guidelines can be ironed out. Your advisor might suggest "caps" on your account. For example, sell if the stock increases more than ten points, or decreases more than fifteen. Most advisors will still try to discuss all decisions, especially downside ones, regardless.

Bonds do not normally fluctuate as stocks do, but they fell 20% in 1995. The best guidelines is not to put yourself into one asset, such as utilities or textiles or technology, but instead have a sensible asset allocation of solid companies whose foreseeable future should be stable or, still better, soaring — "not putting all your eggs in one basket" — kind of situation.

HOUSING

At some point (again, don't rush into this decision unless you are in desperate need of money), you essentially must decide if you want to keep the house which you lived in with your husband. It may be too large, have too much garden and greenery that must be cared for, be too far from the center of your social activities, or it could be just too expensive to maintain.

Furthermore, remaining there would, most likely, contain too many painful memories.

Once you know your money situation, your decision may be made for you. Should you be unable to afford the house, engage a real estate agent and put it on the market. If you can afford the house, but have strong emotional or practical bias against living in it — *sell it!*

As you already know, your home is one of the most important aspects of your life; it's an extension of your personality, and even if you travel a great deal or are out of the house all day and most evenings, you need a warm, comfortable place to come home to, so if you don't like where you're living, leave.

But don't sell until you've decided where to go. Consider the following:

• City vs. suburbs. Do you want the convenience of the city or the peace and quiet of the suburbs? Is fighting commuter traffic worth the fragrance of fresh-cut grass?

• House vs. apartment. Do you like to putter in the yard and watch the bulbs come up in the spring, or is your idea of gardening watering a few house plants? How do you feel about shoveling snow and raking leaves—or paying someone to do it? Are you tired of having someone on the other side of your wall, maybe playing disco music till the wee hours of the morning?

• Detached house with a yard vs. townhouse. How *much* lawn are you willing to mow? How much privacy do you want?

• Renting vs. owning. Are the tax advantages of a mortgage worth the responsibility of a house? Do you want the freedom of being able to pick up and move at almost a moment's notice, or are you willing to trade that for making a profit when you sell?

• An apartment or condominium in a retirement complex vs. a more general neighborhood. Do you want a more structured life style and neighbors who are about your own age, or are you happiest living among people of all ages? Both have advantages, although the former usually appeals to older people.

Your happiness and comfort are the most important considerations in choosing a place to live. If you really want a little house in the suburbs, but all your friends live in the city, buy the house—or stay where you are. Live where it pleases you to live, not where you (or your children) think you *should* live. Consider also proximity to your children. Do you want to see them often? Do they want to see you? Are you your grandchildren's best and favorite baby-sitter? If so, you may want to move closer.

36

If you decide to rent, choose a location first and then look through the newspaper. (You might even decide to place your own ad as a friend of mine did: "Two single ladies, one artist, one Dalmation, seek small but charming country home to rent." She was inundated with replies.) Be sure also to put the word out with friends and call on real estate firms.

If you decide to buy, your attorney will take care of all the legal details of closing and settlement, but a house is not your only option. Cooperative apartments (called co-ops) and condominiums (condos) are increasingly popular.

In the co-op system, you buy shares in a building but do not purchase the apartment itself. As a lessee, you pay a share of the building's maintenance costs such as mortgage, insurance, and taxes, some of which are tax deductible. For this fee, you have sole rights to occupy a designated apartment and are responsible for its maintenance. But you cannot sell or assign (sublet) your apartment without the approval of the building's board of directors, and if a fellow lessee defaults, everyone else is responsible for his or her fees until a replacement is found. (That's one of the reasons why boards of directors go over prospective tenants' financial records with a fine-toothed comb.)

There are fewer purchase and resale restrictions on a condo. In this case, you own your own apartment which, in some complexes, is built so that it is partially separated from other units, providing more privacy. While you are not personally responsible for maintaining the grounds and the outside of the building and common areas, you do pay a share (called a condo fee) for their upkeep. Savings associations and mortgage companies consider a condo a private home, so they're more inclined to lend money for one rather than for a share in a co-op. You can mortgage a condo and borrow on your investment as with a regular house.

If you move into any place other than your own private home, make certain you know at the outset what the rules are about pets if you have one. Many condos and apartment buildings don't allow animals at all and will either force you to get rid of the animal or evict you. Some have rules but will look the other way when it comes to goldfish, hamsters, or even a cat.

If you don't have a pet, consider getting one. They can make an enormous difference in the quality of your life, especially now that you're alone. They provide companionship and an antidote to loneliness, and the responsibility of having to care for them forces structure into your life. The best part, of course, is that they give and receive love and warm feelings—something you're missing right now. Your dog or cat can't respond to your unhappiness with words, but pets do respond in very real and tangible ways, and their fur coats can soak up a lot of tears. A living creature for whom you are responsible can significantly change the quality of your widowhood.

In choosing a pet, you need to decide between cuddly (dogs, cats, rabbits) and noncuddly (fish, turtles), and you must think about how much responsibility you're willing to take on (dogs vs. cats, or fish vs. mammals). In general, the amount of responsibility involved is proportional to the amount of responsiveness; that is, a turtle doesn't need to be walked three times a day, but it's not going to thump its tail with happiness and put its head on your knee when you come home. And you don't have to clean a fish's litter box, but it won't curl up next to you and purr its contentment, and you can't scratch its belly.

4

INSURANCE

Next to the security of having a roof over your head and enough money to live comfortably, insurance is your most important asset. You must protect your health, your home and its contents, and the people for whom your death would be an economic catastrophe.

Both my father, my darling Sam and, I suppose, any man worth his salt, bought his first life insurance policy right out of college or at an early age to cover his final expenses. In my day that would have read as funeral expenses. Today we think of taxes and many other "final expenses." If he is successful during his lifetime, most men will generally buy several more insurance contracts to cover various needs which occur during the normal course of human events (i.e., life policies to cover a mortgages(s), projected educational expenses, to indemnify a business, or to continue his income in case he is disabled, are to name but a few of the reasons).

If he is hugely successful, he will then purchase a single, or series of large policies (one, two, three million and up) to take care of — you guessed it — FINAL EXPENSES! That policy is generally the purchase of raw dollars with which to pay the inheritance taxes that will be imposed upon the heirs of his estate.

Far more than half the wealth in the United States today is in control of women. Although much of this capital is the result of divorce settlements and inheritance, the largest portion stems from proceeds of personal insurance, group insurance benefits, or a combination thereof.

This, most likely, is also true of the majority of the world's industrial democracies.

You are now alone. What should you do? I hope that your husband had the counsel of a well-respected member of the "professional" insurance community. Should this be the case, you are far ahead in the game. If not, read on.

DO I NEED LIFE INSURANCE?

This depends on your age, the way your assets are presently invested, and the ages of your children. If they are minors, the answer is a resounding "yes." If they are adults, the answer is "perhaps" if they are self-supporting and can afford their own children's education.

At this point, you may want to consider some type of annuity as both a current investment, as well as a plan for your retirement years. Insurance annuities offer an attractive return as well as a safeguard of your principal. Let me, however, offer a word of caution. Deal only with someone with whom you have formerly dealt or someone highly recommended by your attorney, your accountant, the friends whose judgement you respect, or all three. There are many scam artists masquerading as investment counselors, estate planners or financial advisors. Sadly, the only financial and estate planning they want to do is their own — and with *your* money. The old "buzz words" still apply here — Caveat Emptor — let the buyer beware.

Never deal with salesmen whom you do not know or solicit you "cold" over the telephone. Although there are many extremely honest young people trying to build a client base with "cold calls" and telephone solicitation, there are an equal number of unscrupulous souls who make their living preying upon unsuspecting widows and lone females. The obituary pages are quite literally "happy hunting grounds," no disrespect intended, for these scoundrels.

If you have an inheritance in excess of six figures, it might be in your best interest to establish a "Financial Planning Team" consisting of your accountant, insurance agent and attorney, as well as a corporate trustee, should your "team" deem the latter necessary.

TYPES OF INSURANCE

Since I am not an insurance expert, let me simply explain what I understand is currently available with a comment or two about each type of of coverage.

Term Insurance

This is used to provide the cheapest form of coverage. It provides no cash accumulation, but assures that one will have money payable to *one's* beneficiary at the time of one's death. Term insurance is generally written for a "term" or specific time period — one year with an option to renew, which some feel is a good buy; or a 5-year or 10-year term, or better still to age 70, 75 or older. There is even a more recent product offering term for life.

Whole Life or Permanent Insurance

These policies create value. They cost more, perhaps, but some of the premium you pay goes into a savings account (cash value) and you receive interest or dividends on your principal after a few years. You can even borrow from yourself at about 6% to 8% interest. Correctly structured, the cash value of these policy contracts grows tax free. In some cases even a withdrawal of money can be exempt from income taxes. A myriad of policies are available in this category. Some of what you earn on your capital invested in these contracts has guaranteed values which are correlated to U.S. Treasury Bills, while some policies are keyed to the investment performance of the issuing company. It should be in your best interest to have an insurance professional explain what the investment record of that particular insurance company has been for the past 10 years, or longer.

These policies come with esoteric names such as Universal Life, Variable Universal, Interest Sensitive Whole Life, Variable Life, Whole Life, etc. The "ordinary" life insurance of yesteryear is "not so ordinary" anymore. Today's insurance policy is a tremendous place to "park" your available dollars which can be used at a later date for other investments, extraordinary travel or unexpected capital purchase. In fact, some professionals use the modern insurance vehicle as their personal banking institution, if they do not feel they have the time nor expertise to invest their savings in other vehicles.

It's important to any decision on an insurance policy to consider riders that can be attached to the modern Life Insurance Policy. Most basic is the "premium waiver." Simply stated, the premiums you are obligated to pay will be cancelled should you become disabled for a specific time.

However, your values and benefits will continue to increase and the death benefit maintains its stability, just as though you were continuing to make payments. Reasonably priced, this should be considered a "best buy."

Conversely, a "double indemnity rider" or the "accidental death benefit" (ADB) appears to be overpriced and is not anywhere near the top of the list of "best buys." It might cost more than it should to protect you.

There are also "term" riders and even "income protection" riders which will pay you a lump sum or a regular monthly payment in the event of your disability.

One of the newest, and most popular riders, is the "Accelerated Death Benefit." Specifically, this rider allows you to use a portion of your policy's death benefit prior to your death should you need the money and if certain conditions are met. These conditions will vary by the offering company. For example, if you are diagnosed as being terminally ill and death is anticipated to occur within a reasonably short period of time, you can elect that a portion of your death benefit to be paid to you immediately. This amount varies between companies and ranges between 25% and 100% of the face amount of your policy. Before electing the accelerated death benefit rider, make certain you have a wise insurance agent explain its details, read the complicated language aloud to you, and be sure you understand it.

Let me remind you that we are all different and our situations vary. Common sense and sound professional advice are the keys to you building a solid insurance portfolio.

My husband was a wonderful provider and thankfully we never wanted for material things. In that respect, I have been most fortunate. At this printing, however, while I am in my 78th year, I am investigating the purchase of a rather substantial insurance policy.

Why? Simply because Sam was so successful and I have had such reliable advice over the years that I could possibly need to purchase additional "dollars-at-a-discount." For what? FINAL EXPENSES to pay increased inheritance taxes! I did not work, save, or invest, only to endow the Federal Government. I would prefer to choose the good causes myself to endow at my death. I have discovered that one is never too old to purchase insurance!

HEALTH INSURANCE

Most widows become well acquainted with COBRA — no, not the slithery (ugh) kind — but a program represented by that acronym which will provide you with your health insurance coverage should you become widowed, divorced, or even become unemployed. COBRA stands for the Consolidated Omnibus Budget Reconciliation Act, which states that as a dependent under health insurance program, you have certain options. They are:

(1) If you are widowed or divorced, you may continue coverage under your former husband's health plan for up to 36 months at 102% of the premium paid by his former employer.

(2) If your husband is disabled from his employment, his coverage and yours will continue under his employer's program for 29 months, at the 102% figure.

(3) In the event of your husband's termination, coverage may be continued for 18 months at 102% of the premium. Most of my contacts in the insurance arena tend to believe that the benefit will become unilateral for the 36-month period, or even longer, in the foreseeable future. There is, however, another option. If your husband was self-employed and not covered under a group plan, you may choose to buy Short-Term Medical coverage. This is temporary coverage, covered and written, for a period of no longer than a year, offering a very reasonable premium payment while you shop for permanent health insurance. There is one catch-all, which exists in most of these policies, and that is that they generally do not cover pre-existing sickness. The Kennedy/Kassebaum bill passed, but rules still vary and are vague. There is, however, pending legislation which would assure coverage despite pre-existing illnesses, and the new bill requires portability of health coverage between jobs.

If you are dollar conscious — and who isn't — a traditional indemnity plan with a high deductible may be for you. With escalating hospital costs, a program with a $1,000, $2,000, or even a $3,000 deductible could possibly be right for you. A $2,000 deductible program shapes up as follows:

(a) You pay the first *$2,000*.
(b) The insurance company pays 80% of the balance up to $5,000. (Plans are available with 50% and 90% co-insurance as well.)
(c) The health insurance company usually undertakes to pay 100% of either *$1,000.000, $2,000,000* or an *unlimited* benefit.

Therefore, on a $100,000 claim, your obligation of the bill is $3,000 (the $2,000 deductible, plus 20% of $5,000, or $1,000 the sum of A and B). Naturally, just as in all other insurance policies, the higher the deductible the lower the cost.

Finally, if you are a younger mother or father or mother/widow and are currently employed, you can insure your risks of becoming unable to work, by purchasing disability income (income continuation). This should be a *must* for a young single parent.

Faced with the decision of which health care program to provide for yourself and any dependents, today's dilemmas are almost impossible to solve. Any insurance advisor worth his/her salt will tell you, up front, that whatever they advise today might not be a wise course of action six months later. Legislation providing any additional health care coverage from governmental sources is pending and may not have passed at the publication date of this book.

HEALTH MAINTENANCE ORGANIZATIONS (HMOs)

Since health care is a life-or-death matter to most people, we must be aware, when thinking of providing for our care, of the large corporations behind it. Managed care, or HMOs, have moved into the mainstream of how we provide for ourselves. There is U.S. Healthcare (recently merged with *A*etna), United Health Care (merged with the Metra Group), and Blue Cross and Blue Shield, which is now owned by a large hospital company. The bigger these "providers" are the better and cheaper your costs should be, but that has not yet happened.

After comparing the offerings of an HMO, see if the top notch doctors in your area are included, and see what you have to pay should your favorite specialist, or primary care physician is not listed. Oxford is the fastest growing HMO operation in the New York area where I live. Its stock has skyrocketed, but that does not mean their health care is better, but I like them because they have found new ways to deliver cost-effective services to asthma sufferers (ME) and to others with chronic conditions. It will remain to be seen if they can keep up this performance, and what other companies will enter the competition. Most Oxford members, according to Dr. Susan Dentzer of Newsweek, are satisfied, even though she points out that certain well-connected enrollees have had the exceptions (what their policy doesn't pay) waived if they are famous or favorite corporate clients.

As a member of the Board of a fine hospital on Long Island, I do know that insurance companies personnel reviewing claims for hospital stays, whether we can keep a patient another day when WE feel that their condition requires it, are told "when in doubt, carve it out" (disallow payment). I have appealed a denial of payment to another large insurance company and collected most of what I had been denied formerly. Few of us can afford the time or money for such an appeal, even though it is usually in small claims court and one can appeal in person without a lawyer. I feel that you should find an insurance professional who can guide you through the choppy waters of the system, so that you are personally satisfied that you have enrolled in a program which will give you as much care as possible for what you can afford to pay. This pertains to those who are seeking a so-called Medicare supplemental care package through a Medigap Managed Care Policy (HMO) or whether you are younger than 60 and just need to provide for all contingencies.

Many people whom I polled are satisfied with their HMO and others are satisfied with the corporate plan they have or have inherited. This is one field in which it is prudent to do some comparison shopping.

The ground rules of insuring oneself against catastrophic medical bills (all those your regular budget cannot pay) will be changing very frequently before we get it "right," if ever. Certainly those who are receiving Medicare as we know it now, should pay a great deal less than those without. "Stay tuned" each week for the latest legislation and the latest best offerings to insure yourself against medical expenses your ordinary income cannot afford.

MEDICARE

Medicare is a federal program, created by a 1965 amendment to the Social Security act, which provides hospital and medical care coverage for people sixty-five years of age or older, some disabled people, and those with end-stage kidney disease. (By the way, do not confuse Medicare with Medicaid, which is a joint federal-state program, also created by the Social Security Act, that provides health services to people who exist at or below the poverty level and have no other way to pay for health care.)

Medicare is *not* charity, anymore than are retirement benefits from Social Security. It is a government entitlement or transfer program, originally designed to provide health benefits for older people who could not afford them for themselves.

Medicare has two parts, both of which are administered through private insurance companies, called carriers. Part A is designed as hospital insurance, and Part B covers Physicians and outpatient services. As a true government entitlements, Medicare is not entirely free; you must pay a monthly premium, and there is a good deal of paperwork involved in claiming medical costs reimbursement from providers (hospitals, doctors, and others who provide health care). However, all hospitals and almost all doctors have plenty of forms available, as does the insurance carrier through which you make your claim.

Medicare covers very basic health care services, such as inpatient hospital care and most of the services provided while you are hospitalized, skilled nursing care, diagnostic tests of most types, emergency care, and some durable medical equipment such as wheelchairs, walkers, crutches and the like.

Medicare paperwork is extremely complex, but all forms must be completed correctly and mailed to your carrier in order for the claim to be paid. In order to expedite matters, try the following:

■ Take a Medicare claim form with you to appointments with any and all health providers (doctors, dentists, X-ray technicians, etc.), and do not leave the office until it has been filled out and signed.

■ Mail the form to the office indicated, and within a week or two, you will receive a return form (with or without a check enclosed) in the mail called a Medicare Explanation of Benefits (MEOB).

■ If, as is usual, the check does not cover the full amount of your medical expense, and if you have a Medicare supplemental policy, mail the MEOB to your carrier in order to receive reimbursement for the balance of your expense.

Medicare does not pay for:
Prescription drugs
Eye glasses
Dentures
Dental care
Hearing aids
Routine physicals
Inoculations

The first three pints of blood for transfusion
ANY MEDICAL CARE RECEIVED OUTSIDE THE U.S.

As of this writing, coverage for nursing home care is even skimpier. If the facility is not Medicare certified — and most of the nicest ones are not — Medicare pays nothing.

Medicare does *not* pay for any private duty nursing. If you are fortunate enough to have had a supplemental care program with the organization for which you or your husband worked which included you, as a surviving spouse, then you will probably elect to continue paying the premiums for that policy. If, however, you compare other supplemental plans to Medicare, and find that the corporate plan you can inherit is much more expensive than others available with the same benefits, you should consider changing. Do not give up a sure thing from which you can receive benefits for an unknown choice without consulting those participating in both.

As an example, I was able to continue as a member of the group plan which my husband carried after his death. The price for continuing with his law firm plan was about $210 per month. However, the AARP Plan F, cost only about $90 per month! The AARP plan did not pay for prescription drugs, but I take very few, so it was worth the switch. It would not have been if I required any expensive prescription drugs. I must point out that AARP offers a somewhat more expensive plan that covers drugs as well. Actually, after purchasing the AARP policy, I have come across several privately issued contracts that are even more reasonable.

If you are under Medicare age, you must REALLY study carefully the health policies available. If you are employed, you most likely have a group health plan, part of an HMO.

Many doctor's on Long Island have formed their own HMO, and say it is much better for the patients than those owned by corporate executives. Even the American Medical Association is sponsoring a Capital Source Program, designed specifically to help physicians secure funds to invest in such an undertaking. About 80% of the HMOs are not doctor owned and managed, are profit-making corporations and, therefore, must be carefully scrutinized. Critics of all HMOs saw that the fierce competition among them is forcing payments to providers below that which would make possible the best treatment required in many cases. One of the big corporate HMOs with more than one million subscribers. One spends 30% of its revenue on administrative costs and profits. A Long Island doctor once said, "Their president makes millions — that is a lot of money — money which should be spent on open heart surgery or extra kidneys." Doctors say they are best positioned to curtail costs as they best understand the delivery of care.

LONG-TERM CARE

By the year 2000, more than 8 million Americans age 65 and older will need some type of long-term care because of disability or chronic illness, an increase of 56 percent over 1980. One study showed that 2.3 million people age 65 and over will spend at least part of a year nursing home, and an additional 4 million people received professional health care in their homes. I don't mean to frighten you — but facts are facts — and this can represent a serious drain on your savings, especially since a stay in a nursing home costs between two and three thousand dollars a month.

Long term care doesn't necessarily mean that you will be confined to a nursing home, but it does mean that you will require some type of professional assistance at home, such as visiting nurses, home health aides, Meals on Wheels, or hospice care, all of which is expensive.

Neither Medicare nor private Medicare supplemental insurance (known as Medigap) policies, nor the health insurance you may have through your employer, will pay for most long-term care expenses.

Medicare does not cover long-term care, nor does it provide nursing home benefits on home health care except in extremely limited circumstances.

Long-term care insurance may be something you want to consider in the event of your disability. It is a relatively new type of private insurance, and most, and most of the policies are indemnity type, which means they can pay a fixed dollar amount per day for nursing home or home health care. No policy, however, provides full coverage for all expenses, and many policies do not increase the indemnity as the cost of care increases over time, so you must read the policy carefully before you buy. In particular, you should check the following points before buying a long-term care policy.

■ You should determine if it makes sense for you to buy a policy in the first place. If you don't have at least fifty thousand dollars in savings, you probably don't have enough to cover the premiums.

■ The policy should also cover skilled, intermediate, and custodial care, the third of which the most crucial because it is the most basic coverage you will need.

■ Make certain that the benefit payouts are not contingent on being hospitalized before receiving long-term care. For many long-term conditions (for instance, Alzheimer's disease), hospitalization prior to long-term needs is highly unlikely. Since about half the patients in nursing homes today are not hospitalized prior to their admission to the home, this is an important consideration.

■ The policy should also cover long-term care in the home, which may be offered as a rider at an extra charge.

■ Look at the clause in the policy that covers "organically based mental conditions." This is an industry term for Alzheimer's disease and other senile dementias.

■ Be suspicious of a policy that has a longer than 21-day deductible or elimination period — that is, the amount of time you require long-term care before the policy's benefits kick in.

■ An "inflation protection" feature is an essential component and covers the rising cost of care.

■ Buy a policy only from an insurance company that is financially sound. Ask the agent to supply the company's rating from any one of several rating services. (Standard and Poor, Duffs, and A.M. Best, just to name three.)

■ Find out the penalties involved if you miss a premium or are late with payment. This is called a "grace period" and should be no less than seven days, but look for a policy with a 31-day period if you can.

■ Find out if any types of nursing homes are excluded from the policy. For instance, some policies will cover the care of only Medicare-approved nursing homes.

Long-term care coverage is also offered as part of some individual life insurance policies. Under this arrangement, a certain percentage of the policy's death benefit is paid for each month the policyholder requires long-term care.

Each type of long-term care policy is priced differently. For example, in 1987, individual policy premiums ranged from about $250 a year to more than $2,500, depending on factors such as the time the policy is purchased, the size of the deductible, the extent of the benefits provided, and the indemnity value. For more information and a list of companies offering policies, write to the Health Insurance Association of America, PO Box 41455, Washington, DC 20018.

This modicum of insight into your "living risks" and how to deal with them might help you plan your future, whether you remain alone or remarry. But, now what about insurance on your valuables, house, auto, et. al.? Let's take a look at them as well.

CASUALTY AND MISCELLANEOUS INSURANCE

You probably already have household insurance, which you ought to continue. The only time you need to think about changing your coverage is if you move or increase or decrease the value of your possessions. If you never had an appraisal made of your household goods, now is the time.

Going from room to room of your house, opening all the drawers and closets to locate and itemize all your assets is a tedious process, but you don't have to do it all in one day. However, when you've written down every single thing you own and the value of each (with purchase records attached if you have them), you will have a complete idea of your net worth, which is important not only for insurance purposes but will be necessary when you draw up a will. It'll also make things a lot easier for your heirs.

If you have items of value, it might be worthwhile to hire an appraiser. If neither you nor your friends know of one, contact the American Society of Appraisers at P.O.Box 17265, Washington, D.C. 20041 (703-620-3828). Ask for the free Directory of Certified Professional Personal Property Appraisers, and include a self-addressed stamped envelope. In addition, it's a good idea to take color snapshots of each room and its contents, with close-ups of items of particular value, including art, china, silver, and glassware. This written and photographic inventory should then be in your insurance agent's or lawyer's files in case of fire or theft. (Don't take the pictures and then just stuff them in a drawer to be stolen or burned up with the rest of your belongings!)

My three wise sons-in-law suggested that carrying a personal property floater in the large amount I did was a useless expense, and it probably is if all my jewelry and other items are added to my household policy. In addition, there are other types of insurance that are a waste of money.

- Air travel insurance. If you have dependents, buy good comprehensive life insurance that covers you in the event of death from ANY cause. Air travel is remarkably safe, so you're not likely to die in a plane, and if you do, your survivors will probably sue someone anyway.

- Mugging insurance. Comprehensive life, health, and property/casualty insurance will cover whatever happens to you during a mugging.

- Contact lens insurance. The premium costs more than a new lens.

- Pet health insurance (unless Fido or Puff is very old and sickly). Vet bills are still reasonable, but if third-party payers get into the act, costs will skyrocket.

51

■ Mortgage or credit insurance. Good life insurance will protect your dependents against economic catastrophe, and it's much less expensive than credit or mortgage insurance.

■ $100-a-day health insurance. The average cost of a hospital stay is a thousand dollars a day. Get good comprehensive health insurance and don't waste your money on other schemes.

■ Rain insurance. This is another scam. If your house is seriously damaged by rain, your homeowner's policy will cover the repair costs.

Some people think it's better to be one's own insurer. That is, you pay a certain amount of money, earmarked for insurance, into an interest-bearing account. In the event of fire or other loss, you withdraw funds from the account to pay for the loss. This scheme is based on the theory that you can invest your insurance protection money as advantageously as an insurance company. The downside is that you must make sure to deposit the money periodically and not to touch it — no matter how tempted. It can be a risky thing to do unless you're VERY self-disciplined, but if it appeals to you and you're up to the challenge, try it.

If you own a car you'll need to insure it. Policies and premiums differ widely from state to state and even in areas within a state. Rates also vary with the kind of car you own, how much you drive, and what your driving record is. You can save yourself a great deal of money if you shop around and use consumer guides. For instance, my broker suggested that I keep my car registered at my Long Island home rather than my Manhattan one — a considerable savings each year. *Consumer Reports,* located in Mt. Vernon, New York, publishes a guide to various types of insurance.

* * *

Before discussing any of your insurance needs with your agent, make a list of the type of coverage you think you'll need — and why. Talk it over with your mentor and ask them what they insure and what she leaves to fate. For example, if your children are grown and independent, do you really need to insure your life for their benefit?

Wouldn't it be more productive to take that money and put it into a fund to help pay for your grandchildren's college education? Or if you have very expensive jewelry that you never wear, keep it in a safe deposit box rather than insured at home.

Don't let yourself be persuaded that expensive policies give you more coverage and better service. Get yourself covered realistically, but don't insure anyting you can comfortably replace. Avoid duplications of coverage. If you work in your home, as I do, you may need insurance to cover employees and/or clients.

Ask your broker for an itemized schedule of each policy you own, what it covers, when it comes due, and what the annual charge is for each. That way you have a ready reference list whenever you want to re-evaluate your insurance needs.

5

CHOOSING AND USING A LAWYER — AND OTHER LEGAL MATTERS

*T*he words "lawyer" and "attorney" can be frightening to many people, especially widows whose husbands have always taken care of the family's legal matters. But one's relationship to a competent attorney can also be reassuring when trouble (or what is first perceived as trouble) looms on the horizon.

Although justice is not always blind, the law does exist to protect us, and we use it many times a day, often without realizing it: when we write a check, buy merchandise, sign a contract, rent an apartment. Unfortunately, most people don't understand the law, and what is poorly understood can be frightening. Much legal vocabulary is confusing and written in such a way that even the most clear-headed among us can't figure it out—and that's not counting all the Latin expressions. So it's no wonder that perfectly intelligent people sit in their attorney's office and feel lost and helpless, wondering what everything means and how to make sense of it.

One of the purposes of this chapter is to sort it all out for you and help you take the process of choosing and using an attorney one easy step at a time.

I will rely on my three decades as a practicing attorney to discuss what we as widows need to know about hiring and working with a lawyer. Chances are, you already have an attorney—most likely one that your husband hired or used in his business—or have used one to draw up a will or arrange settlement on a house, but you have to decide whether to continue with him or her, or to find someone else.

When you "come to" after the initial siege of devastating grief, you as a new widow will need a lawyer to help plan, manage—and eventually dispose of—your own and your late husband's estate. And by the way, don't make the mistake of thinking that just because you don't have pots and pots of money that you don't have an estate; everyone owns something and whatever you own constitutes your estate, and it is very important to you. You may also want or need protection from unscrupulous people bent on moving into your life when you are feeling most vulnerable.

Unless you are an especially litigious person or have a propensity for getting into trouble, you won't need a lawyer often, and when you do, your needs will be varied, so your best bet is a generalist who practices in a large firm (or who has referral access to one) with many specialties. For the most part, you'll need a lawyer for only a limited number of tasks—and those not very often:

- drawing up a will;
- drawing up a living will (also called a health care proxy directive, and you don't really need a lawyer for that) and/or a power of attorney for management of financial matters during a long absence from home or in case of illness;
- an occasional consumer complaint matter that you can't handle yourself;
- involvement in an automobile accident or liability suit;
- being a victim of a crime;
- having to make an appearance in court as a witness;
- representation in a civil suit;
- tax issues (although a good accountant can help here); and
- real estate transactions.

FINDING AN ATTORNEY

If your husband had an attorney, you must decide whether you want to continue with him or her, or find a new one. If you decide to change, try not to feel guilty (unless, of course, the attorney is a close relative, a situation that presents its own special problems of doing business with family members).

An attorney is *your* employee, in a manner of speaking, and although it's never pleasant to fire someone, if he or she is not serving your needs, find someone else. And you don't even have to do it in person; a polite letter will suffice.

But how do you decide if you need a new lawyer or can make do with the old one? Here are some things that might help you decide.

• Do you *like* him or her? Good rapport with an attorney is essential because he or she will be handling some of your most personal and intimate affairs, most likely when you are under an enormous amount of emotional and financial stress. Two single women (one widow and one divorcée) I know well, both very intelligent and practical women, changed their attorneys because they felt patronized and condescended to when their husbands were no longer on the scene.

• Do you *trust* the lawyer? This is something only you can discern—either by experience or by gut reaction, or both. If you don't have *absolute* trust in your attorney, find another.

• Was the lawyer really your husband's and served his business needs and thus is not appropriate for you?

• Are his or her rates fair and can you afford them?

Finding a lawyer may seem like a Herculean task if you live in a big city because there are so many of them. (In Washington, D.C., where I spent the early years of my marriage, one in every fourteen people is an attorney!) Even small towns have more than enough attorneys to go around. And most of them are competent. There is no such thing as the "best" lawyer in town, just as there is no such thing as the best doctor or the best concert pianist or the best actress. You need an attorney who is good at what he or she does, who will serve you well, and in whom you have confidence. Any one of dozens can fulfill this function, so how do you choose?

I'll be providing some specific suggestions, but as you begin your search, keep in mind that you are looking for a person with whom you will be working in a close and confidential relationship for a long—probably indefinite—time. Therefore, you want your attorney to see to it that *your* best interests and desires are served in the most equitable manner possible.

But by the same token, your attorney is not a substitute for your husband, nor can you expect him or her to be a friend or a counselor to you in your grief. If it works out that he or she becomes a friend after you have enjoyed a good professional relationship, that is frosting on the cake (which can have a tendency to go stale, so always beware of doing business with friends).

Now, how do you go about actually finding and hiring a lawyer? Basically, it's the same process as hiring anyone else to provide a service: You do research, interview them, and try them out once. Here's how:

• Ask your friends. Tell three or four people what you're looking for and ask them why they like their lawyers and what they don't like about them. All your friends either have lawyers of their own or know people who do. Seek out people who have problems and potential problems similar to your own. For example, if you have a large and complicated estate with several real estate holdings and a large stock portfolio, you ought to ask people who have similar financial situations. Someone who has only a salary and a small income from her husband's life insurance isn't going to be much help finding you a lawyer.

• If you're new in town and have not made friends you can trust, you can do one of two things: Ask your old friends if they have connections in your new city, or use the legal referral service of the local bar association listed in the telephone book of most major metropolitan areas. The bar association does not charge a referral fee and will provide the names of two or three attorneys of the specialty you seek.

A commercial legal referral service may charge a small fee, but it's worth it to narrow down your choice to a few attorneys who have practices that best suit your needs. (By the way, it is best not to rely on television commercials for lawyers.) Some commercial services provide nothing more than a list of lawyers, and others provide information about specialty, length of practice, and type of experience. You are unlikely to get comparison information about fees from a legal referral service. You might also go to the library and ask for the Martindale-Hubbell Law Directory, which lists attorneys by city, state, and educational background. A rating for each individual is conferred by other local attorneys (an "A" rating is the highest), and in the back there is an advertising section of sorts. If you find yourself in a small town, you may just have to pick several lawyers out of the phone book (or ask the real estate agent who sold you your house) and interview them.

• In any event, you ought to interview a lawyer before you hire him or her—and before you're in a legal mess. You'll be charged for the time, but the investment will ultimately be worth it in eventual satisfaction. Some attorneys will charge a nominal first-time fee if there is no legal work involved. Ask first. It's also good practice to interview several attorneys before you make a final choice.

• Ask where he or she went to law school, although ultimately that might not be as important as where the lawyer's early training occurred. If you want to know, and if you believe it's important (and if you have the nerve), ask where the attorney was ranked academically in law school.

• Ask about his or her tax expertise, as this may constitute the bulk of your legal needs. Find out if he or she is also a certified public accountant (CPA) or if there is one in the office.

This brings up the question of whether you should choose a lawyer who is part of a large or small firm. The large firm may be long on experience and have a wide variety of specialists for immediate consultation, but the disadvantage is that unless you have lots of complex legal work and are bringing a great deal of revenue to the firm, you will be a small fish in a very large pond and may get stuck with a very junior associate who may or may not have appropriate supervision.

In a small firm, you will receive more personalized service, probably at lower cost, but the lawyers may not be as experienced and may not have ready access to the types of specialization you need. In this case, you need to feel assured that the attorney will refer your case elsewhere if he or she cannot handle the intricacies of a highly specialized problem.

• Ask about fees. Many women hesitate to discuss money, either because they have been brought up to think it's less than polite or because their husbands have always taken care of the financial end of things and they just don't know how to ask.

But this is *not* the time to be shy or to hide behind a mistaken perception of etiquette. Lawyers are expensive—everyone knows that, but their fees can range from as low as fifty or sixty dollars an hour in a small town to three to five hundred dollars in big cities. And the client pays for *everything:* photocopying, telephone conversations, messenger delivery service, court costs, even postage. And all this is over and above the actual time spent doing legal work. So find out at the outset what the hourly rate is and what the ancillary costs are likely to be.

Also inquire about the way fees are based. For example, do the rates differ for different types of services? In a divorce, for instance, the charges may be a flat fee or a deposit on account. An hourly rate for professional time spent on your matter, together with out-of-pocket expenses, is another basis for legal fees. A contingency fee is also used, particularly when the attorney asks for no "up front" money but takes a percentage of the ultimate settlement, which is a common fee structure in personal injury cases. The way a fee is set depends on how much work is involved and the complexity of the situation, as well as the way that particular lawyer works. If the lawyer foresees difficulties in the case, he or she may insist on being put on retainer. In probate cases, fees are usually set by the state according to the size of the estate and the time involved. Know at the outset what those charges are likely to be.

The bill you receive at the end of the case will be shocking enough. You do *not* want any rude surprises! You should also ask how payment is expected and when it is due. Are installment payments possible, and if this is a divorce proceeding, will the husband pay all or part of the fee?

• Find out who will be handling the bulk of your legal work: the lawyer, an associate, or a paralegal.

INTERVIEWING AN ATTORNEY

You must interview an attorney before choosing one. You wouldn't take a job without being interviewed, and you didn't get married before getting to know your man. Your relationship with an attorney, although different from a job or a husband, is no less intimate and important in many ways, so make no decisions before getting to know the person who will handle important and intimate aspects of your life.

When you are making the appointment, find out how much the initial conversation will cost, and tell the attorney or his secretary that this will be an exploratory discussion only, that you are talking to several lawyers to see who is best equipped to handle your legal affairs.

Your goals at the initial interview are twofold. First, you want to make a judgment about how the lawyer relates to you, and second, you want to determine if this is the *right* attorney for you. Notice and pay attention to the following:

• Does the office seem efficiently managed? Is the receptionist pleasant or harried?

• When you are with the attorney, does he or she give you undivided attention, or is he constantly interrupted by phone calls? In the future, when you are not paying a flat "initial interview" rate, the attorney may be charging *you* for the time you are sitting in the office while he talks to someone else *and* charging the person on the other end of the phone.

• Does he or she explain things in language you can understand, and if not, why not? Do you feel patronized or condescended to? Does the attorney behave as if your problems are important enough to give them his or her undivided attention, or are you made to feel insignificant?

• Was the lawyer on time for the initial appointment, and if he or she kept you waiting a few minutes (no more than the briefest wait after the appointed hour is acceptable), is an apology forthcoming?

• If you know at the outset that you will have specialized work, find out if your state has certification exams for certain specialties, and if so, ask if the lawyer has taken and passed them.

• Ask him or her for the names of several of his clients (or better yet, find out on your own, if you can) and call them to get the "scoop" on his or her performance.

MAINTAINING THE RELATIONSHIP

It may be difficult for you to speak your mind, especially when you have been used to having your husband take care of business, but you must be assertive. You are now responsible for the matter about which you need legal advice, and it will be *your* name on the contract, will, or whatever document you ultimately sign. And it will be to *you* that the attorney's bill comes, so be certain you understand the process you are about to undertake.

A good attorney should know approximately how long a case or other legal matter will take and what the pitfalls might be, although you must make allowances for complexities that neither of you could have anticipated. He or she should also be able to estimate the ultimate cost. And be certain that you get something more specific than, "This shouldn't be very expensive," or "This will cost you a bundle."

You must understand each and every document you sign. If it seems written in Sanskrit, don't sign unless and until you have the material written in language you understand. Insist on this. You are *not* being difficult, nor does it demonstrate ignorance. Instead, you're being smart enough to know your rights and responsibilities and assertive enough to take control of your life.

If you build a good personal relationship with your attorney, he or she can guide you in a number of business and financial areas. One of my wisest friends, long employed in high-level jobs in the business world, makes it a policy to, as she calls it, "bind herself personally" to her lawyer, accountant, investment advisors, and doctors. To achieve this relationship, my friend invites them to her home for meals and shows them other personal kindnesses. The result is that she becomes a person as well as a client or patient and feels that they have genuine concern for her health, welfare, and future. My friend believes this is a sound idea and thinks that this approach to the professional matters in her life has paid off in the quality of representation and care she receives. In addition, she feels enriched by the friendships of talented professionals.

All professionals would not accept such personal overtures, but you can tell very soon when or if such a gesture would be appropriate. Use your judgment.

Other women may feel as though they want to keep their professional relationships and friendships separate, except in those rare instances when the two naturally overlap. Just as many people feel it is better not to do business with friends, they think it is better not to turn professional relationships into friendships. There is something to be said for both approaches—it all depends on the kind of person you are and how you are used to handling such relationships.

But try not to fall in love with your lawyer! This isn't as far-fetched an idea as you might think. As a new widow or divorcée, you are vulnerable, alone, frightened, and lonely. And your attorney is privy to some of the most personal aspects of your life. All this can add up to an extremely difficult situation in which you both can lose judgment and the professional relationship goes out the window.

But if the two of you absolutely can't help yourselves and a true love relationship develops, find another attorney. You need someone who will operate on your behalf but with strict impartiality and unclouded judgment. And if love withers, you do not want to be left with an attorney who is your ex-lover.

Attorneys are ethically and legally bound to absolute confidentiality, so do not hesitate to be completely open about the matter for which you are seeking advice, no matter how embarrassing or awkward. In fact, if you are not completely candid, your attorney will be handicapped by the lack of complete information and will not be able to do the best possible job. So lying or withholding information will ultimately work to your own detriment.

Even after you have made a choice and entered into a relationship with an attorney, you must constantly evaluate the situation.

- Does he or she return phone calls in a reasonable time?
- Are you kept abreast of all pertinent developments and activity?
- Do you think you receive full information, or do you feel that there are things the attorney is not telling you?

BREAKING UP WITH YOUR ATTORNEY

What if the relationship with your attorney turns sour? This is unpleasant, but it happens. Sometimes one of you dislikes the other (or, if you're "lucky," it's mutual), or you start to distrust the attorney. Should you stick it out if things turn bad? Absolutely not.

No one should remain with an attorney (or any other professional, for that matter) if the relationship is incompatible, but before you look for someone else, tell him or her why you are dissatisfied—perhaps there has been a misunderstanding that can be cleared up with little difficulty. If this isn't possible, request a statement of all fees owed to date and pay the bill promptly.

You must then go through the process of finding an attorney all over again, sadder but—one hopes—wiser. And you have an additional responsibility: You must tell the new attorney that part of the work on the case has been done (surely it would be pointless not to mention that fact, especially since you have paid for the work), and you must give the two lawyers a chance to discuss the case. You will ultimately benefit from their cooperation even if it does seem a bit awkward to you.

Also, remember that you have a right to see the files relating to your case, including a record of unpaid charges owed to your attorney.

SPECIFIC LEGAL MATTERS

As a widow, you will encounter various legal matters that will crop up from time to time. For some you will need an attorney; for others you need only your good common sense and a cool head. For instance, you may want to have work done on your house. For big jobs, like a new addition, you'll work with a contractor and will sign a contract specifying the nature of the work, deadlines, and cost estimates. But unless the new cabinets fall off the wall or the roof slides off and you end up suing for more than the amount allowed in small claims court, you don't need an attorney.

But by the same token, there are legal pitfalls and knacks to dealing with contractors, tradespeople, insurance brokers, and the like, so I refer you to Chapter 7, "Getting Professional Help," for a set of guidelines on negotiating contracts, reading the fine print, and asking the correct questions for a variety of common situations that many widows face.

Your Estate

When it comes to administering your husband's estate, you probably do need an attorney. The legal transfer of or confirming title to those entitled to receive it may or may not require judicial supervision or the filing of federal and/or state estate tax returns, but it is not a judgment you can make alone.

Your lawyer will fill you in on the legal details and explain how probate (the process of filing and adjudicating a will and proving its validity) works, but you should bring certain information with you on your initial visit to the lawyer.

• Data about your husband's life: date and place of birth, Social Security number, information about military service, and the date of death. You will have been given a copy of his death certificate, and perhaps you were too distraught at the time to do more than fold it away in a drawer. Take it out now and have copies made. Although it may sound like a foolish or hurtful thing to say, you need to *prove* that your husband is dead.

• A personal history of both spouses, including the date, place, and circumstance of termination of previous marriages

• Your husband's and your own employment history

• A list of names and addresses of all heirs and beneficiaries, including the date of birth of minor heirs. If you do not know the contents of your husband's will, it will be disclosed to you on this initial visit and you may be asked to provide information about heirs.

• An inventory of all assets owned in whole or in part by your husband. You may not have this information, but you will be requested to furnish it—or you will have to pay the attorney to do it for you.

• An inventory of all property not listed above, including all property acquired during the marriage or claimed by your husband

• An inventory of all property you claim or own

• A summary of income tax returns for the previous five years, or a copy of the actual returns, which is usually easier to prepare

• Data about all outstanding debts (such as a mortgage, car payments, and bank loans)—yours, your husband's, and that incurred by both of you as a couple

If this seems like a great deal of paperwork, it is, which is why it pays to be prepared and keep personal financial papers in good order. And there may be more. During the time your husband's will is going through probate, you may be asked to supply any or all of the following:

• documentation of all purchase transactions, including business interests, contracts, and escrow accounts;
• titles to real and personal property, including bank accounts, stocks, bonds, individual retirement accounts (IRAs), and Keogh plans; and
• interest in partnerships and automobiles.

Don't throw away any paid bills for alterations and other remodeling and redecoration expenses of your house or apartment. You will have to prove what the added asset cost you in order to calculate the capital gain when you sell it. The greater your investment in the asset, the smaller the tax you will pay on the profit you will make on its sale.

SAMPLE CONFIDENTIAL ESTATE PLANNING QUESTIONNAIRE

I. FAMILY INFORMATION

Husband's Name:

Wife's Name:

Address:

Telephone Number:

Occupation(s):

Business Address:

Husband's Date of Birth:

Wife's Date of Birth:

Husband's Social Security Number:

Wife's Social Security Number:

Names, addresses, and ages of children and grandchildren; please indicate if adopted [A], child of husband only [H], or of wife only [W]:

Name and address of any person not listed above to whom you want to leave property:

Names and addresses of individuals or bank you are considering as Executor or Trustee under your will, with alternates:

Names and addresses of individuals you wish to name as guardians of any minor children, with alternates:

II. ASSETS

	VALUE		
	Husband	*Wife*	*Joint*
Home			
Mortgages (outstanding balance)			
Other Real Estate			
Stocks			
Bonds			

	VALUE		
	Husband	*Wife*	*Joint*
Certificates of Deposit			
Mortgages			
Savings Accounts			
Checking Accounts			
Furniture, Jewelry, Autos			
Location of Safe Deposit Box			

Brief description and approximate value of any unusual or valuable tangible property, e.g., works of art, stamp collection, gun collection, etc.:

Brief description and value of interest in any closely held corporations or partnerships:

III. LIFE INSURANCE

Policies on husband (include name of company, policy number, face amount, beneficiary, and cash value):

Policies on wife (include information as above):

IV. OTHER ASSETS—list amounts and beneficiary of death benefit:

Pension Plan:

Profit Sharing Plan:

Keogh (HR 10) Plan:

Individual Retirement Account (IRA):

Other Assets:

V. CURRENT DEBTS AND LIABILITIES—list amounts and lender:

VI. TRUSTS AND EXPECTANCIES—describe briefly, including approximate amounts:

Your Own Will

If you don't already have a will of your own, you should. As soon as possible after your husband's death, you need to prepare (or have rewritten, if your husband was your only beneficiary) a will to protect your assets as well as those of your children and other family members.

Although it is perfectly legal to write and execute your own will without the help of a lawyer—as long as when you sign it, your signature is witnessed by two people who are not your beneficiaries—if you have anything more than the simplest estate or if you want to avoid unnecessary probate and death taxes, you should hire an attorney to help you draw it up.

Laws about estate planning and taxation change often, so if you have any assets at all (and everyone has more than they realize), ask for legal advice, if only on a one-time basis for a general discussion of your needs.

Probate can be costly (fees are usually based on percentage of assets) and, depending on the nature of the will and the jurisdiction in which you live, it can be time-consuming. In fact, probate cases can go on for two years or more. The other drawback is that once a will is submitted for probate, it becomes a matter of public record, and you and your beneficiaries might want to keep your financial business to yourselves.

There are several ways in which an estate can be handled.

• If you have no will, you are said to die intestate, and the court will distribute your assets, possibly in a way you would not have found pleasing. Your estate will go through administration.

• If you have a simple will, probate becomes only a formality to determine if it is indeed your last one and if it is valid. You will need to choose an executor (and an alternate) who is the person you appoint to execute or perform the instructions contained in your will. You must trust this person completely and be sure that he or she is willing to serve.

You can provide in your will that your executor is protected from legal fees and other costs and expenses incurred in the performance of his or her duties, which include locating heirs, paying outstanding debts, perhaps mediating squabbles among beneficiaries, and seeing to it that real and other property and assets are managed in such a way that their value increases and produces income. He or she must also oversee the preparation of your estate tax returns.

An executor is in a position to make choices—for example, where to get the money to pay for and deduct expenses to administer your assets. This could involve significant tax savings, which in turn affects the size of your net estate, so again—be certain that you trust your executor and know that he or she will do as you wish and is capable of these tasks.

(For my widowed readers, this parenthetical note comes too late, but I must add a cautionary word to women who are still married— and to widows and divorcées who will marry again—to discuss with your husband what he has arranged for you in his will. This is *not* a "money grubbing" or rude thing to do, because when he dies, *you* will be left with the financial residue of his life, so it is in your best interest to know in advance what and who you will have to deal with in the administration of his estate. In other words, you must know *who* will be in charge of your financial future.)

In choosing an executor, think carefully about asking a family member to serve. Such a person will usually serve without charge to the estate, but you would be doing yourself and your heirs a disservice if your executor knows nothing about investments or estate management or doesn't know how to obtain good counsel. It is advisable to have your attorney act as co-executor if the person you choose is not an attorney or experienced in executing wills—as few people are. If you choose a bank as executor, it's best to have the bank serve as co-executor or co-trustee. I know of too many estates that have been frittered away by incompetent or lackluster care at the hands of a bank officer.

• You may set up a trust fund in which you place cash in trust for whomever you wish. This system avoids a certain level of taxation and often carries out your instructions well. Discuss with your lawyer every aspect of what you want done with whatever is left of your assets after taxes.

• You and another person, usually a spouse, hold joint titles to property and other assets. This usually confers the right of survivorship and means that when one person dies, the assets automatically become the property of the survivor.

• A testamentary trust takes effect after death and is a system in which assets are held for protection and/or investment for other individuals, usually minors. (You may also provide for the guardianship of children or elderly parents this way.) This system avoids taxation.

• A living trust (called an inter vivos trust) takes effect during your lifetime. You choose a trustee to manage assets for your benefit (and/or that of others) while you are alive, which gives you the opportunity to determine if the trust is being managed efficiently and will continue that way after you die. The money you have placed in an inter vivos trust avoids probate, but it has disadvantages.

You do not avoid taxation if you own and control the trust. The advantage is that you can get someone (the trustee) to manage your money and property, and if a friend or relative wants you to lend or give them money or property or invest in a business, you can always say, "I'm sorry. My assets are tied up in a trust." This is a revocable trust.

You can avoid the latter consequence by careful drafting of the trust language, but it *is* something to consider and requires a highly skilled, experienced, and trustworthy attorney whose specialty is estate planning and trusts.

Setting up a trust is more complicated than writing a simple will, but it may be the best answer for you. You will need an executor and a trustee. They are entitled by law to receive commissions, but they are not obligated to take the money. They can also waive such compensation if they do not need the money and wish to help you in this way. You are the owner of the trust and the beneficiary *is* the trust. After three years, it is not taxable in your estate.

• You may also designate someone as beneficiary of an irrevocable life insurance trust in which insurance policies are placed, thus removing them from the probate procedure.

Your present will, including codicils

Any trust agreement you have created and any trust agreement or will under which you: (a) are now acting as a fiduciary; (b) are presently a beneficiary; or (c) have a power of appointment

Any prenuptial agreement, separation, or divorce papers

Any power of attorney you have given to anyone

Any outstanding promissory notes owed by or to you

Any proprietary lease and stock certificates relating to your cooperative apartment; a deed to your real estate (including a condominium)

Any employment agreement

Any life insurance policies on yourself and others, and latest premium notices

Any casualty insurance policies covering fine art or jewelry

Any buy-sell or other agreement concerning any business enterprise

Any document concerning tax shelters

Income tax returns (last three years), gift tax returns, and any estate tax return of an estate in which you are a beneficiary

Any documents relating to pending litigation

Any other documents you think would be helpful

Your Financial Future

The subject of finances may be frightening to you—as it was to me. I think this is because we all fear the unknown, and many women haven't the slightest idea of the state of their husband's finances.

You'll sleep better knowing that you've done some financial planning, so before going to your lawyer, make out a list of what your assets and expenses are so you will have an idea of what you will need to live. You will already have made a list of your assets and their value, but

71

don't forget things like tangible personal property such as clothing, jewelry, furs, antiques, cars, and the like. You will also need to bring with you the list of all debts and liabilities that you drew up in preparation for settling your husband's estate.

Every widow, no matter what her assets, is afraid of, even panics over, her financial future. The fear is probably mostly unwarranted, but some widows are in for a rude shock when they discover the true nature of their situation. Your life style may have to undergo some modification, and the sooner you realize that, the better. Some of the budget cuts may be serious—for example, moving to a smaller home.

At some point (try to wait at least a year if you can to make this decision) you will have to decide if you want, and are able, to keep the home in which you lived with your husband. It may be too large for you, and it may be too expensive to maintain, even if the mortgage has been paid. Your lawyer or financial advisor will advise you about the financial aspects of where you ought to live, but he or she cannot advise you on the emotional part of that decision.

Rose Lewis said she wanted a place that was entirely her own. "I married when I was eighteen and had *never* lived by myself. I wanted to see if I could do it."

So she sold the house she and her husband had lived in and raised their two children in, and rented a garden apartment. "As soon as I moved in, I knew I would love it. I wasn't any more lonely than I would have been if I had stayed in the house. In fact, maybe I was less so. This place was all mine, and I hired a decorator to help give me a completely new look with my old furniture."

She said she had always wanted to live in the city, but the real estate was too expensive there, so she found a suburban neighborhood she liked, and rented. And when the apartment development converted from rentals to condominiums, she decided to buy. "I've never regretted it, and I believe that living alone helped me adjust to widowhood because it forced me to be even more independent than I would have been ordinarily."

Don't ask a real estate agent for advice about whether or not to move. Wait until after you have made that decision. A real estate agent has a vested interest in selling your house and finding you a new one.

You have many options about where to live, and even if you have only limited means, you still should take the time to think through the best decision.

Although you may have personal and emotional reasons for wanting to rent instead of buy a home (there's less responsibility for maintenance, and moving out is no financial hassle), there is little financial advantage in doing so. Depending on the part of the country in which you live, rents are skyrocketing, and because of the tax advantages of home ownership, rent often turns out more expensive than a mortgage payment even though the amount of cash you have to lay out the first of each month may be smaller.

There are other financial aspects of your future that you will have to think about, some of which are unpleasant to contemplate.

• Should you buy or lease a car? Although buying a car for outright cash is the cheapest way to obtain personal transportation, few people can get their hands on $14,000 or so to buy "wheels." The question, then, is whether to lease the car or finance the purchase. There are advantages and disadvantages to both.

Leasing a car does not require a down payment, and you don't have to use credit for the transaction, thus saving it for another purpose. The monthly payments for leasing are sometimes lower than purchase payments for the same car, but this varies from dealership to dealership and often depends on the deal you manage to strike. Also, if the car you have leased doesn't work for some reason or is clearly unsatisfactory, you can always exchange it for another.

But leasing gives you no equity, and if you plan to keep a car for a longer time than the length of an ordinary car loan (three or four years), then purchasing makes more sense because when you send off the last payment voucher, you own the car. Alternatively, most leasing companies allow you to buy their car at very favorable terms.

People tend not to maintain a leased car as well as a purchased one, so if you want to buy it at the end of the lease, you may end up with something in worse shape than if you had negotiated the purchase price right from the start.

But if you should choose to lease instead of buy, negotiate just as hard and as shrewdly as you would over a purchase price. There is no automobile dealer in America that has a fixed price on anything on his lot. Everything on wheels is negotiable!

• What will you do in the event of a protracted illness? Do you have the resources to pay for continuing long-term care, or will you ultimately have to rely on the kindness of family or on public assistance?

• You must decide now who will be responsible for you in the event of a short-term, life-threatening illness, such as a heart attack or stroke. I am assuming that you have adequate health insurance (to neglect that is utterly foolhardy), but you need to designate someone to take over your financial and domestic affairs until you are better.

• In the event that you are completely mentally and/or physically disabled, who will provide custodial care and who will pay for it? Painful as it is, you must discuss this eventuality with your children or other close family. You need to know if you can count on them

Managing Your Finances During a Long Illness

If you should fall seriously ill to the point where you cannot manage your own affairs, someone else will have to do it for you, and it might as well be the person of your choice. The only way to assure this is to arrange for it before you are sick.

If you fail to make such provisions beforehand, your family or your lawyer could instigate an incompetency or conservatorship proceeding. This means that a court assigns someone the authority to act on your behalf until you recover. This is expensive and time-consuming, and the court might appoint someone who would not have been your choice and who may not have your best interests at heart. So don't let it happen. Plan ahead.

Power of attorney allows you, when you are competent, to appoint one or two people of your choice to act on your behalf in case of illness or absence. These people can

• conduct real estate transactions;
• transact business in personal property, banking, or securities;

- operate your business;
- deal with insurance matters;
- file claims or otherwise go to court on your behalf;
- prepare records, reports, tax returns, etc.; and
- conduct other matters that you specifically designate.

You probably do not need an attorney to fill out a simple power of attorney form. Many legal stationers have blank forms for this purpose, although if you do not understand the language or its meaning, then certainly you ought to ask a lawyer's advice.

You can also limit the powers you assign to only those specifically designated, and you may specify that two people of your choice, who need have no relationship to each other, must act jointly to execute the power of attorney. This is a wise procedure to institute on your own behalf. Arkansas, Delaware, Florida, Idaho, Louisiana, Texas, Utah, Virginia, and Wyoming all authorize the appointment of a health care proxy.

Living Will

Many women ask me about a living will, which is a statement made while one has one's full faculties of how one wishes to have one's life conducted after one has become totally and irrevocably incapacitated. (Technically, "living will" is not the correct way to refer to the document; it is rather a "health care proxy directive.")

It is common to fear being kept artificially alive when, if natural processes were allowed to take place, we would ordinarily be dead, and now that medical technology has advanced to its present state, more people are aware of just how long one can be kept alive. The general public is also becoming more aware of how much emotional and financial stress is placed on those who love a person who has had the bad fortune to have fallen into such a state.

Many people, out of religious or personal conviction, want to have everything possible done for them and want to avail themselves of every form of life-sustaining treatment. This is fine and should be entirely one's own decision. Unfortunately, often it is not—if one has not taken the forethought to state a preference before it is too late. Very often families and medical personnel make decisions that may or may not be in one's own best interest and may or may not conform to one's philosophy of life and stated or unstated wishes.

If we are irrevocably comatose (yes, it is true that some people in this state wake up and recover sufficiently to lead relatively normal lives, but that is not usual and is a subject for another book), or in what physicians call a "vegetative state," decisions must be made for us *unless* we have stated our preferences beforehand. This is where a living will comes in.

If we do not want to prolong a terminal illness indefinitely, it is best to sign a living will, which is recognized as legally binding in most states. This means that although health care personnel are not obligated to abandon treatment, they will not be prosecuted if they do as long as you have signed a living will.

All states recognize a person's right to refuse *any* medical treatment for him- or herself, even if that refusal will ultimately result in the person's death. You may refuse treatment at the time it is proposed or in advance of the possibility. Here is the statement of a living will, the wording of which may vary slightly:

> To my family, my physician, my lawyer, my clergyman, to any medical facility in whose care I happen to be, to any individual who may become responsible for my health, welfare, or affairs: Death is as much a reality as birth, growth, maturity, and old age. It is the one certainty of life. If the time comes when I, ———, can no longer take part in decisions for my own future, let this statement stand as an expression of my wishes while I am of sound mind.
>
> If the situation should arise in which there is no reasonable expectation of my recovery from physical or mental disability, I request that I be allowed to die and not be kept alive by artificial means or "heroic measures." I do not fear death as much as the indignities of deterioration, dependence, and hopeless pain. I therefore ask that medication be mercifully administered to me to alleviate suffering even though this may hasten the moment of my death.
>
> This request is made after careful consideration. I hope you who care for me will feel morally bound to follow its mandate. I recognize that this appears to place a heavy responsibility upon you, but it is with the intention of relieving you of such responsibility and placing it upon myself in accordance with my strong convictions, that this statement is made.

Even this very specific statement can fall through legal loopholes. On October 14, 1988, the New York Court of Appeals overturned the legality of a statement like the one above. So I had the following statement drawn up for myself, which you may want to follow:

> I, ———, residing at ———, desiring to designate health care agents and provide direction regarding my medical care, hereby execute this Health Care Proxy and Directive in recognition of my legal right to make important decisions about my life, including those regarding health care treatment, and, in particular, my legal right, if I do not desire to receive certain forms of health care treatment, to be protected against their administration to me. I expect my family, doctor, and all those concerned with my care to regard themselves as legally and morally bound to honor my decisions.
>
> 1. *Appointment of health care agents.* I appoint ——— my agent(s) to act on my behalf to make all decisions regarding my health care, including (but not exclusively) decisions regarding my admission to and discharge from health care facilities, the administration of X rays, tests, examinations, and anesthetics, and medical, surgical, or other procedures or treatments.
>
> I specifically authorize each of my agents to consent to decisions to withdraw or withhold any or all life-sustaining procedures (other than those procedures I have either checked and initialed or written in below) if I am in a terminal condition or in a state of permanent unconsciousness unless their administration is necessary to alleviate my pain or discomfort:
>
> > ——— cardiopulmonary resuscitation
> > ——— respiratory support
> > ——— surgery
> > ——— artificially administered feedings and fluids
>
> 2. *Consent to withdrawal or withholding of life-sustaining procedures in agent's absence.* If ——— is unable or unwilling to exercise the authority I have given in this document, I consent to the withdrawal and withholding of any and all life-sustaining procedures (other than those procedures checked and initialed or written in above) if I am in a terminal condition or in a state of permanent unconsciousness, and I express my intent that those procedures then be withdrawn or withheld, unless their administration is necessary to alleviate my pain or discomfort.
>
> 3. *Consultation and records.* I authorize ——— to consult with any physician or other medical personnel who may treat me, and I instruct that my medical records be made available to each of my agents as part of any such consultation. I further authorize each of my agents to visit me in any hospital, convalescent home, or other facility where I may be receiving treatment or care, and I direct that each of my agents be given first priority in visitation if I am unable to express a preference because of my illness or disability.

4. *Release.* I release each of my agents from all liability for having exercised in good faith the authority I have granted under this Health Care Proxy and Directive. I release all persons, including (but not exclusively) my physicians and all health care professionals attending me, and any hospital in which I am a patient, as well as any person employed by or under contract with such hospital, from all liability for having honored the consents and followed the instructions given by any agents and for having in good faith complied with my directions. I direct any person entrusted with the care of my affairs or who at any time represents my interests in any capacity, including (but not exclusively) the interests of my estate, to honor this release.

The statement is then signed and dated with at least two witnesses in attendance. You may also designate someone to act as a backup, that is, give him or her the power—in writing—to make such a decision on your behalf if you are unable to do so for yourself. This designated power is generally legally recognized in most jurisdictions. In fact, in 1984 the Special Committee of the Legal Problems of the Aging of the Association of the Bar of the City of New York reported that, "A durable and properly limited power of attorney may be used to delegate specifically to an agent the responsibility to communicate preferences concerning life-sustaining treatment through a companion living will."

There is, however, little point in having a living will if no one knows about it. Therefore, when you have made the decision to sign one, give a copy to your physician, your close family members, and your attorney. If you should enter the hospital—even for a routine procedure from which you expect to recover fully—bring a copy of your living will and ask that it be placed in your hospital chart. One never knows what can go wrong.

Taxes

Unless your financial affairs are so uncomplicated that you have income from only one job that automatically deducts the correct amount of state and federal tax, the best advice for any woman who finds herself suddenly alone, through the death of her husband or through divorce, is to find a good certified public accountant (CPA) or tax attorney (often the same person). Many retirees, mostly men I admit, prepare their own tax returns. If you have only tax-free bonds, social security income, and a monthly pension, tax preparation is not all that difficult if you are not frightened by such a task. As two widowers I know said, "Our tax returns get easier and easier to do."

You will want your CPA or tax attorney to prepare your tax returns in the early spring and to give you tax advice the year round. The preparation fee is tax deductible only with applicable limitations.

Whether you are preparing the returns yourself or hiring someone to do it for you, documentation is everything, and a CPA cannot do a good job on your behalf unless you provide him or her with correct and complete documentation. You must record and keep a file (including invoices and canceled checks) of all expenses such as

- income-producing property, for example, real estate that you own and rent;
- all income from all sources and from investment transactions;
- medical expenses, including physicians' bills, private duty nurses, home health aides, prescription drugs, hospital charges, ambulance, and a log of all travel expenses to and from medical appointments;
- if you are over age sixty-five, copies of Medicare reimbursement forms;
- charitable activities (cash contributions, travel expenses, telephone, postage, entertainment if you are doing fundraising, and expenses incurred as a result of holding meetings or parties in your home); and
- all expenses related to the production of income.

Retirement

Do you have the financial resources you will need to live comfortably in retirement? This question makes many women nervous because either they are not sure of the answer and don't know how to go about finding out—or they know they won't have enough to cover expenses, and the thought is so distressing that they prefer to put it out of their minds.

This is not only silly, it's dangerous. It is no fun to be old and poor in America. In fact, it's an outright tragedy, but if you plan *now* for your old age, you can live comfortably, if not luxuriously.

As soon as you feel emotionally strong enough, you should get together with your family and your attorney or financial advisor to discuss how vital it is for you to have a realistic picture of the income you can anticipate for your future needs. Social Security monthly payments are unlikely to be enough to sustain you, so you must plan to be able to draw funds from an IRA, a Keogh plan, stock dividends, other pension funds, and anything else you have or can add to your investment portfolio. And you also need to know whether you have to continue to work—or to find a job.

By the way, the Employee Retirement Income Security Act (ERISA) requires that employers inform employees of their rights and obligations under the company's pension plan, so be sure to ask your (or your late husband's) personnel manager for a written statement of what your retirement income will be. While the language of retirement plans may seem like Greek to the uninitiated, such plans are actually written to protect the beneficiary, so be sure you understand what payments are due you and when they are payable. You must also know when and how to apply for your retirement benefits, because in many plans, payment is not automatic. (Wives automatically have rights to husbands' qualified pension plans, unless they have specifically waived it in writing.)

Civil Suits

Civil law pertains to the private rights of individuals or groups and is generally distinguished from criminal law, in which government is a party—usually as prosecutor.

If you find yourself a party to a civil suit, you may or may not need an attorney. It depends on the nature and monetary value of the action. If you have been hit by a car (or if you have run over someone else) or if you have been a victim of medical or legal malpractice, you'll need a lawyer. However, if it's a small matter, such as a dry cleaner ruining a dress or an automobile mechanic selling you a new transmission when the old one was fine, you can probably do well on your own in small claims court.

The amount of damages you can claim varies from jurisdiction to jurisdiction, but in many places it is as high as $15,000. Small claims courts have a long and honored history of equal justice, regardless of the education, sophistication—and bank account—of the plaintiff and defendant. Besides, it's an interesting (but sometimes discouraging) experience.

The "smallness" inherent in the name of the court has nothing to do with the importance of the case to the parties involved—or to the way that judges view their roles there. It simply means that the financial amount of the damages incurred is small enough not to warrant hiring an attorney (besides, most attorneys are unwilling to take their time with "small potatoes" cases).

If you feel you have been cheated or dealt with unfairly, and if money is involved, don't stand around and complain. Try to get justice. At least you will have your day in court.

The process is very simple. You simply go to the Clerk of the Court's office, which is listed in the city or county government section of the phone book, fill out the form, and pay the nominal filing fee. The clerks are used to dealing with legal amateurs and are most helpful in showing you how to fill out the form, which is terribly easy. You don't need to know legal terminology; you will simply be asked to describe, in a sentence or two, what happened.

You will receive written notice of the date of your hearing; it usually takes about two weeks to two months, depending on how busy the court is. While you are waiting for your case to be called, marshall your evidence and rehearse your plan.

Let's say you've been ripped off by a mechanic. You'll need to prove that not only did you have the work done but that it was unsatisfactory. Dig out the repair bill and have several copies made. Did you write to the mechanic complaining of the bad service? Make copies of that letter and add them to your file.

What was the mechanic's response? Nothing? Good, then he will be able to produce no evidence of trying to make things right. Did you have trouble with the transmission after the mechanic installed a new one? Find a way to document that fact; perhaps you called the American Automobile Association and had to be towed. Perhaps you had your car serviced at another garage. Collect proof of everything, including the letter you will now write to the mechanic explaining that even though you are suing, you are still willing to be reasonable and that if he fixes your car or returns your money, you will drop the suit.

Everything you can do to persuade the judge that you are a reasonable and fair person will be to your ultimate credit in court. You also want to appear to have tried everything possible before resorting to a law suit.

When your day in court arrives, dress conservatively. You don't have to look like a million dollars (and you certainly don't want to appear rich), but showing respect for the court by dressing properly can't hurt.

Small claims court is informal—but not lackadaisical—and you and the defendant will be asked to tell your sides of the story in your own words in plain language. This is not the place for fancy legal jargon, so if you know some, don't try to impress anyone by using it. (And by the way, if one party does not show up for court, he or she automatically defaults. In other words, if the mechanic doesn't show up, you win.)

The judge will listen to each side and will call witnesses if there are to be any. Then the judge will make a decision—usually right there on the bench with no waiting. Once in a while, the case is complicated enough for the judge to need to think it over, but it's much more common for you to know the outcome right then and there.

Most sessions of small claims courts have calendars (agendas) two or three times longer than can be heard that session. (And, by the way, many jurisdictions hold small claims court in the evening for the convenience of those who work during the day.) Your case may be postponed—sometimes more than once if the docket is very busy. Unless you are willing to return several times, you may decide to submit your dispute to arbitration.

Some jurisdictions have instituted arbitration hearings, and you may be asked if you are willing to submit to arbitration before your hearing date. In a successful arbitration hearing, everyone gives in a little, so there are no real winners or losers. For instance, you may agree with the arbitrator and defendant to take half the value of the repair job if you drop the suit. Or the mechanic may agree to fix the transmission again for no charge. However, if you don't want to go to arbitration or if you can't agree to settle, trial in small claims court is there for you.

If the judge rules in your favor, you still have to collect the money from the mechanic, and that's usually the hard part, even armed with a court order that says he owes it to you. If the mechanic does not pay voluntarily, there are various legal remedies, which the Clerk of the Court will describe.

If you lose, you can either shrug philosophically and walk away, having added another life experience to your sense of independence, or you can appeal. The choice is up to you, and again, it depends on how much the case means to you—financially and otherwise. An appeal requires an additional fee and takes much more time.

Credit

Many women have never had a credit rating in their own name, some because they have no private source of income, others because they never had the need to go into major debt (for example, a mortgage or an automobile loan) and the rest because their husband earned the income and paid the bills. And by the way, having a charge card at Bloomingdale's or an American Express card with your name on it does *not* mean that you have your own line of credit. It only means that your husband authorized you to sign charge slips for which he was financially responsible.

But you're all alone now and need your own credit. It's not enough to say that your mortgage was paid off years ago and that you have enough money to pay cash for a new car (in which case you certainly have enough to establish a healthy line of credit with Visa or Master-Card).

You need credit because you never know when you will be in a situation that costs money you don't have instantly at hand, for instance, stuck in a strange city needing a hotel room for the night and perhaps a rental car the next day. Both are available *only* if you present a major credit card. Or what if you're traveling late at night and your car breaks down? You forgot to renew your membership in the American Automobile Association, and the only open gas station won't even send a tow truck if you can't guarantee payment: "Lady," says the guy with the greasy overalls, "I don't know you, so why should I take your check?" He has a perfectly valid point, and you're left sobbing and scared by the side of the road.

And have you ever tried to pay cash (not a check, actual greenbacks with pictures of presidents on them!) for an airline ticket at the airport counter? You often can't because the clerks who work there are trained to accept *only* credit cards.

Or what if you're meeting a friend for dinner and stop off at the bank machine to get cash and something goes wrong? The machine sucks in your card and won't give it back. You have $2.53 in your purse, and your friend doesn't have enough to pay for both meals. You probably will be able to explain your situation to the maître d', and if he's a nice guy, he might take your check. But he doesn't have to, and if you had a credit card, you could have saved yourself a major embarrassment.

You need to apply for credit—at the minimum, two major credit cards: American Express and either MasterCard or Visa. Once you have those, department stores, oil companies, and everything else is easy—as long as you pay your bills on time. Or you can do it in reverse and open department store charge accounts first. Most major stores will give you two to three hundred dollars' credit automatically when you apply for credit. When the first bill comes in, pay it in full right away and establish your ability and willingness to pay on time. Do this in several large stores, and presto! You will have an established credit rating.

Then when American Express or Visa checks your application with one of several national companies that maintains credit records, your name and account will be in the computer files in good condition.

When you apply for credit, you will be asked to provide information about your bank accounts, employment history, residence (whether you own or rent and how long you have lived at your present address), income, outstanding debts, and other established credit. The company is looking for employment stability or some other indication that you will pay your bills.

If you are denied credit, you will be notified in writing and given the name of the credit reporting company, also known as a credit bureau, that supplied the information. This company, which does not make decisions about credit, compiles information about you and provides it to credit-granting companies (banks, stores, mortgage companies, and the like). The credit reporting company must comply with your request to examine your file. They must do so free of charge if you have been denied credit; otherwise they can charge a small fee, usually twenty-five dollars or so.

If you believe the information is inaccurate, contest it in writing. If you believe you have been discriminated against without cause, contest it. It is against the law to discriminate on the basis of sex, age, marital status, or race, and with a few exceptions, a company may not discontinue a line of credit simply because marital status changes.

Once you have established credit, you must protect it. All this requires is paying the minimum balance on your statement each month. This minimum depends on how large a balance you have accumulated, how long you have had credit with the company, and what their rules are. For instance, American Express requires payment in full each month, although they do have a plan to extend payment for several months for big-ticket items like airline tickets; bank cards like Visa and MasterCard allow you to pay as little as ten dollars a month. But don't forget that interest charges have a way of accumulating quickly, so pay as much as you can each month.

And try not to make the mistake that so many people do: running up credit card bills that they cannot possibly pay. It is so tempting to buy clothes and gifts, not to mention restaurant meals, with the handy little plastic cards. But the shock at the end of the month is almost never worth the pleasure of an expensive new dress—unless you can truly afford it.

One woman, who lives on only her salary and a very small pension from her former husband's company, has made a few rules for herself so she doesn't get into credit card trouble. First, she *never* pays for food with a credit card. "It's too dangerous," she says. "My rule is that if I use my card to pay for something, I want to still have it when the bill arrives!" Her second rule is that when she runs up a balance that is half what the credit company provides, she takes the card out of her wallet and lets it "cool down" before using it again. That way she doesn't run the risk of going over her limit, and she always has an emergency cushion of credit if disaster strikes and she needs quick cash.

Prenuptial Agreements

You may not want to read this section right away, and you may never have need of it, but if you do decide to remarry, the information it contains may be useful.

People disagree about prenuptial agreements. Those who oppose them say that people who are about to be married suffer from impaired judgment, presumably as a result of being severely bitten by the love bug. Therefore, they are in no condition to enter into a binding contract. In addition, they claim, the commitment to marry implies placing complete trust in one's partner, which makes a prenuptial agreement superfluous—and indeed carries with it the implication of ulterior motive for the marriage.

I disagree, especially when one is contemplating a second marriage. One can always tear up the agreement later, as several of my clients have done. But it is impossible to know how you will feel five years after the wedding; that is, will you be more or less in love? Will you trust your spouse as much as you do now? And will you be more or less willing to share your assets?

One attorney friend of mine said that he did not have a prenuptial agreement for his first marriage because he didn't think it was a proper way to begin a "till death do us part" enterprise, and besides neither he nor his wife had any money. But his wife died, and when he chose another woman to marry and to be mother to his three children, he wrote an agreement. He wanted to be sure that his children would get what he had when he died and to assure his second wife that she would be well provided for. In fact, his second marriage didn't work, and the divorce involved some legal snarls, but he ended up paying less alimony than he would have if there had been no prenuptial agreement.

There are many types of prenuptial agreements. Some cover only financial matters: who pays for what during the marriage and who gets what in the event of divorce. Other agreements cover the most de-tailed arrangements of married life: who does the dishes, how many

"nights off" the husband and wife get, how many vacations they take together and how many separately.

The ideal agreement lies somewhere between these two extremes, and although your lawyer should help you draw up the actual contract, I offer here some guidelines to think about before the two of you sit down with your attorney.

• Be honest with each other about how much of your assets you are willing to share and how much you insist on controlling yourself.

• Think of the agreement, at least in part, as an avoidance of bitterness if you divorce—not as a guarantee of being able to get as much money as possible out of the estranged spouse. That is truly no way to begin a marriage.

• If you expect to have children in your new marriage, the prenuptial agreement must make provisions for child support, including education through college. There is no way to avoid custody battles before a child is even conceived, because you do not know what will cause the divorce.

• You need to protect the children you already have and ensure that they are not jeopardized by your new marriage, and you also need to protect yourself against having to involuntarily support someone else's children.

• Be honest with each other about why you want or need to draw up a prenuptial agreement. If there is a serious lack of trust before the wedding, you may want to think long and hard about the person you say you want to share your life with. If you suspect secret Swiss bank accounts, if you feel you are being pressured into signing something (or are afraid you might later be accused of coercion), don't do it.

We all want to believe that we marry for something on a higher level than money and security, but not one of us is immune to the fear of being taken advantage of. And most often it's the woman who gets the short end of the financial stick. Rich men marry women who are not strong bargainers (and some women *do* marry for money, as do some men), and many wealthy women are seduced into marriage by younger men (who are still called gigolos in some circles) and are talked into signing away their estates.

I'm not saying that this will happen to you, but in your new role as an independent woman, the stronger you are, the more prepared you will be to face life—with or without a new husband.

Miscellaneous, But Important, Legal Matters

• You must apply to Social Security for your survivor's benefits. They do not come to you automatically upon your husband's death. You will find your nearest Social Security office listed in the federal government section of the phone book.

• If your husband was a veteran, you may have benefits coming from the Veterans Administration. They too are listed in the federal government section of the phone book. Call for an application. Again, benefits are not automatic.

• Write letters to your husband's union, professional organizations, alumni associations, and any other groups to which he belonged. There may be death benefits (for instance, group life insurance) of which you are not aware.

• If you are dunned for payment by a funeral home, hospital, physician, nursing home, or other creditors, and if the bills are too large for you to pay all at once, you will have to work out some sort of payment schedule. Write to all of them, explain your circumstances (or have your attorney do it if you can't face the chore and are willing to pay for the service) and ask for extended credit.

The creditors may tack finance charges onto the bill, and it may be worthwhile to borrow a large sum of money at a lower rate of interest, pay all the creditors at once, and then pay off the "bill payer loan" gradually. However, this method may or may not be in your best interest. Do not make any decision immediately; investigate all the ways you can to pay your debts and then choose whichever is the cheapest and fastest.

But don't ignore debt. It won't go away, and creditors can make life extremely unpleasant if they believe you are trying to "stiff" them.

Most creditors are reasonable and will agree to a set monthly payment if you take the trouble to explain your circumstances (use the word "widow" as many times as you have to if you are trying to enlist sympathy to gain time)—and if you stick to your promised payment schedule and demonstrate that you are making a sincere effort to pay your debts.

• If you need to buy or sell property (your house, other real estate, your husband's business, and the like), don't do it without the advice of an attorney. Even though the terms of the sale may *seem* uncomplicated (and perhaps they are), there are enough legal pitfalls in such arrangements to make even the most sophisticated person wary.

• You may not need an attorney to sign a lease for an apartment or house, but *do* read the entire thing before you sign. Apartment leases are usually less involved than house leases because they are standard forms, especially if you are moving into a large building owned and operated by a commercial concern.

A lease for a house is more flexible because you are usually renting from an individual (perhaps someone you know, which can cause additional complications) rather than a corporation. But you also need to do more negotiating. For instance, who is responsible for maintenance and repairs? Who has to shovel the snow, rake the leaves, and mow the lawn? Who carries the liability insurance? You *must* get all such issues straightened out before signing the lease.

• Learn how to deal with moving companies and find out *first* what your rights are and what the company's responsibilities are. For instance, federal law (administered by the Interstate Commerce Commission—the ICC) requires that a moving company provide you with a written estimate, and if the actual cost of the move comes out to be more than 10 percent above the estimate, you do not need to pay more than that 10 percent overage.

The company may or may not come to your home to give the estimate. It depends on how big your home is, what you have in the way of belongings, and how well you are able to describe what you have. For instance, a friend of mine moved five years ago from an apartment to a small house. She had moved many times before and was experienced. She was able to describe—on the telephone—exactly what she owned, how many cartons of kitchen utensils and books she would have, and how many wardrobe cartons she would require. The company mailed her the estimate, and on moving day, the actual price came out slightly less than the estimate.

But this is unusual, so you should insist on a written estimate from at least three moving companies, and you must get an agreement *in writing* that the truck and a certain number of moving men will be at your house at a certain hour on a certain day. You also must have a written promise of when your belongings will arrive at your new home, whether you will share the van with other people's property, and how much it will cost to insure the load in the event the van goes over a cliff.

6

FINDING A JOB

---

*N*ow that we are grown up, we are a little, but certainly not entirely, free from carrying the total emotional burden of our family. Younger husbands are now helping bear the formerly exclusively mother-wife burdens. It's good for them, the children, and the wife to have the father share in the joys and disappointments all children have.

But now that your husband is gone from your life, you must batter it out alone. A wise friend of my mother told me when I was most pulled and tugged in various directions by my job, my responsibilities at home, my children, and my community, "Phil, the best intellect is frittered away by constant interruption."

Every mother and many childless wives have felt that they just couldn't persevere through life with these constant daily, even hourly, interruptions of managing a family. No desk or office job can compare to a homemaker's tasks.

Now you might be at the stage where, once the immediate tasks of settling your husband's estate—or if divorced, sorting out your share of communal assets—is over, you can focus on your own future. Perhaps you had training that was interrupted by marriage and children. Often this interruption is a blessing; now you have matured and are more able to sort out your priorities. World War II did that for many men who said to themselves, "I didn't really want to spend the rest of my life doing what I did before the war," and they redirected themselves.

The important thing is not to set your goals too high. One of my role models, Dr. Beatrice Berle, went to medical school after she married Adolf Berle. They had three children while she studied, interned, and did her residency. She told me that she would not have finished if she had not been content with Bs and maybe some Cs in medical school. This was a big compromise for her, Phi Beta Kappa in her junior year at Vassar, whose scholastic goal had always been straight As. She agreed with a physician relative of mine who said, "Settle for what you can accomplish and keep your private life in order. The A medical student goes into research, the B student teaching, and the C students take care of the patients." (When I screamed, "I don't want a C student for my doctor," my relative reassured me that a creditable C means that you know a lot of medicine and you'll learn a lot more as an intern and resident—enough to take care of your patients very well indeed.)

Should you redirect yourself to a job (paid or volunteer), know that there is a lot to learn and it will nourish you to learn it. You'll acquire new colleagues and friends in whatever you decide to do, and you'll make your peace with a goal attainable at your present state of grief, physical stress, and health.

Speaking of goals, think of them generally, but don't set ones that are too lofty or too definite. Goal-oriented people (it's a favorite present-day phrase for yuppies or those ascending the business or professional ladder) often know their exact destinations, and those who have high aims often find themselves arriving at quite different, perhaps better, situations. The important thing is to have direction in your life's journey, especially in your newly begun journey alone. Anne Morrow Lindbergh says she looks at life as a "journey toward insight." Maybe that's what's so good about your new status in life—having the maturity to have realistic aims toward helping others while growing yourself, whether you are trying to make your town a better, cleaner, safer place to live or are involved in an effort on a national or international basis. Today's problems are so diverse, menacing, and difficult to analyze that the mature wisdom that you can offer a cause is doubly important.

Most mature women, either widowed or divorced, have already lived through their educational process, their marriage and childrearing, and early professional years. Now you can concentrate on productive years. So many women manage to be productive up to eighty or ninety years of age, some beginning after their husband's death or after a heart-rending divorce. Think of Margaret Mead after her divorce. A neighbor of mine in New York, now ninety years old, began a life fascinating to her and helpful to all those in need of orthopedic care, when she began working as a volunteer at the New York Hospital for Special Surgery. That institution gave her several large dinners at the Waldorf Astoria Hotel honoring her contribution when she was ninety!

Georgia O'Keeffe and Agnes De Mille (who never married) kept on producing wonderful things in very late years. Ms. De Mille accomplished much after a crippling stroke, which she fights valiantly while working on choreography and writing books.

•   •   •

Many widows must face the realization that they don't have enough money to live and have to find a job—soon. This presents a number of serious problems that you'll need to cope with, especially if you are "older" (over forty-five or fifty) and/or have not worked outside the home, ever in your life or for a long enough time that your skills are too rusty to be of immediate apparent value on the job market.

There are some women who don't need the money, but the time, energy, and intellectual challenge that a job requires can be a tremendous help in healing grief. Rose Lewis, whose husband died twelve years ago when they were both only forty-nine years old, said, "My job saved my life." She was teaching in college at the time her husband had a massive stroke and died nine weeks later, and the necessity of having to meet her classes every day and fulfill all her other faculty functions kept her going.

"Nathan died in January," she said, "and the following August, I was encouraged to apply for the chairmanship of the department, and I did."

She got the job and threw herself so totally into her work that she was too exhausted to have much time left over for self-pity.

Another friend, who was on the editorial staff of a large daily newspaper, doubled her output, changed her area of specialty, and became much more prolific and well known. Her friends worried that she was burning herself out by burying her grief in her work, but her answer was that it saved her life.

This chapter will not, and should not, be a primer on job-hunting because there are many good books available for that purpose; rather, I shall outline what you need to do and how to go about doing it.

Good-paying, interesting jobs are not easy to get—for anyone. For a woman "of a certain age" who has just been widowed and is still going through the first throes of grief and who may have few, if any, marketable skills, finding work that will pay the rent and buy groceries can be a difficult task indeed.

Job-seeking may be your most difficult challenge. You are still a very slow study of any material, and you are probably still trembling inside. Many friends report that for several years, their hands were shaky, they constantly dropped objects—too often for comfort—and they were not up to their usual well-coordinated performance.

Before you will have the strength to look for a job, you need to recognize the anger and resentment directed at your husband for leaving you in this predicament in the first place. You may be furious because he left too little life insurance or angry because he either didn't or couldn't have the foresight to provide for you (and your children) after his death. And perhaps you're angry at yourself for depending totally on someone to provide for you, and now you feel left in the lurch.

But whatever your feelings, you will have to put them "on hold" while you look for a job. Taking care of yourself and your children will have to be your first priority, especially if you will shortly be in serious financial trouble and have no other way to find some income to tide you over for the several months it can take to find a job, and especially if you need vocational training.

If you are in serious financial straits, you must look for sources of income. Try the following:

• Make certain that you exhaust every possible benefit to which you are entitled as a widow. Was your husband a veteran? Have you applied for Social Security survivors' benefits? Have you made certain to apply for the life insurance provided by his job? Do you have a life insurance policy that you can cash in? (Don't do this if you have children.)

• Ask family and close friends to lend you money, but be very careful about borrowing cash on the line of credit that you have with bank credit cards. Borrowing money can be embarrassing—even humiliating, depending on the relationship with your family—but if your survival depends on it, don't hesitate to ask. And be certain to do it in a businesslike manner. Write a promissory note and *do* pay back the loan when you are on your financial feet again.

• If you have real estate or valuable material assets (furs, jewelry, silver, an extra car, or art) consider selling them. This can be a wrenching experience, but you have to eat—and you don't have to tell anyone.

• If worse comes to absolute worst, go on welfare. This is truly an awful situation to be in, but do *not* think of it as charity. You and your husband have been taxpayers for years, so try to remember that it is simply another government benefit, like police protection and interstate highways. It's not going to be easy, but it's better than living on the streets.

You may think I'm sounding overly melodramatic, talking about being on the streets, but for a woman alone with no source of income and no man to protect and provide for her, homelessness is all too common a "solution."

LOOKING FOR WORK

Once you have gotten your financial situation in order, you need to find a job. And if you are over forty-five or fifty and have few skills, that's not going to be easy. You will have to decide what type of work you want to do and are suited for. I suggest you buy or get from the library two or three books that deal specifically with this subject, but there are a few preliminary questions you ought to ask yourself.

• What do I *like* to do?

• Where do my talents lie?

• What sorts of experiences do I have that can be turned into a paying job?

• What types of work are practical for me to look for?

• Do I want to work alone or with others?

• What kind of company do I want to work for: a huge corporation, a retail store, a small office?

• What fringe benefits are important to me? If you have been married to someone whose medical and pension benefits are still available to you as a widow, you can offer to waive these benefits, thus saving your future employer a part of your salary. He or she may, as a result, find you more attractive than other applicants.

• What barriers are there to my getting a good job? For instance, is transportation likely to be a problem and are my health and physical condition good enough to provide the stamina to work all day?

The first thing you must do is write yourself a résumé (see Chapter 2 for my comments on the necessity of having one), which means sitting down with a pencil and paper and taking stock of every shred of talent, skill, and experience you have ever had, including

• education, from high school and after, college degrees and honors, honorary sorority and fraternity memberships;
• volunteer work for charitable organizations, which probably required more managerial skills than you realize;
• any paid job you have ever had—as long as the skills are still useful in today's market;
• sales work in stores or other places; and
• typing, shorthand, dictation transcription, and other secretarial skills, even if they are very rusty. (Once you know how to type, working back up to speed is only a matter of practice for you, as this is a very specialized skill.)

If you feel as though you lack the confidence and ability to write a résumé, hire someone to do it for you. Look in the employment section of the Sunday newspaper and find listed, usually right on the front page, a number of agencies that will sit down with you, listen to your experiences, and write you a credible and attractive résumé. In major cities there are dozens of these services, so get estimates from a few before committing yourself, but most of them are not expensive.

You might also ask the help of friends in business. Write your own résumé and then ask someone to review it and offer suggestions about how it can be strengthened. You might also explore the possibility of having several versions of your résumé, emphasizing different skills. For example, one friend of mine who had spent the first twenty years of her life as a nurse wanted to switch careers and become a writer. She had done some publishing when she was on a nursing faculty, so her résumé emphasized her publications in the area of health and medicine, and she put her nursing accomplishments in the background. She is now a successful and highly paid medical writer—and no one taught her how to do it.

· · ·

There are several ways you can go about getting a job, and again, these suggestions are only sketches of ideas. First, tell *everyone* you know that you are looking. This is *not* the time to be shy or reticent. If you need a job, say so. Don't make yourself into an object of pity or ridicule and don't dominate every conversation with job-hunting sagas, but do mention casually to everyone you talk to that you are in the market. You never know when someone will know someone who needs a person with just your talent and background.

In particular, ask to meet people who are in the line of work that you want to join. Don't ask your friends to get you a job—they won't be able to and you don't want to place that kind of burden on the friendship. Rather, say something like, "I'd love to meet your friend Mary who works for XYZ newspaper just so I can pick her brain about how to go about finding a job in journalism. Do you think it would be all right to call her and ask her to have lunch with me?" Your friend will probably be delighted to help and may even offer to place the call to Mary to make the introduction.

Go through the help-wanted section of the paper every Sunday before you do anything else. Read every section that would be even remotely interesting and apply to every single position that you think you have even the slightest chance of getting. Paper the world with your résumé!

Send your résumé with a cover letter that is specific to that particular job. (A computer is helpful here, if you have access to one, so you can write essentially the same letter with details tailored to fit without having to type dozens of letters every week.)

Spend a few hours in the library going through the jobs materials. Ask a librarian to help you find what you need and then read trade papers and magazines, pore over the federal and state jobs register, and go through the associations directories.

Write to your college or graduate school and ask if there is a limit from the time of graduation that you can register with their placement office. You might also register with the local state employment office.

Get part-time work through a temporary agency. There are dozens of them listed in the yellow pages. You may end up doing boring and menial secretarial jobs, but many agencies will train you to do word processing and other computer skills, so do not automatically discount this valuable source of free training. Moreover, you may find that there are other job opportunities in the company for which you are doing temporary work, or your temporary boss may know a colleague who needs your skills.

In any event, temporary jobs bring in money; they keep you occupied and out of the house during a depressing and frustrating time of your life, and they are another opportunity to make contacts. In addition, temporary employment isn't just for secretaries anymore. There are all types of part-time or temporary jobs available: accounting, nursing, engineers, draftspeople, health care technicians, telemarketing representatives, survey takers, people who hand out samples in supermarkets, and all manner of sales jobs.

Temporary agencies can also provide experience interviewing, which is a skill in itself. Again, there are many books available that detail ways to behave on an interview, and almost all of them tell you that the first minute or two (some even say the first thirty seconds!) are crucial enough to make or break the rest of the interview. So I have included only the most basic tips here.

• Get a good night's sleep before the interview so you look rested and alert. If that's not possible, drink coffee and fake it!

• Dress neatly and attractively in an outfit appropriate to the job. Leave your flashiest jewelry at home, and this is not the time to wear the sable coat your husband gave you for your twenty-fifth wedding anniversary!

• Be on time; be polite even if you are dealt with rudely; and send a thank-you letter afterward—even if you are positive that you didn't get the job.

• Show self-confidence even if you feel like weak tea inside, but try not to be brash or overconfident.

• Employers are prohibited by law from asking your age or from discussing age unless it can be directly related to the work you are being evaluated for. But the reality is that in all likelihood you will be interviewed by someone younger than yourself (often by as much as twenty or twenty-five years!), and unless you spend all your time having plastic surgery, that difference will be apparent.

Should you or should you not bring up the issue of age? That's up to you, but if you do, be positive. Point out that older workers have valuable experience and a work ethic that is not often found in younger people. You might also mention that studies have shown that older employees take less sick time than younger ones and, in most jobs, are among the most productive people in the American work force. And the maturity, judgment, and life experience you can bring to the job may more than compensate for the lack of direct job-related experience.

• Try to see yourself from an employer's point of view and rehearse the types of questions you are likely to be asked: Why did you choose this company? What can you do for us? Have you done this type of work before? How will you fit in with our work style? How much will it cost me to train you?

• Always critique your performance, and ask yourself why you didn't get the job. Were the reasons within your control or outside them, or as most often happens, do you have no way of knowing? If the last, don't dwell on it. Learn what you can from the experience and go on to the next interview.

AGENCIES AND OTHER REFERRAL SOURCES

Another way to increase your chances of finding a job is to sign up with a variety of employment agencies, or, if you have marketable skills, you can work through a "headhunter."

An employment agency can be fairly impersonal, and they do charge a fee. Sometimes the employer picks up all or part of the agency's charge, and sometimes you must agree to pay a flat fee or a percentage of your first month's salary.

Employment agencies almost never charge "up front" money, but employment consultants do, and their fees can run into the thousands of dollars.

Some job-search consultants/agencies are little more than résumé-writing services, and most do not guarantee that they will find you a job. However, almost all of them offer a free one-time evaluation visit, at which they will try to sell their services. Do *not* sign up for anything on the spot, but listen carefully to what they have to offer and compare their services with those of similar agencies. Also, see how much free advice you can worm out of that one free visit.

You might also consider the various types of vocational training available to women entering or re-entering the job market. There are dozens of sources, including

- your local community college;
- university extension programs;
- county or municipal adult education courses that have an emphasis on practical skills;
- the American Association of Retired Persons—request a copy of the AARP's *Working Options* by writing to them at P.O. Box 2400, Long Beach, CA 90801;
- Displaced Homemakers, 1010 Vermont Avenue, NW; Washington, DC 20005; and
- Operation Able, 36 South Wabash, Chicago, IL 60603.

Investigate them all and ask everyone you know what they would suggest if you want to obtain low-cost, relatively fast training.

THE SEARCH

Once you have decided the type of job you want and know the skills you have to sell, you need to develop a strategy for finding, if not the perfect job, one that is satisfying and pays enough for you to live on. In order to avoid a good deal of frustration—not to mention time, effort, and shoe leather—that a job search entails, you might want to consider a few approaches:

• Conduct a planned, *focused* job search. That means market only the skills you want to use in your job. In other words, if you *can* type and take shorthand but don't want to be a secretary, don't admit to those skills. If someone asks you a direct question, don't lie. Rather, say something like, "I can peck at a typewriter for my own use, but I see you have good support staff here."

• Keep your goals set on the type of job you really want, but don't close your mind to a good "stepping stone" job that comes your way. It may pay a few thousand dollars less, but the experience, contacts, and professional credibility that it provides may be valuable—especially if the job is offered now and the dream job is not right around the corner.

• Make job-hunting a full-time job until you find one. You'll never find what you want if you approach the problem in a half-hearted, sporadic way. You must devote forty or fifty hours a week to the search.

• Use each job interview, in person and over the phone, as a source of contacts. Turn each rejection into something positive. Say, for example, "I understand that you don't need someone with my skills now; but can you give me the names of two or three people that you think it would be helpful for me to talk with?"

•   •   •

STRIKING OUT ON YOUR OWN

If you have a skill but are having a hard time selling it full time, perhaps because of the state of the economy or the lack of job opportunities in your area or because you are a victim of age discrimination (a practice that is, of course, illegal but very common and difficult to prove), you might want to try free-lance work.

Most people think that free-lancers are writers or artists, but there are all types of work that can be done on a part-time free-lance basis, among them:

- cooking or catering;
- public relations;
- flower arranging;
- party planning; and
- shopping for career women who have neither time nor energy to do it themselves.

Although it takes an enormous amount of time and energy (as well as at least some start-up capital), you might consider going into business for yourself. It doesn't have to be a major operation, and it ought not be very diverse—at least at first. But there is money to be made in selling an item or a service that you do well.

For example, do you have a recipe for a dessert that you're famous for? When you serve it to friends, do they swoon with joy and beg for the recipe? Then people who eat at restaurants might have the same reaction. Take the idea (along with a sample piece of the cake or torte) to local restaurateurs and offer your services as a free-lance dessert chef. This means that you agree to bake so many things each week in your own home and deliver them on time. All you need is two or three restaurants to accept your offer (and a definite talent for making delicious desserts), and if you are reliable, you will soon have all the business you can handle. Word of mouth is the best advertisement of all—and it's free!

Two friends of mine have taken lots of cooking courses. One is dessert and bread chef to a seasonal resort's restaurant. This is exciting to her, and she is now a professional even though it means limiting her free time for the beach. Another with the same cooking skills has taught cooking courses and has now written two cookbooks. (By the way, a publisher friend says he is amazed that so many cookbooks are in such demand.)

Try selling prepared foods (homemade mustard, chutney, relish, flavored mayonnaise—whatever you do well) at consignment shops. Do the same with hand-knit garments or needlework.

Several friends have offered party giving, arranging events, and gift shopping for business executives who have a long Christmas list of business obligations and no time or talent for coping with it. Others are well-versed in antique and art collecting. Many businesses, when they move to new quarters, buy valuable lithographs and original water-colors and art to decorate their new offices. They have realized that they are buying assets as well as décor for their firms—assets bound to increase in value. Women of good taste in art and accessories can offer their services either directly to the organization involved or to decorating firms hired by them on an ad hoc basis.

Are you handy around the house? Can you repair clocks, rewire lamps, hang wallpaper, paint stencils? Then sell your services. It's easy and very inexpensive to make up a single-paged handbill and stick it in the doorway or fence of everyone in your neighborhood or leave in the lobbies of apartment buildings. Again, if you're good and reliable, word of mouth will soon set you on the path to money-making.

You can sell other services: be a pet and plant sitter, transport children to school, pick up and deliver laundry, grocery shop for people who are too busy, prepare tax returns, keep the books of small neighborhood businesses, care for children or invalids, run errands, escort an elderly person or an adolescent on a trip to Europe.

Start a bed-and-breakfast and turn your spare rooms into cash; provide an after-school service for the children of working parents; take care of two or three elderly people in your home.

(You should note that some of these occupations may require operating licenses and/or other regulatory papers, so find out from your state office of occupational licensing what the legal restrictions are, but do not let them deter you from following through on a good idea.)

. . .

Many of the types of work that fall into the realm of private entre-preneurship are done at home, either out of necessity or because renting and furnishing an office is out of the question until you start making a profit. There are advantages and disadvantages to working in the same place where you eat and sleep, and you should be aware of them.

Here are the plusses:

- you don't have to commute;
- you can wear whatever you want and thus save money on clothes;
- you can set your own hours;
- there's no one hanging over you to see if your work is done;
- there are no office politics to distract you so that work time is pure work; and
- you can deduct a portion of your rent or mortgage, utility bills, insurance payments, etc., as a business expense.

But some of these advantages can also be disadvantages, depending on the type of business you run and your own personality quirks and work habits. For instance:

- living, working, eating, and sleeping in the same abode can be tedious and can lead to boredom;
- most people who work at home don't bother to get dressed to the nines (and a few don't bother to get dressed at all!), and working in sweat pants, jeans, or a bathrobe all day, every day, can be demoralizing;
- setting your own hours is good for only the most disciplined (many people find that remaining in bed late becomes an overwhelming temptation, as are long afternoon naps);
- because you are unsupervised, there may be a tendency to miss deadlines, to procrastinate, or to simply not bother to work;
- there may be no office politics, but neither is there the pleasure of office interactions, gossip, establishment of contacts, and the sharing of ideas that is one of the pleasures of collegial work;
- deducting mortgage payments is a bonus, but being self-employed requires much more paperwork (and if you're smart, the expense of

an accountant) than does working for someone else, including tax forms, and finding out about and obtaining the appropriate licenses and permits;

- self-employed people have to pay their own health insurance, which averages $2,500 a year for reasonable coverage;
- no one hands you a pay check every two weeks—you are responsible for sending out all your own invoices and collecting all accounts receivable yourself, and often free-lancers are the last people to get paid; and
- many people who work at home find that their friends don't take their work seriously, and they are put into the position of having to fight an uphill battle to "prove" that they really do serious work and are not free to socialize during the day.

Self-employment can be one of the most fulfilling ways to earn a living, perhaps because it is the final and ultimate proof that you are a successful and independent woman. But it's tough. It can be depressing and lonely, and until you establish yourself, which can take up to five years, it can be almost paralyzingly frightening.

So think twice about striking out on your own at home, but if you do—good luck!

LEGAL PROTECTION

Whether you plan to work for yourself or for others, you are protected by law from a series of abuses often suffered by older workers, especially women. The federal Age Discrimination in Employment Act (ADEA) sets age seventy as the mandatory retirement age and provides protection against age discrimination. Many states, however, have gone beyond the minimums of ADEA and have set stricter standards, and some have even eliminated mandatory retirement altogether.

Title VII of the Civil Rights Act of 1964 outlaws discrimination based on sex in all aspects of employment, including hiring, fringe benefits, transfers, job opportunities, promotions, and discharges. It also prohibits labor unions from excluding members because of sex.

The Employee Retirement Income Security Act (ERISA) is a comprehensive employee benefits law requiring that employee benefit plan sponsors design and administer their plans according to legal standards—for example, mandating pension coverage for employees who work a thousand or more hours a year.

The Consolidated Omnibus Budget Reconciliation Act (COBRA) ensures that if you should be fired, your health and pension benefits will not be automatically cut off. If you work for a firm with more than twenty-five employees and if you are willing to pay the group rate yourself, your benefits will continue for up to eighteen months.

The Job Training Partnership Act (JTPA) is a federal job training program, administered by the Department of Labor, that provides funding for older workers. It places heavy emphasis on training for private sector, unsubsidized jobs.

The Senior Community Services Employment Plan (SCSEP) is funded under Title V of the Older Americans Act and provides part-time community service jobs for low income individuals age fifty-five and over.

Information about all these programs and laws is available from the office of your representative to Congress.

7

MEN — AND HOW TO FIND THEM

*W*hether you have been married ten years or forty, the prospect of being single again can terrify even the most socially secure woman. The condition of being single is going it alone, whether widowed or divorced. It takes most of us several years before we can even bear to think about the continuous company of an eligible man, but the time eventually arrives when we do crave the companionship of someone wearing trousers and a tie.

It takes effort and determination to avoid leading a ladies-only life, and one important lesson I've had to learn is to *unlearn* one drilled into me as a young girl: to wait patiently by the phone for men to call. Since I have been widowed, I have found that it is most assuredly not true that "nice girls" don't initiate phone calls to men.

Fortunately, my close friends didn't wait for me to tell them that I was ready to be introduced to single men, because I probably never would have. They knew I was lonely, but they also knew that I was used to a nonstop social life and to spending time with interesting people—including men. They didn't want me to lose all that just because Sam had died (and to be perfectly honest, after a certain amount of time had passed, I didn't want to either), so whether or not I was ready to make an appearance as a single, my friends pushed me into it.

ENTERING THE WORLD OF DATING

When you look back on the your first dating experiences as a young girl, you remember them with a good deal of pain, some embarrassment, and a lot of chagrin. Starting the dating experience as a new widow is not much easier, although of course the problems are different. Some of what will happen to you is funny (perhaps more so in the telling afterward than at the time), some is highly insulting and unpleasant, and some will be boring and stupid. But in this chapter I shall try to smooth the way a bit by covering the following points:

- how to meet men and where to find eligible ones;
- taking the initiative in your male-based social life;
- getting your friends and family to "fix you up";
- how to recognize and avoid the "man about town" who is determined to avoid commitment but will shower you with compliments and gifts when you are lonely and starved for affection;
- avoiding predatory married men;
- getting into the "dating scene" after you have been married for so long (things have changed and you may find yourself depressed and out of your element);
- who pays for what when you go out;
- going away for weekends or longer trips;
- beginning a sexual relationship and what that means;
- affairs with married men, God forbid;
- the pros and cons of remarriage; and
- who suggests the date and makes the arrangements.

As soon as I got over the shock of realizing that I was "in the market" for a man, not to marry but to have as a friend, I was actually grateful to my friends for forcing me out into the co-ed social scene. I had always enjoyed being part of a mixed group at friends' homes and have always been flattered—I still am—when someone invites me to even out her guest list. (My children tell me that the balanced table is passé. Maybe it is in their age group, but it certainly is not in mine.)

Whether the extra man was a teacher, businessman, doctor, lawyer, or church music director, I always used to enjoy sitting next to someone who could provide an evening's masculine conversation. I never considered it as "dating" (whenever I write that word, it seems to have nothing to do with me and is more like something teen-agers do) but more as a way to spend a pleasant evening that included people of both sexes.

As I look back on those first experiences with men, realizing that I was alone, I am aware that almost all the men with whom I have developed strong friendships I have met at the homes of my friends who dragged me out of the depths of widowhood into the light of a social life with men. My advice to anyone so situated is: *Force* yourself to accept invitations that are either obviously or covertly "fix-ups." It's only an evening, and if the man proves to be horrible, talk to the other dinner guests. If the whole thing is horrible, plead a terrible headache or an early morning appointment and take a cab home. And *do* try again.

Just yesterday I was actually too exhausted after a month's absence from my home and affairs to go to a postfuneral reception of an old friend. However, I had been out of circulation for a month and knew that many friends would be there, so I plowed my way through the traffic to attend. Being there gave me a chance to touch base with and make plans to see three friends whom I had not seen for a year. What luck! Without pushing myself to make that effort, three interesting opportunities would have been missed.

Believe me, I have had my share of ghastly evenings, and not every dinner party has resulted in a new male friendship. Furthermore, not every friendship has run smoothly. For instance, one day I was surprised to receive an invitation to a dinner party from a woman who was not a particularly close friend. When I arrived, I was touched to see that she had included several single men, and I was the only single woman there. Obviously, she had asked me with the specific intention of having me meet those men.

It turned out that one of the men and I knew a lot of the same people and shared a similar professional background. After I had gotten to know him better, I asked him to be my escort at a dinner dance that was to take place not far from his home on Long Island. When I arrived at his house, I was greeted by three enormous, aggressive, and incredibly noisy poodles. I'm embarrassed to admit that I am afraid of dogs, and those huge, friendly, leaping, licking animals scared me half to death in their attempt to make friends with me.

The gentleman and I remained good friends until his remarriage, but we always met for lunch in the city or had dinner at my apartment. I *never* again ventured near those dogs!

Meeting men has never been a particular problem for me because I have such a wide and varied social life, but not everyone is so fortunate, and not every widow lives in a major metropolitan area where the sheer numbers are apt to work in her favor. So here are some places that you might look—and *don't* dismiss any of them out of hand until you've given them some serious thought:

- Parents Without Partners, a national organization that has local chapters just about everywhere;
- other such organizations in which you have an interest and can do things, such as the Sierra Club (whose members you can hike with), your bowling league, or the American Association of Retired Persons;
- adult education classes, university extension courses, and the like;
- at the museum (don't be afraid of starting a conversation with a man alone who's staring at a picture that you are drawn to also);
- classified advertisements in magazines and newspapers (don't laugh—many people find many evenings of pleasant socialization that way, and many other people find much more);
- commercial dating services;
- organized volunteer work;
- clubs and professional and other associations;
- in business (it often pays to get a job, even if you don't need one); and
- singles groups of various kinds, although this last is difficult for most women.

My friend Sarah said that one morning, after her husband had been dead for about eighteen months, she "woke up and realized that there are other things in life besides work."

She had been working night and day, because she had just been promoted and wanted to prove herself in the new job, and because hard work took her mind off her misery. So she set out to find a man. "I went to a few singles evenings and *hated* it," she said. "I hated being on display; I hated the fact that everyone knew why I was there because we were all there for the same reason; and I hated the feeling of being picked over like a piece of fruit at the market."

Most of the evenings that she went to the singles events she met men who asked her for dates, "But they were losers, and I've always thought of myself as a winner. I would have had a better time staying home reading a good book."

She decided to relax and not try so hard, and about six months later she met a man with whom she has had a relationship for the past ten years.

I think it would be pleasant, and much more convenient, if men took the social initiative more often. But the fact is that interesting, attractive single men are usually so besieged with invitations, so sought after for parties, concerts, theater, and dinners, that they practically have to fight off the dozens of single women who claim their attention.

I have one friend whom I invite to dinner about once a year. Each time I see him we have a delightful evening, and I know he enjoys my company as much as I do his. Yet he never picks up the phone to arrange for us to get together. A few months ago I asked him why. He looked a little sheepish when he answered. "Phil," he said with some embarrassment, "I have to admit that I never call women. In fact, I have to fight to have an evening to myself once in a while!"

Another reason that men don't contact women is that, with widowers anyway, they were used to having their wives make all social arrangements for them. Divorcés and men who have never married are so much in demand that they don't have to take the initiative, so they don't. Many of them don't know how.

When Sam was alive, each morning before leaving the house, he always asked what was on the evening's calendar and I would tell him where we were going, with whom, what time we had to be there, and how he should dress. He never had to worry about social engagements, and the only scheduling he did for himself was golf games and business meetings.

I think that many men are grateful when a woman calls with an invitation, but that doesn't mean that it's easy for a woman to ask.

Recently a friend mentioned that the wife of an acquaintance of Sam's had just died. Although I hardly knew the couple well enough to send a condolence letter, I said I was sorry to hear the news. "Phil," said my well-meaning friend, "you'd better get yourself over there to borrow a cup of sugar every morning. Otherwise you'll be standing in line with a lot of other eligible women."

This wasn't advice that I felt I wanted to follow, given that I hardly knew the man, but many men, especially those who have been happily married, are lost without someone who will send their shirts to the laundry, handle their social life, and generally minister to their needs. They usually find—or are found by—someone very quickly.

If you want to find a man, you probably will. There are plenty of them out there, so you might want to remember a few things when they cross your path.

• Keep the fragility of the male ego in mind at all times. Most men believe that all the women they meet want to get married—to *them*. This makes them wary and skittish, so even if you are desperate to get married, never, never let it show.

• Give men lots of praise. There are always good things to say to men (if you can't think of any, you shouldn't be in their company) about their personality, their looks, and their achievements.

• Provide men with the security that you like them and want to be with them. All grown men are a lot like little boys or adolescents trying to get up the nerve to cut in on a girl at a dance. They never get over their fears of rejection, so you will probably have to take a lot of the initiative in the relationship, such as suggesting things to do and places to go.

• When you know you will be in male company, dress in an appealing but tasteful way. Be sure you look "scrubbed" and fresh—even though you may spend hours over your makeup. Wear becoming clothes that do something for you and that accentuate your best features. Wear soft, feminine fabrics even when you are dressed for the most conservative type of business, and don't, under any circumstances, try to look younger than you are by the way you dress. Few things are more depressing and pathetic than a sixty-year-old woman wearing a sequined T-shirt over too-tight pants.

• Learn how to approach a strange man in a friendly fashion without being too forward or flirtatious. If you're traveling, ask advice or directions. If you're in a museum, make a comment on a painting. If you're at a party or other gathering, introduce yourself—and then keep the conversation going by asking questions of the man. Find out what interests him, where he's from, what he does for a living (but try not to sound like you're "interviewing" him).

• If you're interested in a man, don't let him slip through your fingers because you don't know how to make the next move. Be direct but not pushy. If he's from out of town, offer to be a tour guide. If you're both traveling, suggest each other's company over dinner. Ask for his phone number; offer your own card. Say you're having a few people in soon for an informal supper—then go home and madly phone six or seven friends for a date that he says he has available.

• If you've been keeping company, get to know what he's really like, what his values and beliefs are. Ask him if he believes in God, how important money and security are to him, what he likes to do, how he plans to spend the rest of his life, what his goals were as a youth and how he has met them. Find out what he detests and the kinds of people he likes to be with. Does he have close friends, and if not, why not? This is just as valuable for you to know as it is for him to know that you are interested. You might not like him after all!

• Gradually tell him things about yourself and find out if he's interested. If not, try to find out why. Is he terribly self-absorbed, or is he not interested in *you?* The answer may hurt, but it's better to find out sooner than later.

• Avoid conversations that are calculated only to please. Most people can see right through that type of subterfuge and it only scares men away. There are many sincere ways to compliment men: remembering their birthdays and other important occasions, sending cards and flowers, and being considerate of their values and feelings.

• Don't let on that you're bored to tears. If you really are and can't stand to be in his company, end the evening as soon as you decently can and don't go out with him again, but don't let on that you're having anything less than a delightful time while you are in his company. Charm always works and if one man is not for you, perhaps a friend of his will be.

KEEPING A RELATIONSHIP GOING

If you have a special interest in someone who seems eager to settle down, throw a chicken in a pot and make some soup. Call him up and say something like, "Supper's ready, why don't you come over and share it with me?"

This method worked for at least one young friend of mine. Determined to nab an attractive man who was a hard-working associate at a law firm, she came up with a solution to the problem of his having to work late night after night. She arrived at his office one evening with two delicious sandwiches, a bottle of chilled white wine, a gingham tablecloth in a pretty country basket, and two napkins. "You have to eat somewhere, some time, and with somebody," she announced to the astonished man.

My friend continued to bring her beau a picnic supper every other night until he finally popped the question six months later. I am not at all sure that their wonderful marriage would have happened if she had been more bashful or less imaginative.

Younger women seem to have more confidence in themselves when it comes to relationships with men—or at least they give that impression. Also, I think society allows young women more leeway in what is acceptable, although again, this may be my imagination and my years of training to take a passive role where men are concerned. I am still shy about calling men, and I've had to work hard to overcome that part of my upbringing. I've been able to do it, in part, by reminding myself that social life today is a whole new ballgame, and for older women, the choice is to be lonely or to adjust to our new lives.

Now when I meet a man who seems intelligent and kind, I hand him my card and say, "I've enjoyed our chat this evening. I hope we'll see each other again." Or you can try: "Here's my card. Call me sometime and let's go to a museum or a movie."

As a working woman, I have always had a business card, but I think that every woman, working or not, should have one. All you need printed on it is your name, address, and telephone number. Then when you meet someone whom you would like to get to know better, you can give him or her your card as a reminder. It's so much easier than fishing around in your purse for paper and pencil and so much more convenient for the other person to have a card than a little scrap of paper that is easy to toss out or misplace.

If you are too shy to take such a direct approach, don't force yourself. Often a less straightforward appeal works just as well. I'm always amazed at the shortsightedness of single women who head straight for the men at social gatherings and ignore the women. They forget that it is the women who structure the social life and decide who is invited to dinner.

But it's not always easy to finagle dinner invitations either. Just last week I entertained twelve couples, and I am positive that every one of the twelve men present knows several interesting single men. My upbringing forbade me to say to one of the women, "I would love you to invite me to dinner with some of your husband's unmarried colleagues." But I was thinking it!

And by inviting those couples to my house, I have paved the way for them to reciprocate, along with a single man of their acquaintance. I doubt that they will, but I enjoyed their company and perhaps one of the women will someday think of me if a lone man appears in their lives.

GETTING BACK INTO THE SOCIAL SWIM

About a month or so after Sam died, I looked at my calendar and realized that I had two tickets to an upcoming concert of the New York Philharmonic. I was at a loss as to what to do with the second ticket. I wanted to go to the concert because I have always found that classical music instills a sense of peace, and I felt that I badly needed to immerse myself in its beauty. But I didn't want to go alone, and it seemed a shame to waste a perfectly good ticket.

I finally decided to invite a man whom I had known for many years and whose company I had always enjoyed. I'm sure that some eyebrows were raised when I was seen in the company of an eligible man so soon after Sam's death, but this gentleman and I understood each other well, and we both knew that nothing more was expected than each other's company at the concert. I soon realized that many men are happy to do the same.

It is difficult to be single again and in the company of a man who is not your husband. For most of us, it's been a long time since we have flirted or sat listening raptly to what our companion has to say. But you can ease your way into what my granddaughter, who goes to school at Princeton, calls the "dating scene" (she doesn't seem to like the phrase any more than I do) by spending time with single male friends. Whether you invite them over for a drink or an informal supper, or suggest a lecture, movie, or concert, they will most likely be happy to join you. If not, don't be discouraged; try someone else.

Some single men seem to make things especially difficult, perhaps because they are shy, or they have too many invitations already or because they still operate on the principle that the man should always call the woman. But if it's a man you're interested in, remember that you will probably have to do it. Find something that you think he'd like to do and then invite him to share it with you. Talk about things he's interested in, or use your shared professional or avocational interests to put him at his ease.

Draw him out about his current enthusiasms and future plans. Ask him what bothers him most about the politics in your city or in the federal government (*that's* a subject to keep you talking for years!). Ask him what he would do if he could be "king for a day" and wave a magic wand to solve the problems of the world.

Not only will these kinds of questions give you something to talk about over dinner or during intermission, the answers he gives will provide a clue as to whether or not he is interesting enough to devote time and energy to.

But you can carry all this too far and come to be known as a woman who makes a nuisance of herself. I know one woman who calls a mutual friend of ours at least every other day to invite him to dinner or a concert, to find out if she can pick up something for him at the store, or to ask his opinion of a newspaper article. "Is there anything I can do for you?" she always asks.

The man once confessed to me that only the tightest rein on his manners prevents him from responding, "Yes, leave me alone for a month!"

Women who behave this way rarely develop the type of friendships I have been discussing, which is not to say that they may not develop something else.

I can hear some of my readers wondering where in the world I manage to find so many single men. One close friend told me that in the ten years of being a divorcée, she hadn't met as many single men as I had in the two years I had been active on the social scene after I had recovered from the initial grief of Sam's death. "Men just seem to come out of the woodwork looking for you, Phil," she said to me in some exasperation.

I reassured her that I had no "secret stash" of single men, that they didn't fall all over themselves at parties trying to get dates with me. I told her that I worked hard at getting and keeping friendships with single men, that I had just as many rejections as anyone else, and that I spent just as many evenings alone with a book as she did—well, almost as many!

I take advantage of all situations in which I am likely to find men— for instance, through out-of-town visitors. Whenever I have friends visiting from other cities, I invite people over for a small, informal get-together. I serve drinks and a large platter of raw vegetables with a dip or a tray of cheese and crackers. My guest list includes both mutual friends and friends of my guests whom I don't know but would like to meet. I do not hesitate to say, "If you know any extra men, I'm always dying to add some to my list." That may sound a little opportunistic, even bold, but I have made several new men friends that way.

You are bound to be faced with occasions, as I have, when you absolutely have to have an escort—for a sit-down dinner or dance being held by your church, synagogue, or charitable organization in which you are very active. You've looked everywhere and have gone through your Rolodex three times, but everyone is unavailable for that evening. When you think you'll have to send your regrets to the organization, go through your address book once again. Perhaps you overlooked a name, perhaps there's someone you have just met and don't know well, or perhaps you could ask your friends if they know of someone who would escort you.

And if worse comes to worst, and there's no one at all, go alone. There are times when it is better to go out with just any man. However, some evenings it is more pleasant to stay home with a book. The only trouble is, it's almost impossible to tell beforehand when that would have been the case!

I must admit that since I have been a widow, I have said yes to several men with whom I was not thrilled to spend the evening. Sometimes it was a mistake to accept those invitations. But more often than not, even if I don't enjoy the company of the man I'm with, the other part of the evening—the opera or play or party—has been a success, and I usually run into a few people I haven't seen in a while.

I suspect that several of the invitations that have followed such evenings came from people who were reminded that I was again "on the scene" because they saw me out and about. And—even if you are bored to tears by a man and there is no one to come to your rescue, all evenings come to an end, and there are sudden headaches and alarms that will ring very early in the morning to give you an excuse to get home before you resort to screaming in frustration.

I have told several of my women friends that if they are giving a sit-down dinner party and one of their guests has to cancel at the last minute, they can feel free to invite me without the slightest bit of embarrassment. Don't ever hesitate to let your friends know that you are open to last-minute invitations to any social gathering. You never know who will be there. There are four or five of us in New York, all women alone whom I like very much, with whom I have the above relationship. In other words, up to a half-hour before you sit down to dinner, try me. If I'm not doing anything else, I'll come.

AMITIÉ AMOUREUSE

An *amitié amoureuse* is a relationship based on shared affection and respect, often seasoned with a dash of flirtation, that is not romantic love in the usual sense and usually does not lead to anything more than a deepening friendship.

I first discovered the idea years ago through dear friends who each year reprinted one of their favorite essays on their private printing press and sent them out as little pamphlets along with the season's greetings. I was so charmed by the one titled *"Amitié Amoureuse"* that I tucked it away in a special place for safekeeping. I have since reread and consulted it many times.

Margaret Lane, the author of the essay that originally appeared in the British magazine *Punch*, said,

> Everyone knows that falling in love causes the adrenaline to flow. . . . Looks improve, the weather brightens, wits sparkle, the sound of the telephone is interesting, a delicious buoyancy sets in. . . . At the onset of an *amitié amoureuse*, the symptoms are milder, of course, but they do one good. There are no sleepless nights; nothing, in fact, but a subtle gilding of all the edges of life, comforting in the heart, the spirits and the digestion.

How do you go about developing such a relationship? You don't really; it just happens because, in its own way, it is as special as a romantic love attachment—and that, as everyone knows, is impossible to predict.

What you must do is let your friendships blossom to encourage intimacy without sexuality—not the easiest thing to do. But when you are able, it is one of the most precious things in the world. You really care about one another but are not devastated when the telephone doesn't ring when you wanted and expected it to.

When the *amitié amoureuse* has developed into its full potential, you can do things and say things together that are impossible with others. For instance, one friend gives me little marbleized pillboxes for my desk, and I send him funny paperback books. You can exchange articles, poems, or new items. Stick a newspaper clipping in an envelope with a note saying, "I thought of you when I read this. Let's get together soon and talk about it." Or send him a review of a movie you think he might enjoy and suggest that you might see it together.

As long as you are clear in your own mind that you are not interested in or ready for a sexual relationship, you can send that message by way of thought, word, and deed. Sensitive, intelligent men will understand that you are interested in a loving, nonsexual friendship that does not go beyond good talks and reassuring hugs.

One friend of mine has such a relationship with a gay man. They are each other's best friends and probably are in some way in love with each other. But, naturally, there is no thought of a sexual relationship. Only her most intimate friends know that Albert is a homosexual, because he has squired my friend to many social occasions, and he has taken her to dances and dinners at the large teaching hospital where he is an important member of the staff. In addition to being best friends, they are each other's occasional escort, and no one need be the wiser!

And this brings me to the subject of women who are concerned with appearances and feel they need to follow the convention they were raised with even though the same "boy-girl" rules don't seem to apply any more.

Ten or fifteen years before I was widowed, eyebrows would have been raised if I had gone traveling with a man. At times they still are, but I do it anyway. I do try to make it clear to everyone that sharing a vacation with a man does not mean I am sharing his bed, but sometimes my message isn't loud enough. Too bad! People will think what they want anyway, and I don't have the time or energy to worry about it.

Fortunately, society no longer frowns so much on an unmarried woman who chooses to travel with a man. If a mature person decides to have an affair—or not have one—it is no one's business but her own.

At a recent conference I was attending out of town, one of my women golf partners turned to me as we were walking to the next tee and said, "Phil, everyone is wondering what you and Joe [the host of the conference who had invited me] are up to."

"Nothing," I replied, "but we're having a lot of fun doing it."

Men have many ways of staying unmarried while having a rewarding social life. Only a few months ago, I was on a trip outside the United States with an *amitié amoureuse* with whom I have traveled a great deal. He doesn't really want to be married, although he has always said when we part, "Goddamn, don't marry anyone else."

We have been guests in each other's homes often and in homes of other friends. On our most recent trip, our luncheon hostess commented on his attractiveness. I replied that we were "only friends." She replied to that: "The maiden doth protest too much!"

I just shrugged and let her think what she wanted. But I reported the exchange to my friend and he said, "Phil, it doesn't matter what people think. After my years alone [he had long since been divorced], I think I'd be a pain in the ass to be married to."

SITUATIONS—AND MEN—TO AVOID

My greatest misadventure since Sam died was partly the result of a business card that a most attractive man gave me. I had met him at the annual meeting of an organization in which I am active.

About six weeks after Sam died, I presided at the meeting as I had for years, and while introducing me, the president of the organization mentioned Sam's death and expressed condolences. Afterward, as I was packing my briefcase, a man whom I had seen before but didn't know, came over to tell me how sorry he was to hear about Sam. He invited me to dinner that evening, but I had other plans. He gave me his card and said that any time I needed an escort, he would be honored to be on call.

A couple of months later I was cleaning out my briefcase and came across his card. I put it in my desk and forgot about it. While I was attending dinner parties by that time, I was nowhere near ready to go out on a date.

Seven months after that, I found myself at the last minute with an extra concert ticket because the woman I had invited was ill. Not one of the several people I called was free, but as I rummaged through my desk, there was Alex's card. I called him, half thinking that he might not remember me and said, "You told me to call if I ever needed you, and now I need you."

He wasn't free for the concert that evening, but we had lunch the following Saturday, and thus began my misadventure.

We started with champagne at his apartment and then had lunch at a beautiful, romantic restaurant. "Tell me the story of your life," he said over the antipasto. I did and then asked the same of him. I didn't find out until much later that much of what he told me wasn't true.

After our third date, he introduced me to his three grown children, professed love, and proposed marriage. "Phil," he said, "I want you to know that I want to marry you. I know it's still too soon, but I'll be waiting whenever you're ready."

How wonderful I felt to think that this very desirable man, several years my junior, was in love with me! How splendid to be showered with lovely gifts and loving attention. What a terrific lift to my ego it was to have this attractive and intelligent man care for me.

But shortly after that, it all fell apart. I found out that he could not be believed, was proposing marriage to another woman at the same time, and was a confirmed womanizer. He had been married four times, had had many affairs, and was at that moment being introduced by a woman twenty years his junior, who lived out of town, as her fiancé.

It was obvious that a permanent love relationship was out of the question, and my own common sense (not to mention two of my best friends!) told me never to see him again. But Alex was so terribly attractive to me that I was able to fool myself into thinking that I wouldn't be hurt. "There's something good in all of God's creatures," I rationalized—and went on seeing him.

Some time later he presented me with another problem: a beautiful fur coat for Christmas. Now, I am a woman who loves clothes. I needed a new coat, and I'm a little weak-willed when it comes to beautiful things to wear. I kept it.

I was not proud of myself for accepting such an expensive gift from such a man, with whom I knew there was no future. In fact, I was downright ashamed of myself, as I should have been. I had never done anything like that before in my life. And I amazed myself with all the convoluted rationalizations and justifications I was able to devise just because I really wanted that gorgeous fur. One of the most inventive, I thought, was seeing the coat as a special farewell gift to commemorate what had been a lovely relationship. Since I wouldn't marry him, I told myself, this was his way of saying, "Whenever you wear this, remember me and all the wonderful times we had."

My daughters were disappointed with me, of course, as well they should have been, and eventually I was furious with myself. But I have since learned that this kind of experience is common among widows. A man enters our lives when we are most vulnerable, and because we crave the affection and physical contact he offers, we are blinded to his faults. Taking advantage of people when they are weakened and hurt is one of the most heinous things that people do to each other, and you must do your best to guard against it. But how? How do you detect bad qualities in people before your emotions get you tangled up in something that becomes very difficult to extricate yourself from?

It's hard, believe me, but you might think about some of the following when you meet and start dating men.

• How long has he been single and why is he single? A man who has reached forty and has never married may have a problem with commitment, and you're not going to change him. A man who has been married several times is also subject to question. He may also be homosexual, and you owe it to yourself to find that out right away. You might end up being best friends with him, but you need to know if romance is a possibility.

• What does the man want? Is he looking for love? Is he looking for an appointments-and-social secretary? Does he want a woman to wash his socks and get supper on the table on time? Does he want your money? (Does he have any of his own?) Does he want what *you* want?

• Although I don't want to sound like a "hard-hearted Hannah," and I certainly don't see myself that way, my experience with Alex taught me that you ought to know a great deal about a man before you become permanently involved with him. I'm not suggesting that you hire a private detective (although I'm not suggesting you don't, if that's where your inclinations lie), but someone of your acquaintance ought to know something about the man, and you ought to ask questions.

• Make sure you understand your own motivations before you begin a serious relationship. Why are you attracted to this man? What do your friends think of him? What do your own instincts say about him?

What does the community think of him? How does he stand in his field of work?

Now that my episode with Alex is long in the past, I can think of it as a cautionary tale for myself and others. When I decided to continue seeing him after I had learned about his character, I told myself I was smart enough not to get hurt. But of course I wasn't and I did. I thought I was strong enough not to care about his other women—past and present—but to this day I feel a twinge of jealousy when I hear about whom he has been seen with.

It was a hard lesson to learn that not all men are as honorable or hold to the same standards as Sam, but I do think that the relationship gave me something valuable that I needed at the time: a lift to my spirits. He helped me believe in myself, to feel as though I wasn't an ugly duckling and that I was, and still am, attractive to men. I hope he is still my friend, as I am his. And the coat is still gorgeous!

SEX AND WIDOWHOOD

It used to be that one of the reasons people got married was to have a steady supply of sex. This is no longer true, of course, and the need for sex is no longer a reason to marry. But by the same token, women are different from men when it comes to a physical relationship, and they still take sex far less casually than do men. Said the poet Lord Byron, "Man's love is of man's life a thing apart; 'Tis woman's whole existence."

Having had one very exciting relationship since Sam died, I know that it is still possible for me to be physically attracted to a man, and I don't think I would marry someone without first sharing a physical relationship. But since I cannot separate physical satisfaction from my emotional needs, I would need to believe that a man shares my desire for a serious commitment before I could share his bed.

And this brings me to a subject that many of you will find uncomfortable—perhaps even immoral: affairs with married men.

Let's face it, coveting thy neighbor's husband and adultery are not right. They are, in fact, wrong. Personally, I would find it impossible. But so many people do it and it has become such a common part of our social fabric that, while not condoning it, I think we should discuss it. There are many practical reasons why it is a temptation to consider an affair with a married man when one is totally alone.

• They are *there* and they are in abundant supply, much more abundant than single men.

• They will probably shower you with love, affection, compliments, and gifts because you are new, different, and not their wife.

• Some women who go into an affair with a married man with the understanding that he will not leave his wife for them (don't believe it if he promises to divorce her) may be able to have a pleasant, uncomplicated relationship.

• He will never pressure you to get married, and you can maintain your independence.

• Once you set aside the adultery taboo (if you cannot do this, then an affair with a married man is not for you), you may be able to get past sexual inhibitions that have plagued you—many women find that sex with married men is far more open and passionate than what they had with their husbands or with single men.

But affairs with married men have disadvantages other than the morality issue.

• Often what starts as a friendship—even a friendship with sex—turns into romantic love, which results in pain when it's over.

• Your lover will not be able to spend holidays, Saturday nights, and other important occasions with you.

• You and he may not be able to go out in public in your own city.

• His wife may find out.

• You or he or both of you may begin to feel guilty.

125

I am seeing a wonderful man whom I care for a great deal, and my friends can hardly believe he has never made a pass at me. His wife died a few years ago and we both speak freely and often about our late spouses. He kisses me good night, and if he were to suggest it, I believe I would sleep with him. But I think this intelligent, sensitive man is waiting for me to make the first move and probably assumes that when I am ready for that kind of relationship, I will let him know. Right now, to complicate our love with an affair might result in ruining our present lovely relationship.

But we are both cautious, and we both suspect that our present loving friendship would be transformed into something else, something from which we could not completely return if the new, changed relationship did not work out. I think we would either become a formal couple and get married, or we could no longer see each other. It is these considerations (perhaps you might justifiably see them as fears) that have kept me from becoming more deeply involved with this very dear friend. Many widows have similar problems and resolve them in this way to the satisfaction of both concerned.

TO REMARRY OR NOT

Most of the men I know don't think in terms of marrying again. If they had a wonderful marriage, they may worry that the second won't compare favorably with the first. If they were unhappily married, they seem to feel they will make another mistake and are afraid. There are some, however, who want to be taken care of and will do whatever they can to find a wife. Beware of those!

If you do consider marrying someone you know well and have seen a lot of, do not hope for a perfect love relationship. If you find it, fine. However, if you find someone with whom you enjoy exchanging thoughts, daily doings, joys and disappointments, and whose confidences you want to hear, that's a great deal.

Orgasms have little to do with the real beauty of lovemaking, and I believe the happiest couples, particularly if they have been married for a while and are mature in the best sense of the word, do not spend a lot of time in bed worrying about how often, how much, and how long they make love. Cuddling and making love in a spiritual sense is "letting it all hang out" to one another.

Merle Shain has written a book called *Some Men Are More Perfect Than Others* (Charterhouse Books, 1973). She says,

> Once we couldn't speak of sex and now we can't speak of love. Love is lonely and poetic and mysterious. We climb in bed not knowing what we want from each other and with a lot of anxiety, especially if we are older. It's more important that we feel and smell good and cheer each other with affection. Most women would rather have someone whisper their name at the optimum moment than rocket with contradictions to the moon, and ten minutes in bed with someone who appears to really know you has been known to change a life.

I have had C. S. Lewis's book, *Being in Love* at my bedside for 30 years. He says,

> Being in love is a good thing, but it is not the best thing. There are many things below it, but there are also many things above it. You cannot make it the basis of a whole life. It is a noble feeling, but it is still a feeling. Who could bear to live in that excitement for even five years? But, of course, ceasing to be 'in love' need not mean ceasing to love. Love is a second sense, love as distinct from being 'in love' is not merely a *feeling*. It is a deep unity maintained by the will and deliberately strengthened by habit; reinforced [in Jewish and Christian marriages] by the graces which both partners ask, and receive, from God. They can have this love for each other even at those moments when they do not 'like' each other; as you love yourself even when you do not like yourself. They can retain this love, even which each would easily, if they allowed themselves, to be 'in love' with someone else. 'Being in love' first moved them to promise fidelity: this quieter love enables them to keep the promise. It is on this love that the engine of marriage is run; being in love was the explosion that started it.

For myself, the longer I am on my own, the more independent I feel and the less interested I am in finding another husband right away. I have become accustomed to not having to consult anyone about my plans for the day or the month. I am used to planning my own life, and I like exploring my varied interests. I like not having to look my prettiest possible self the first thing in the morning; I don't even have to get dressed until noon if I don't feel like it! This is, particularly after you have been married, a very selfish existence indeed.

Some of my women friends have told me that I ought to think about getting married again, but others take the opposite view. "Why get married again," they ask, "if you're not so inclined? You certainly don't need to trap yourself into becoming some man's housekeeper just to have a little love and companionship."

I am afraid I am guilty of wanting too much if ever I should give up my single status. Men my age, or even a little younger, will never change their patterns, any more than I can change mine. Will I ever be someone else's wife? I am a lot less sure of the answer eleven years after Sam died than I was three years after his death.

I know that some of you reading this book cannot imagine life alone. You worry and wonder about how you can possibly structure your life without your husband—without a man. My advice to you is to spend some time analyzing yourself—your health, your interests, your prejudices, your hopes and dreams for the future. Try to understand who you are and what makes you happy. If you absolutely hate to live alone, then do everything in your power to find someone else as soon as you can.

Otherwise, make the most of being alone. You may find, as I have, that you can relish your independence. You also will find that you can have perfectly satisfying sexual relationships without being married. Don't think for a single moment that just because you have passed age fifty or fifty-five or even sixty that your sex life is over.

Beverly Johnson, an assistant professor of nursing at the University of Vermont, interviewed 164 men and women between the ages of fifty-five and ninety about their sexual attitudes. Here are some of the things she found out:

- about half of both men and women say that their interest in sex is less than it was when they were young, and more than half say they participate less in sex; but
- fewer than half of the men and a third of the women say they are less sexually satisfied now than when they were young—many say

their sexual satisfaction has not changed at all; and

• the vast majority say they are still interested in and think about sex.

Not too long ago, while having dinner with three successful, unattached sixty-ish women, I asked them to describe their lives alone. "It's wonderful," they said. "It's fulfilling, it's independent, it makes you feel like a really grown-up person to make decisions about how you're going to run your life."

I thought I detected a little hypocrisy in their comments, feeling as I did after more than ten years without Sam. I was positive that if a man they could love, respect, and depend on wanted to marry them, they would leap at the chance.

But I was also sure of their sincerity. They had all been divorced, not widowed, and had made financial successes of their lives—on their own. In fact, they had succeeded in their respective careers despite a lot of discrimination along the way, and had overcome many obstacles to build happy lives for themselves.

So their perspective of living alone was very different from mine *at that time.* Now I'm not so certain. True, life and the way we look at living alone is still different for widows and divorcées, but I now, a decade after losing Sam, feel more like those women than ever before.

Don't for one minute think that I "have it made." Although I don't fall prey to self-pity often, it does happen (let's face it—it happens to everyone, widowed or not). Just last week I was at a party where two of the other guests were men with whom I had been spending a lot of time lately. I had wonderful chats with both of them, but neither one offered to take me home. Neither one of them had come to the party with a woman, and both could have afforded to take a cab home and drop me off.

But neither did!

One of the prices that truly independent women pay is that not only do they *feel* independent, they project that image to others, who sometimes feel that they can do *everything* for themselves, which everyone knows is not true.

"Damn it," I thought. "Here I am alone. It's three degrees below zero in the middle of the night, and I'm standing on the sidewalk trying to hail a cab."

I had to force myself to stop feeling sorry for myself, but I wasn't entirely successful until I had gotten into a cab and had been deposited safely in front of my nice, warm house. Even then, it took a while. It *is* sometimes frustrating being single and having to arrange everything for yourself, and not every hostess is thoughtful enough to provide transportation for her guests, and sometimes I forget to arrange it for myself beforehand. But even through my tears of self-pity that night, I knew I would never, never marry just for the sake of being taken care of!

8

GETTING PROFESSIONAL HELP

PSYCHOLOGICAL HELP

*S*ometimes we feel overwhelmed, drowning in sorrow, rage, and despair. Emotional paralysis becomes more than a way of describing how we feel; it turns into reality, forcing our lives to a virtual halt. At those times even closest friends and family can't provide the comfort to get us through the darkness.

One woman said she felt so utterly alone and isolated that even her sister, with whom she had shared the greatest intimacy over the years, couldn't help. If she hadn't found a psychiatrist she trusted, she thinks she might have killed herself. "The walls were closing in on me," she said. "I don't know what I would have done if I hadn't had my doctor to call that night."

Another friend of mine said, "You're allowed to talk about the grief for a while but not for as long as you *need* to. I'm not sure at what point people's patience with your loss begins to wear thin, but it does, and they make it really obvious that they think you ought to snap out of it and get on with your life. The only trouble was that I wasn't ready when everyone thought I should be."

Most widowed people agree that the sense of grief and emptiness lasts far longer than it "ought" to, according to their friends, family, and even physicians. But research is beginning to corroborate actual feelings.

The first documented study of grief was done by Erich Lindemann in the wake of the 1944 Coconut Grove nightclub fire in Boston in which 491 people were killed because they were trapped inside the burning building by locked fire exits. Lindemann erroneously concluded that it was possible to reconcile the death of a loved one in four to six weeks.

But a 1987 study done at the University of Michigan belies what Lindemann thought. Researchers there found that the long-term effects of losing a spouse, especially if the death was sudden and unexpected, as in an accident or fire or a sudden devastating illness, lasted four to seven years.

A 1985 report on bereavement by the Institute of Medicine of the National Academy of Sciences in Washington, D.C., blames society's ambiguity about appropriate grieving behavior and the privacy of mourning in Western countries. The report concluded, "The lack of social prescriptions concerning mourning and bereavement may result in serious adjustment and recovery problems for the recently bereaved."

Peggy Eastman, a Washington, D.C., writer whose husband was killed in a plane crash, put it in more human terms: "Grief is an untidy and overlapping process. The griever takes two steps forward and one back, or one step forward and one back, or gets stuck in one place for a while. There is no correct way to grieve and no time limit."

Since the agony of grief is so universal, seeking professional help is not a shame or a failure of strength. In fact, it shows the opposite. Making that phone call for help is a strong, positive statement about determination to feel yourself again.

How to Get Help

There are a variety of ways to reach out for help, not all of which are right for everyone. There are also a variety of frustrations that most people don't realize at first. But if you think of psychological counseling as purchasing a service, a very special and unique service, but a service nonetheless, you will begin to see yourself as a consumer and some of the obstacles will be evident.

For instance, when you shop for a dress, an important but certainly not crucial purchase, think of how many you try on before you find just the right one. Now compare the importance of buying clothes with the importance of pouring your heart out to a professional counselor. Think too about your experiences of finding the right physician, lawyer—or carpenter to hang your kitchen cabinets. You didn't sign up with the first one you met.

But don't let the frustrations deter you. It's true that you may have to shop around for a while before you find someone whom you like, who likes you, whom you feel comfortable with, and whom you believe to be a competent practitioner. All four components are absolutely necessary for a successful relationship with a therapist. But when you finally find someone, the relief of being able to come to grips with your pain and anger are well worth the trouble.

I shall first discuss the various sources of help available and then some of the procedures you might want to follow to find and screen a therapist.

As in finding help of all kinds, one of the best ways is to ask around and tell your friends that you need to see someone. However, in this case, the whole thing might be too personal to do that, and you may not want to either see a friend's therapist or even call that therapist for a referral. Divulging your need for help to friends and family is entirely up to you, but if you do decide to tell someone, be sure it's a person you can trust. Telling the "whole world" that you are in therapy should be your own decision—you do not want to be a source of gossip.

Where to Go for Help

If you choose to look for counseling entirely on your own, or if your friends have no practical suggestions, there are a variety of people and places that can serve your needs.

• Your minister or rabbi. Sometimes you can get actual help from a member of the clergy him- or herself if you feel comfortable with the inevitable spiritual component that is bound to be part of the process and if the religious director of your church or synagogue has training in pastoral counseling.

In any event, he or she can surely serve as a source of referral, because you are not the first member of the congregation to need help, nor will you be the last. Almost all congregations of any size have referral lists of community resources of all types, including counseling services.

• A psychiatrist (a medical doctor). There are dozens of schools and theories of psychiatry, one or more of which may be right for you. The practice of psychiatry is similar to the practice of any medical specialty in that the practitioner has been to four years of medical school and has probably done a few years of general medical residency. He or she then does a psychiatric residency of four or five years before taking the certification examinations and hanging up a shingle.

The length and complexity of psychiatric training has advantages and disadvantages for you. He or she has a well-grounded basic understanding of all types of mental illness, which may or may not be of practical use to you. Grief, unless it takes a very unusual course, is not a sickness. You are *not* mentally ill because your husband has died. Therefore, if you choose to see a psychiatrist, he or she may tend to view all your reactions as if they were symptoms of a mental illness—just as a cardiologist views all chest pain as though it were symptomatic of heart disease.

On the other hand, if you are severely depressed and unable to function at your usual level, or if you can't function at all and are in what is known as a clinical depression, a psychiatrist may be the best equipped to treat you, especially since he or she can prescribe a variety of psychotropic medicines like tranquilizers and antidepressants.

Too, psychiatrists tend to charge more than other types of mental health counselors, although in major metropolitan areas there is often not much difference between psychiatrists and clinical psychologists. Psychiatric fees now *start* at about a hundred dollars for a fifty-minute session—often more in large cities like New York, Los Angeles, and Washington.

Psychiatrists, because of the nature of their training and the way they view people's temporary diminution of mental health and/or functioning, often want to institute long-term therapy that can last five years or more. You probably need only short-term counseling of a few weeks to a few months.

But if you think you want to investigate the possibility of finding a psychiatrist, where do you start? You can ask your doctor, your friends, or the local medical society's referral service. However, there is no way to know whether he or she will be right for you until you spend a few hours in each other's company.

Sometimes it's easy to know right away if you're *not* going to like the doctor; knowing whether the relationship will work takes longer—which can be an expensive proposition. (Most health insurance policies pay no more than 50 percent of outpatient mental health costs, and all have an annual limit of what they will reimburse.)

A relationship with a psychiatrist or other mental health counselor is one of the most intimate you will ever develop. You may end up telling him or her things you would never dream of telling your best friend, perhaps things even your husband didn't know. So be certain you trust the person to whom you will entrust the most private part of yourself before embarking on a course of therapy.

• A psychologist. A psychologist holds a Ph.D. and fills many of the same functions as psychiatrists, with the exception of prescribing drugs—and many charge about as much! Psychologists function in many capacities (testing, administration, research, and the like), but you will want one who does clinical work—that is, working with patients in both individual and group settings. Although psychologists also tend to see human behavior in terms of healthy or unhealthy, many are trained in more nontraditional ways than are psychiatrists, so you are more likely to find a psychologist who will see your pain as a case of grief gone awry rather than true mental illness. But as there are exceptions to any rule, you can find as many psychologists who are as anxious to label you "sick" as there are psychiatrists who are not caught up in traditional Freudian or Jungian molds.

I cannot tell you if it is better to enter therapy with a psychologist or a psychiatrist because it is so individual. Neither can I tell you that it is better to seek help from a woman than a man. It all depends on how you feel, what your needs are, and most important, on the relationship you establish with the therapist.

But you go about finding a psychologist the same way you do a psychiatrist: ask around and call the local branch of the American Psychological Association for referrals.

You might also look in the yellow pages of the telephone book under "mental health." Most cities of any size and almost all counties (some sparsely populated areas have regional consortia made up of several local and county jurisdictions) provide mental health services to residents, for which they charge on a sliding scale. They also run referral services for private practitioners. You might also look in the government listings of your telephone book under "Health Department."

• Social worker. This is a person who holds a Master's of Social Work degree and has had training in clinical work. Social workers often do not have the depth of theoretical background that psychiatrists and psychologists do, but they have the advantage of being very health-oriented and are therefore more likely to see your problems as situational rather than pathological. In other words, they're less likely to view you as sick.

Also, many social workers are highly experienced in crisis intervention, that is, being able to help you compartmentalize your life and deal with the problem at hand—getting through this difficult period—rather than seeing your whole mode of functioning as unhealthy and insisting that you change your entire behavior.

Social workers also charge less than psychiatrists and psychologists, but some health insurance policies do not cover their services as a reimbursable expense, so be sure to ask at the beginning—unless, of course, money is no object.

• Support groups. The support group concept developed two or three decades ago and has proved so successful that there seems to be a group for every possible life situation. In a widows' support group, you will meet regularly with men and women who share your experiences, and that in itself is a comfort. The group provides the freedom to express feelings, sometimes strange ones that come as a surprise to the mourner.

In a 1987 study by Harvard researchers, 15 percent of the people they interviewed said that they "felt just like" the dead person, 9 percent reported feeling the same pains or other symptoms experienced by the dead person in his or her terminal illness, and 12 percent at some point thought they had the same illness. A full 40 percent of grieving people were worried at one time or another that they were losing their minds.

A good support group helps grieving people to share these feelings and provides an outlet for the commonality of feelings. The group meets on a regular basis, usually weekly or biweekly, and requires a commitment of attendance from its members. In other words, once you decide to become a member of the group, you are expected to attend each meeting and to be an active participant.

One man who has been a member of his group for about a year says, "This is not a social get-together over wine and cheese. In this group you must have some willingness to stay with the pain and convert it into meaning."

He explained that most people enter a group after the initial denial and shock has worn off and the reality that the spouse has gone forever has set in. "There is a lot of hard work between recognizing that and beginning to rebuild," he said.

The two best ways to find a grief and loss support group in your community are to look in the newspaper in the section where such activities are listed, or to call the local chapter of the American Association of Retired Persons and ask for the Widowed Persons Service. You can also ask other widows you know for the names of people who have participated in such groups.

NONPSYCHOLOGICAL HELP

Everyone knows that plumbing is no respecter of feelings, and pipes burst and toilets back up just as easily during the depths of depression (and more easily on the day you're giving a sit-down dinner for twelve!) as they do when you are feeling on top of the world. Therefore you must know how to find help of all sorts, and once you have found a reliable professional, keep his or her name in your address book or Rolodex and guard it with your life.

There are so many types of workers that you will have to hire during the course of your widowhood—from auto mechanics to podiatrists to gardeners to electricians—that I cannot provide a guide to hiring all of them. What I will do is give you general rules of thumb about how to find reliable people and the kinds of "tests" you should put them to when you are interviewing them to do work for you.

• The first, and usually the most foolproof, way of finding someone you will be happy with is to ask a friend or professional colleague for a reference. If a couple you know had their kitchen redone, and they spoke highly of the contractor and loved their new kitchen, get the name of the person who did the work—and tell that person you were referred by Mr. and Mrs. So-and-so.

If your friend Katie raves about her plumber and says he is always there when he says he is going to be and has never overcharged her, write down his name.

One friend of mine drives a ten-year-old car that is in perfect working order. One day at lunch she said in a joking sort of way, "Nasko [her mechanic] has as much of an interest in keeping this car going as I do. It seems to be a matter of pride now with him to keep my geriatric car on the road."

That was no joke to me. Good auto mechanics that deal honestly and competently with single women are a rare commodity, and I have been taking my car to him ever since.

The referral doesn't even have to come from a friend. Elizabeth, one of my closest friends, was widowed two years ago, and a year and a half later she decided to sell the big old house that she and her husband had lived in for thirty-eight years. But she liked the idea of having a "real" house with a yard in the suburbs and went shopping for a small house that wasn't so far out in the country.

She eventually found one that was perfect—except that the yard and garden were a disaster. "It looked like something out of your worst horticultural nightmare," she said. "It was as if no one had cared about the green things for an entire decade."

Elizabeth had always prided herself on maintaining her own garden, but this was too big a job. "I needed help getting the mess straightened out," she said, "and then I would be able to take care of it myself."

So she drove around her new neighborhood, and when she came to a yard that looked particularly lovely, she rang the bell, introduced herself as a new neighbor, and asked for the name of the people's gardener. Not only did she get the mess in her yard taken care of, she made friends with several people in her neighborhood, joined a bridge group, and is now on the board of the local civic organization. "I'm turning into a political animal," she said with a laugh.

• You must make certain to find out if the professional or other workman you are thinking of hiring is licensed or certified by the appropriate body—and, preferably, belongs to a society or organization of his or her fellows.

For instance, let's say you need a new gynecologist. You ought to know if the physician is board-certified in obstetrics and gynecology. This means that he or she has had postgraduate medical education in gynecology, has done a three- or four-year residency in the specialty, and has passed an examination at the end of that time. The training program and examination are administered by the American College of Obstetricians and Gynecologists, and the doctor should have a diploma hanging prominently in his or her office attesting to certification. If the diploma isn't there, ask if he is board-certified. If he says he's not—or worse, if he says that certification isn't necessary, choose another doctor.

But what if you just want a small repair service to trim some tree branches that have grown out along your roof? There's not much harm they can do as long as you tell them exactly what you want done, and the whole job probably won't take more than an hour. Your state doesn't require a license for this type of work, so there's nothing for you to check. Right?

Wrong! What if one of the workmen falls off your roof and hurts himself? Who is liable for his injuries? You are—unless the workman has his own liability insurance, and you won't know that unless you ask. And make sure you see the certificate of insurance. Don't just take his word for it. Too many people will tell too many stories to get work.

• Ask questions that require evidence that the workman knows what he's doing—and can explain it to you in language you understand.

Take a plumbing job, for instance. Last year the little button you push to make the water in the tub faucet come out through the showerhead stopped functioning in my bathroom. Now, I'm ashamed to admit that I can't even change a washer myself and have my friend Jack do it whenever the drips get too serious. (Actually, I probably *could* do it; it certainly doesn't look that difficult, but I'm not interested enough to learn, so I feel helpless whenever something like the shower incident happens.)

So I got estimates from three plumbers, and I ended up hiring the one who charged slightly more because he was very careful to explain what he needed to do, how the faucet-shower mechanism worked, and why he advised replacing the entire system instead of just repairing it.

Perhaps the other two knew their work, but they weren't willing or able to explain it to me, and I always like to know exactly what I'm paying for.

But let's go back to the gynecologist for a moment. Say you're thinking of taking estrogen, now that menopause is upon you. Ask the doctor questions that show whether or not he or she knows much about the current research on hormone replacement therapy, for example, "Would you tell me what the statistical risks are of endometrial cancer if I take X or Y brand of replacement estrogens?" Or, "Why exactly do you recommend X brand instead of Y brand of estrogens?" Or, "What precisely causes hot flashes, and why do I hear that replacement estrogens can get rid of them?" Or, "Should I take progestogen along with estrogen? Why?"

These kinds of questions all require specific knowledge *and*—this is crucial—the ability to impart that knowledge to the patient so that questions are fully answered. In other words, you shouldn't walk out of the doctor's office with more questions than you had when you walked in.

If a doctor (or anyone else you hire to care for your body or your possessions) can't or won't answer specific questions, he or she is not doing the job you're paying for.

• Learn to rely on your judgment and instincts even after you've done reference checking and license verification. The professional or workman is theoretically in the best position to know the benefits and potential problems of this or that treatment or repair, and you probably will want to follow his or her advice *if* you trust your judgment.

And the only way to develop judgment is to work on it by trusting and testing your instincts. For instance, if you feel patronized and mostly ignored by the person you have hired, ask yourself why. Are you being too demanding, or are you really being patronized and ignored? If it's the former, change your behavior and see if the other person changes his. If it's the latter, get a new electrician.

Both negative and positive feelings have to originate somewhere, and people don't fantasize unpleasant experiences—especially when it comes to dealing with service people, because unpleasant experiences are all too common these days.

• Don't let yourself be overcharged. This is sometimes difficult because there are such wide variations in price estimates for a particular piece of work, and sometimes it makes a difference. But sometimes it doesn't.

I once needed to have a small tree taken down in my backyard out on Long Island. It was a straightforward and uncomplicated job, and I asked four people to give me price quotes for the job of cutting down the tree, cutting it into fireplace-size logs, stacking them, and hauling away the branches. The estimates ranged from eighty-five to three hundred and sixty dollars! I chose the cheapest because I didn't have to worry about the quality of the work or replacement parts or the fact that the workman needed a great deal of arcane knowledge.

But sometimes the cheapest way is not always the best. For example, Nasko, the auto mechanic I mentioned earlier, is not the least expensive one in town. But he has never cheated my friend, and he has never cheated me. He guarantees his work, and if something isn't just exactly right, he works on it until it's perfect—for no additional charge.

That's why I trust him implicitly. If Nasko says I need a new gizmo or whatchamacallit, I tell him to go ahead. My friend says that when

Nasko tells her that it's no longer worth fixing her old car and to get a new one, she'll go out and buy one immediately.

• Get references and talk to people who have used the service. If a professional or service person hesitates to provides references, go elsewhere immediately.

• Check with your local Better Business Bureau and county or municipal consumer affairs department to see if there is a history of complaints lodged against the company.

• Read the fine print on whatever contract you sign. Read *every word* and don't sign until you are certain you understand your rights and responsibilities and those of the person you are hiring.

What to Do When Things Go Awry

If you have been cheated, ripped off, or dealt with unfairly in any way, don't just stand there, do something. Take charge of your life and stand up for your rights.

Your ultimate recourse is a lawsuit, either with an attorney or by yourself in small claims court, but there are many things you can do before filing legal papers. Here are some of them:

• Write a letter of complaint to the person *in charge.* Always find out who's in charge and write to him or her. Your letter may be sent back "downstairs," but it will come from the president's office and will therefore receive the attention it deserves.

If you have a problem with a department store, get the name of the general manager of the store, or the president of the chain and write a coherent, cogent letter describing exactly what happened and what you want him or her to do for you. Do not sound like a crank or a whiner, and be certain that you are specific in every detail. Don't sound unreasonably angry (you are, of course, outraged at being cheated but keep your anger in proportion) or sarcastic, and never make threats. Include copies of all relevant documents (bills of sale, warranties, etc.) and be specific about dates. Allow a reasonable time for a response and then take the next step if you have not been satisfied.

• Contact the appropriate municipal, state, or federal agencies. You can find their addresses and phone numbers in the government listings of your phone book, although it is sometimes difficult to wade through the maze of bureaucratic-sounding offices to find the right one, and you can waste a morning on the phone trying to find the correct place to direct your complaint.

A much better idea is to request the *Consumer's Resource Handbook,* which is available free by writing to the U.S. Consumer Information Center, Pueblo, CO 81009. This is an invaluable compendium of information about how to resolve consumer complaints, and contains sections on corporate consumer contacts; automobile manufacturers; Better Business Bureaus; trade associations; third-party dispute resolution programs; state, county, and city government consumer protection offices; state agencies on the aging; state banking authorities; state insurance regulators; state utility commissions; state vocational and rehabilitation agencies; weights and measures offices; military commissaries and exchanges; federal information centers; and selected federal agencies. In short, everything you need to know about what to do if you get ripped off.

• Keep up the pressure. Sooner or later you will get a response to your complaint, and more than likely you will receive complete satisfaction. Companies have no way of knowing how far you are prepared to go, how much delaying tactics will ultimately cost them (in legal fees and customer good will), who else you will pull into the act, and how many friends you might have in high places.

9

YOUR PHYSICAL
AND
EMOTIONAL SELF

Being sick and alone is no fun and we all dread it. It's not that we think we're going to die if left alone, but illness means vulnerability and the possibility of succumbing to depression and self-pity. It also can dredge up memories of your husband's last illness or the times when he was sick and you took care of him or when you were sick and he took care of you.

We want someone to hold our hand, feed us chicken soup, drive us to the doctor, change the sheets, and provide an unlimited amount of sympathy and cluck-clucking. Thus, people who live alone tend to try to get better faster because we have no one dancing constant attendance, and if we're not going to be pampered, there's no point in prolonging the agony. It's a bore to be sick, and the novelty of lying in bed all day (especially if you've just conquered the difficulty of getting *out* of bed after a long depression), reading, or watching television wears off quickly.

Coping with being sick depends on the severity and length of the illness. If you have a week-long case of the flu, all you need is a neighbor or friend to go to the grocery and make sure you have enough to eat and drink. But if you're recovering from a heart attack or major surgery, you may need professional help and/or a home health aide for a while. There are many agencies (listed in the yellow pages under "Nurses") that can supply either or both, and many health insurance policies will foot at least part of the bill if your doctor says you need the service.

If you have family or a close friend who will take care of you—at least for a while, so much the better. This may be the time to call your children or accept their invitation to recuperate in their home and let *them* mother *you* for a few weeks.

Naturally, it's impossible to predict illness, but you can protect yourself against some disasters and minimize others.

• Always keep a phone by your bed in case you're stricken in the night. Have enough phones in the house so in case you break a leg or have a stroke, you won't have to drag yourself too far.

• Tape your doctor's number to the telephone and *do* have a doctor you can call in case of emergency. Many healthy people think they don't need a physician and then have no one to call when they fall ill. Choose a doctor, have an initial examination, and get yourself on his or her patient roster—even if you don't show up in the office for a year or so.

• Give your house key to a close neighbor in case you're too sick or injured to come to the door. *Do* call if you need help.

• If you know you're coming down with the flu or a bad cold, go to the store before you're too sick. Stock up on aspirin, orange juice, and the kinds of foods you know you'll feel like eating.

• Keep a well-stocked emergency medical kit within easy reach.

145

• If you're sick but don't need help, tell someone anyway so they can check on you once or twice a day by phone to make sure you're all right. Some illnesses have a way of turning nasty without warning.

• Know where the nearest hospital emergency room is.

• Keep your health insurance identification card in your wallet at all times, and if you have potentially fatal allergies, keep a card describing them in your wallet attached to both your driver's license and your health insurance card. Better still, wear a medic alert bracelet or necklace.

Maintaining Your Physical Self

In the days immediately after my husband's death I felt physically numb. I had no appetite, no energy, and got what seemed like no sleep. The physical problems continued for a long time (I still sometimes have trouble sleeping), but if I had known then what I now realize, I would have felt better sooner.

What I now know is that it's never too soon to begin taking care of your health, to pay attention to what you eat, how you look, how many hours of sleep you're getting, and how much exercise you take. Much of the time you won't care what you look like and won't feel like cooking for yourself, let alone go on a two-mile walk. But you *have* to. Some mornings, just getting dressed will consume all your energy, and it'll seem too much to actually care what you wear. You'll even stop going to the hairdresser. But if you wait too long to start (or continue) a diet and fitness program, you run the risk of slipping into a rut of not caring so that it'll take that much more energy to snap out of it when you finally decide to—or your friends make you.

• • •

The first foe is fatigue. Grief is exhausting; sobbing can leave you drained for hours, and chronic insomnia can make your waking hours hell. One friend described the feeling as "swimming through a vat of Karo syrup."

Many of my widowed (and divorced) friends report feeling "bone tired," and I'm convinced that this is due in part to avoiding the reality of the loss (denial is not always as unhealthy as some experts say it is, and it's a natural part of the grieving process—but it's tiring). I recommend leveling with your doctor. Tell him or her exactly how many hours you're sleeping at night (you might want to keep a written record for ten days or two weeks before your appointment) and see what he or she advises.

But there are things you can do on your own to prevent insomnia.

• Avoid frenetic, stressful activity in late evening. Try "winding down" for an hour or so before bedtime by doing something pleasurable and relaxing.

• Establish a regular sleep schedule and stick to it—even on weekends.

• If you can't get to sleep, don't force it. Turn the light on and read or listen to music.

• Don't drink caffeinated beverages in the afternoon or evening. Experiment and establish a cut-off time for caffeine.

• Avoid strenuous exercise in the evening, but do establish a regular daytime exercise program.

• A warm bath before bed can relax tense muscles, though some people find that an evening shower is too invigorating.

• Make your bedroom as conducive to sleep as possible: darken the room, shut out noise, change the sheets often, and make the bed before you get in it. If you're cold in winter, wear socks or get an electric blanket. Use earplugs, an eyemask, or a white-noise machine if necessary.

• Wear beautiful and/or comfy nightclothes.

• Sex before sleep can be a wonderful hypnotic—but not if it leaves you tense and frustrated.

• Don't take daytime or evening naps.

• Drink a glass of warm milk or eat a small high-carbohydrate snack before bed. Don't go to bed hungry, but neither should you get between the sheets right after a heavy meal.

• Try not to take the day's worries and tensions to bed with you; deal with whatever you can before bedtime and make plans to fix the rest the next day.

• Learn relaxation techniques (consider buying relaxation tapes to keep by the bedside) and do them in bed.

• Don't do office work in bed.

You have to eat properly. You're depressed, wallowing in self-pity, and maybe even bored. These are all invitations to either overeat or undereat, depending on your psychological makeup and how food has always fit into your coping mechanisms. This is not the place to tell you how to lose, gain, or maintain weight—there are about a zillion books in stores and libraries to do that—but this is the place to discuss the problems of suddenly having to cook only for yourself and eat alone every evening. There are ways to make that more pleasant and to avoid doing it all the time. You do *not* have to live on frozen food heated in a microwave, slapped-together bologna sandwiches, or take-out Chinese food. Neither must you eat in restaurants every day.

The important thing is to learn not to dread dinner hour, and I'd be lying if I said this was easy. But try to set aside a time with "real" food that you've cooked yourself; eat at the kitchen or dining table set with nice dishes and a flower or candle. This is a psychological and nutritional necessity. In addition:

• Create a pleasant interlude between the day's and evening's activities (even if it's only staying home to watch television or read). Many people like to read or watch the news while they eat. Others enjoy listening to a favorite record. Still others like to do nothing but concentrate on the food. If you've put effort into cooking something delicious (or even if you've stopped off at the deli on the way home for a juicy corned beef on rye), take the time to enjoy it. But whatever else you do besides eat, if the phone rings, let your machine answer or say you'll call back after dinner.

• Don't eat alone every night. Invite friends over for an informal supper, or call someone and suggest going out.

• Prepare meals that are well-balanced and interesting, but that don't require you to spend hours in the kitchen every evening. For instance, cook a pot of stew or hearty soup one weeknight or Saturday afternoon, divide it into single portions, and freeze them. Combine it with a salad or lightly steamed vegetable. Buy food that lends itself to single portions instead of large lumps that you'll tire of before you finish: a few Brussels sprouts instead of a whole cabbage, broccoli stalks instead of a head of cauliflower, cut-up chicken parts instead of a whole roaster, and small steaks or packages of ground beef instead of an entire roast. If you like cakes and pies, make one and cut it into individual portions and freeze for future pleasure. Keep plenty of pasta and rice in the house to combine with cheese, vegetables, and meat or chicken. Or keep it simple: a grilled cheese sandwich, raw zucchini and carrot sticks, and fruit or a store-bought dessert takes about ten minutes to prepare but is as nutritionally sound as a full meal that took hours.

Exercise is an important component of feeling physically fit. Again, there are many books and tapes to teach you techniques, or you can join a fitness center or the Y. (Most such places have classes geared to older women where you won't have to compare your sixty-year-old thighs with a twenty-two-year-old's. Also the exercises are different.)

Walking is one of the best and most recommended forms of exercise. Get a comfortable pair of shoes, find a partner if you're bored doing it alone or need the impetus, dress in warm layers in cold weather—and get out there and do it. Make it a regular part of your life three or four times a week for two or three miles.

Exercise is one of the best ways to reduce stress and lift depression. It boosts your spirits, enhances energy levels, and combats fatigue. And you might even meet some potential friends in exercise class.

• • •

I discovered that one of the most important parts of my recovery strategy was becoming as attractive as I could. It took an effort, but it was worth it. Here are some things you might consider.

• Get a facial and take a makeup lesson. No matter how long you've been "putting on your face," there are always new tips and new techniques.

• Get your hair restyled. Have it highlighted or frosted or lightly colored. Make sure it's flattering and easy to care for.

• Go through your closet (or hire a wardrobe consultant) and throw out everything you haven't worn in two years or you don't really like.

• Go shopping. Splurge on one or two really good things and perhaps some new jewelry and accessories.

• Buy some *really* slinky underwear and feminine sleep clothes.

• Have plastic surgery if you can afford it and have always wanted to do it.

YOUR EMOTIONAL SELF

Exploring Your Potential

Understanding your strengths and weaknesses is one of the biggest gifts you can give yourself, now that your life has changed so drastically. Self-appraisal is never easy, and it will be particularly difficult now, but in the end you'll be better equipped to begin your new life if you understand the skills you have to cope with it. Ask yourself some of the following questions:

• What are you doing to improve your world or your community?
• What are you doing to improve yourself?
• What are you doing to stretch your mind?
• How can your work have more meaning and be more satisfying?
• Are there ways you can make your family and friends happier?
• What are the best things about you? Why do some people like you?
• What are the worst things about you? Why do others not like you?

I decided to sit down with a pad of long yellow paper—we lawyers always have them ready for making lists—and write down all my assets and faults. No one will ever see it, so you can be totally honest. In fact, you *must* be honest. A friend of mine, who has built a constructive and successful life, titled her list "Things I Like and Things I Don't Like." She started doing this when she realized that she was seeing people she didn't really care about and doing things she didn't enjoy.

You might also consider planning or updating a résumé—even if you've never had a job and don't plan to get one now. A résumé is a one-page statement of your education, work experience (including nonpaid work), and abilities.

Putting a résumé together was not as easy as I had thought it would be. I had not had a "real" job for years and saw only selected, privately referred clients in my home office, and now Sam, always my best press agent, was gone.

I had no piece of paper listing my qualifications, so how could anyone decide if I was an appropriate employee, volunteer, committee member, or part of a corporate board of directors, which I had always wanted to be? Friends in the executive-search business offered to help me prepare a résumé, and this is what they suggested.

• Keep it short: one or two pages only.

• Put your name, address, and phone number at the top.

• Leave as much white space as you can—including only the most important data shows discipline and organization.

• Include only education that pertains to your present goals.

• Don't include references; wait until you're asked for them when a job is offered.

• Include pertinent experience: jobs, volunteer work, relevant travel, workshops and seminars, special courses, and honors. Start with your most recent experience and work backward.

A good résumé is one of the best aids to finding a job or volunteer position, and you never know when it'll come in handy.

A calling card is also essential. We're all familiar with seeing business people whip out their card at every occasion; they do it so they—

and their phone number and business name—will be remembered. You can use your card for the same purpose: exchanging it with people you want to see again or whom you want to remember you.

Another friend, after her husband died, had cards printed with her name, address, phone number, and underneath, "Have golf clubs, will travel." She has dozens of friends and now a new husband.

Find Something to Do

You can't sit home and do nothing but watch television from now on. Even if your entire life revolved around your husband, you must now find another interest. If you *need* work, that should be your first priority and you might want to turn now to Chapter 5. Even if money isn't a problem, a job can be a satisfying way to spend time and contribute to society.

On the other hand, try not to make too many changes too quickly, and understand that restructuring your life shouldn't be confused with undermining an already shaky sense of self. One woman moved out of a beautiful apartment she loved because "my children felt I was still waiting for my husband to come home from work every evening." Five years later she regrets having given up her home—"And I still expect my darling Joe to walk through the door at the end of the day." Even the new door!

Volunteer work offers much satisfaction, interesting hours of labor, and new friends. Every town in America offers such opportunities, and all you have to decide is what arena is best for you. Volunteer work need not involve a tremendous outlay of money, although don't forget to keep track of tax-deductible expenses, such as getting to and from the organization, and supplies and equipment you buy.

Try some of the following:

- a hospital where you can deliver flowers and magazines, visit patients who are alone, read to and play with children, and generally make yourself useful;
- a library where you can participate in literacy programs, literary friends' activities, reshelving books, and the like;

- foster grandmother programs;
- shelters for the homeless and/or battered women;
- your neighborhood civic association where you can write the newsletter, get involved in zoning fights, or organize services for shut-ins;
- Meals on Wheels or similar programs that bring outside life to shut-ins;
- symphony, opera, theater groups, and public broadcasting companies always need people to stuff envelopes, call potential donors, and organize volunteer usher programs;
- political candidates, constantly on the lookout for free help.
- the Girl Scouts and other youth organizations.

Investigate your hidden talents. Did you play the piano as a child and give it up even though you were good? Take piano lessons or train yourself to play seriously for an hour every day. Have you always had a hankering to be an actress? Then join a local theater group. You may not get a starring role the first year and you may have to collect tickets and paint scenery, but you'll be "in the theater" with other people with similar desires, and you'll see your social life blossom.

Do you like to sing? Join a choir or chorus. Do you like to read and discuss books? Join a reading group. Your library can steer you in the right direction, or ask your friends. Do you have a murder mystery or a short story ready to be told? Write it down—and be disciplined about it. Set aside three mornings a week, put your answering machine on, and get to work. If you have artistic talents, buy paints and an easel, throw a drop cloth on the floor, and get busy.

But *do* something. Don't let your mind turn to mush. Your brain is in a pitiful state after a major trauma, and some days you'll be convinced that you're losing your mind. You're not, but you can't neglect your brain. You must use and stretch it to keep it limber and interesting. Make certain you read the newspaper every day and at least one quality magazine every week. Join a current events discussion group and check out the lecture series at local colleges and Ys. Take a course at a university extension program or community college. Learn a foreign language.

Come to Grips with Your Psyche

One of the worst moments during the healing process is when time begins to weigh heavily, and you develop anxieties about aging, your emotional stability, and mortality. It happened to me after I had contacted all the people who had written and called after Sam died. My social responsibilities had been fulfilled, or so I thought, and there I was asking myself what Peggy Lee had asked in the song, "Is That All There Is?"

Is my life, which had been so exciting, fulfilling, and fun, now going to consist of sitting around waiting for my children to call and going out with my single friends? Would I ever enjoy traveling without Sam? Would I be invited to dinner parties? Would I want to *give* a dinner party?

"No!" I told myself. "I will *not* turn into a boring old lady with no interests and no life outside her own unhappiness. If I don't *feel* happy, at least I'll pretend to be, and maybe that will take the edge off my misery."

I began by looking for and making pleasure out of even the most insignificant daily routine. Take breakfast, for instance. I ate it in bed and set the tray attractively. Even when I "graduated" to activities outside the house and had to leave early, I set the breakfast nook table with my pretty placemat and napkin and used my best cups for morning coffee. It made me feel special, as if I was worth doing nice things for.

I also decided never to go out of the house without looking my best, even if it was only to run to the grocery or the shoemaker. In the first place, you never know who you'll bump into, and second, aren't you worth the time it takes to look nice? And if I didn't have to go out, I always got dressed at home. Sometimes it was just slacks and a blouse or sweater, but I always had my hair combed and light makeup on. The day always seems so much better for having made this small but crucially important effort.

Alan Lakein, who wrote *How to Get Control of Your Time and Your Life*, suggests making a "To Do" list every day, and I've found it an excellent idea. Each evening, or early in the morning, list the tasks you want to accomplish that day. Cross things off as you do them, and add new ideas as they occur to you. Rewrite the list at the end of the day.

When you grow more confident, start a weekly planner where you block out your volunteer time and biweekly bridge games or monthly reading group, and then develop long-range goals, such as beginning an exercise class or taking a course in art history. Keep the lists and look back over them when you're feeling a bit down. You'll be amazed at how organized you've become and how much you've been able to accomplish.

Schedule the most difficult jobs for the times when you're at your physical and mental best. If you're a morning person, practice the piano right after your early coffee. I reach my peak in late morning, so I try not to schedule anything that requires a great deal of heavy thinking for late in the afternoon. That's when I try to meditate or do deep breathing exercises. I sometimes even recharge my batteries by running up and down the fire stairs in my apartment building.

Combating Depression

A widow's helpless feeling of aloneness is different from that of a divorcée. The latter surely feels a sense of abandonment and rejection, but the former's soul, especially if her marriage has been good, is wracked with loss. But both may be bitter, guilt-ridden, and depressed, albeit for different reasons.

You're depressed now, you will be so in the future, and the feeling will wax and wane for the rest of your life. You've been through one of the most devastating experiences there is, and you wouldn't be *real* if you weren't depressed. You must expect it, but you must not allow it to overtake your entire being. And the only way to do that is to fight it every step of the way.

You may not believe this now if you're still in the early stages of grief, but one way to "liberate" yourself from depression is to take off your wedding ring. Perhaps you're shocked that I suggest this, and you should not do it until you're truly ready, but the reality is that you are no longer married, and removing the symbol of the marriage that no longer is can be freeing in a way that nothing else is.

Many of my friends advised me to put my ring on my right hand, but that didn't seem right. After all, it's not just any piece of jewelry, and anyway, it wouldn't come off. I had never taken it off—not for childbirth, not to do the dishes, not even for major surgery, and now it was stuck!

I believed that I'd never be able to restructure my life if I still felt married to Sam, so one day I marched into a jewelry shop and had it sawed off. The jeweler put it into a neat little plastic envelope, and I felt so naked on the walk home—and a little like a traitor to Sam. But I put it in so safe a place that now I can't find it!

Another thing I did to cope with depression and ease many lonely nights was put together a scrapbook of Sam's life, and our life as a family. I did it to give to our daughters, but I spent many hours of my own poring over the pages—and the memories. I included eight or ten of the condolence letters that I found most comforting, copies of letters Sam had written that expressed his philosophy of life and the law, of course dozens of photographs, memorabilia of his military, professional, and community life, and other personal mementos. I wrote an introduction about his youth, how we had met, our early years together, his goals, and a few anecdotes that shouldn't be forgotten.

Many evenings that scrapbook served to release the tears that I couldn't seem to shed without it, and that helped immensely. One Sunday evening, almost two years after his death, I went to the corner shelf where I kept the book and reached for it. My housekeeper, who by that time was familiar with my frequent forays into tearful memories, said, "Nothing doing, Mrs. Gates. You can't cry over that book anymore."

I didn't look at it for a long time after that, and now when I do, I don't cry but am able to immerse myself in the remembered love and pleasure of Sam.

The symptoms of depression are easy to recognize: sadness, bouts of crying for no apparent reason, irritability, insomnia, lack of appetite (or eating compulsively), restlessness, boredom, lack of interest in sex, inertia about one's appearance, and a general malaise and decrease in energy. If the symptoms are so serious that you stop functioning, it's time to get yourself to a psychiatrist—there are many highly effective drugs that relieve the symptoms of depression and allow you to get on with your life.

But before things get that bad, there are things you can do for yourself.

• Dress in bright, cheerful colors and *do* get dressed every day. Long gone are the days when bereaved women had to walk about for years in "widow's weeds" in slowly lightening shades of black, gray, and purple.

• Make sure you have plenty of green plants and fresh flowers in the house. Living things (here's where a pet can help) force you to think of life.

• Get out of the house at least once a day. Plan social activities, go shopping, see a play or movie, go to the museum. It doesn't matter what you do as long as you get out.

• Exercise every day. You don't need to run the four-minute mile, but you do need to move.

• Stay in the light as much as possible, especially in winter. Take advantage of sunny days by going outdoors (protect your skin from long exposure to hot sun) and keep your indoor environment well lit.

• Never do anything for more than an hour at a time. Keep your mind engaged with external activities so it doesn't have a chance to dwell on depression. Depression characteristically feeds on itself, and if you wallow in it, pretty soon you're depressed about *more* than just the death of your husband.

• Plan advance activities that you're obligated to do: buy season tickets to concerts, theater, opera, or ball games. Invite people over. Accept all invitations. Register for a course. Do them all with other people. The obligation forces you to do what you had planned and won't allow you to disappoint others. And as a special bonus, you'll probably enjoy yourself!

• Spend as much time as you can with children—your grandchildren, other people's children, or strangers' children, as in Foster Grandparents or the pediatric unit at a hospital. Although little kids can be naughty and irritating (they can also be lovable and charming), they force you to vacate the gloomy recesses of your own thoughts and concentrate on their needs.

• Learn to structure your day so you don't have huge blocks of time with nothing to do. Incorporate your list of things to do into an actual *written* hour-by-hour schedule if necessary. Busy executives do it to make sure they get everything done and don't waste time, so you can do it for the opposite reason. Schedule everything, from exercising to grocery shopping to afternoon tea to a museum exhibit. You may feel silly at first, formally planning a trip to the dry cleaner around the corner, but no one has to know, and the important thing is that you'll *feel* purposeful and soon, with enough planning and filling your life with activities, you *will* have a meaningful and fulfilling life.

• If you haven't written thank-you letters for condolence cards, letters, gifts, and contributions, do it now. It's not as depressing as you think, and you don't have to do it all at once. Set a goal—say, four first thing in the morning and two after dinner.

• Get rid of your husband's clothes, accessories, and other personal things. This will be hard and it may make you feel "unfaithful," but you must clean out his closet and drawers to avoid turning them into a "shrine" or other unhealthy memorial. Ask your children what they want, keep a few sentimental treasures for yourself (one friend of mine saved an old cardigan of her husband's and wears it as a bedjacket on chilly evenings), and give the rest to the Salvation Army or Goodwill or your church or synagogue rummage sale.

You will also have to learn to deal with loneliness. The problem with occasional bouts of loneliness is not that they occur, because they are not unique to being a widow; it is how you cope with them. Sometimes it's enough to just wait it out, but other times loneliness grabs hold and turns to serious depression.

Thinking of widowhood as a temporary arrangement, even though it may eventually turn out to be, or as an interlude between husbands, is thinking of yourself as at the mercy of others, which can lead to deep psychological hot water. Instead of developing a satisfying single life style and learning to like the way you live, you could begin to think only of ways to get out of what you see as a predicament—and often wind up with people you don't really care for, doing things you don't want to do—or with a husband who is less than desirable. Human relationships spawned by desperation and loneliness rarely provide lasting pleasure to either person.

You can shorten or forestall bouts of loneliness with some of these activities:

• Perfect some of the antidepression strategies described above.

• Keep a few escape routes handy. Buy a VCR and rent movies. Keep some escape books (murder mysteries, trash novels, or whatever is your pleasure) ready to absorb your attention without requiring deep or serious thinking.

• Call a close friend and tell him or her that you need some human company for a while and suggest an activity, even if it's only quiet conversation. This doesn't mean that you ought to whine and complain to your friends every time you feel a little down, but in an emotional emergency, feel free to ask for help.

• Get to know the times when you're most likely to be lonely—for instance, when you and your husband had private times alone—and plan an activity that will fully engage your attention. Take yourself to a movie or play, weed and fertilize your garden, *really* listen to records that have been gathering dust for months, or cook something from an intricate recipe that requires time and attention.

• Develop a network of other single people, but don't spend your time together complaining about the vicissitudes of being alone. Do things with them and have fun. You don't have to belong to a crowd that always does things together, but get to know other widowed, divorced, and single people whose company you enjoy, and create a coterie around whatever interests you. Form a theater or reading group, or go birdwatching once a month with the same people. Take architectural walks around the city, going to a different neighborhood each month. Use your imagination and combine your intellectual interests with a social activity.

• Help someone. Giving of yourself never fails to ease the pain of loneliness. It replenishes your spirit and erases self-pity when you compare your life to those who have less. Read to the blind, clean out cages at the local pound, tutor children in inner-city schools, visit the elderly at home, become a regular visitor or play the piano at a nursing home, organize a fundraiser for your church or synagogue.

10

DEVELOPING FRIENDSHIPS AND LEARNING TO LAUGH AGAIN

*T*he first time I heard myself laugh after Sam died, I looked around in amazement to see who it was. How could I be so fully enjoying a moment when Sam wasn't there to share it with me? I felt guilty to be having a good time when my husband had just died, and that first little hint that life *could* be enjoyable after all (although of course I didn't take the hint at the time—I didn't even see it for what it was) jolted me and created all sorts of feelings that I wasn't prepared to deal with at the time.

Most widows go through this type of guilt, and in this chapter I shall discuss why some of us resist pleasure and why we think things like, "How can I travel, buy new clothes, or even enjoy a movie when my husband will never again have that pleasure?"

Many of us are angry ("How can I enjoy myself when I'm all alone because he refused to quit smoking?"). The anger of widowhood is one of the most difficult emotions to deal with because somehow it doesn't seem appropriate. After all, it wasn't Sam's *fault* that he died, so why should I be angry with him? But I was, and first I had to understand it for what it was and then deal with it.

Then there's remorse: "If only I had taken better care of him . . . if I had insisted he slow down, or had eaten more sensibly, or not driven so fast. If only . . ."

161

Nothing, of course, will bring your husband back, and now your job is to learn that asserting your right to live and accepting your husband's death does not constitute a betrayal. These are some of the ways we can do this, which I shall elaborate on in this chapter.

• Learn what gives you pleasure and pursue those things.

• Avoid the things that either don't provide pleasure or cause pain. (For instance, one friend of mine sold her vacation home on Cape Cod because the memories of the wonderful times she spent there with her husband were too much to bear.)

• Cultivate the friendships that enrich your life and get rid of the ones that do nothing for you—or at least put them on the back burner. There are also old friends who need you whom you must not abandon.

• Learn to accept the fact that some relationships you thought were friendships turn out not to be, once your husband has died. This is a painful lesson, but you must learn it.

• Form new friendships that are based on new activities and that have nothing to do with the memories of your husband.

• Join associations and develop interests that will provide contact with people who are potential friends.

• Learn to do things for people that enhance friendship: encourage intimacy and confidentiality, develop trust, avoid hurtful gossip, and give of yourself.

• Go out of your way to meet people of all ages so you develop a variety of friendships.

The absence of an intimate physical and love relationship is a serious emotional road block to survival because we need such attachments. We are a social species, and no matter how self-sufficient we believe we are, we cannot survive (at least with a semblance of emotional balance and happiness) in isolation.

Widows are not the only ones who are lonely. Loneliness, that most common of all forms of human despair, happens to everyone from time to time. Children go off to college, close friends move away, parents die, and some friendships may fade if you are divorced and feel abandoned, bitter, and alone. Bereavement and loneliness in all its forms is a universal phenomenon, and the problem is how to keep it at bay so that it doesn't become overwhelming. Developing friendships is one of the best ways.

In her book, *In Search of Intimacy,* Dr. Carin Rubenstein says, "The lonely tend to be self-focused and self-conscious, instead of focusing on the other person. You cannot support a relationship unless you consider the other person's needs. That is the basis of making and keeping a friend."

Nothing provides a greater blessing in life than a real friend. "Friendship is a sheltering tree under which we find sustenance and comfort unavailable from any other source." I once embroidered a sampler with that quotation when I was eleven years old. Little did I know at the time the true implications of those words.

But as a tree takes a long time to grow and develop to the point where it bears fruit and provides shade, so a friendship takes time to establish trust and intimacy. Be patient. Don't expect friendships to blossom in an instant. Enjoy the development of the relationship and the increasing sense of trust and closeness.

Of course, honesty is one of the bases of any good relationship (and no real relationship can flourish without it), but be careful about being too honest.

We all flourish in an atmosphere of approval and positive feedback, and although false cheer and false compliments are almost worse than nothing (perhaps worse than anything to the truly perceptive), beware of unsolicited "honesty." We all cringe at statements like "I'm only telling you this for your own good" or "I know you won't like this, but . . ."

Most of the time these statements precede unnecessary messages, communications that are none of the listener's business, or direct efforts to hurt and insult. Don't do it to others, and if people insist on saying such things to you, drop them—without insult if you can manage it.

Do compliment your friends on their clothes, their accomplishments, their cooking—whatever is admirable about them. And express genuine interest in their lives, their children, their activities, their careers. Even if the style your best friend is wearing is very unbecoming, perhaps you can say what a flattering color it is.

But do *not* give unsolicited advice. No one likes to be preached to, and that's almost always what advice sounds like. If someone asks your advice, respond with a question: "Do you really want to know?"

This gives them an out, a chance to change their minds, especially if it's likely that they won't enjoy what you have to say. But if they insist on advice, give it if you can and give the best you can—and do it as tactfully as possible. That's one of the obligations of friendship: to find out what your friend's needs are and then to meet them to the best of your ability. And try to take the sting out of whatever negative message you have to impart. Instead of saying, "That dress isn't flattering at all on you," try, "With your hair and your beautiful skin, you'd look good in red and other bright colors instead of pastels."

If the matter is something serious, you are obligated to provide a serious answer and to try to solve the problem. If your best friend says, "I think my son is taking drugs at school because such-and-such happened. What do you think I should do?" you cannot wave the situation away or help your friend deny it. You have to listen and try your best to provide a practical solution to the problem.

One of my best friend's sons, many years ago, was using marijuana and urging young friends of mine to do so. I never at any time told her and his father what I knew. I did call him at his college and asked him to come see me. In *very* strong words I told him he was committing an illegal act—disgracing his upbringing—and about to ruin his life. So far as I know, it worked. His parents were wonderful friends and still are.

This situation created something of a dilemma for me. On the one hand, my friends might have been devastated to know that I knew that their son was smoking marijuana. But on the other hand, the boy was doing something illegal, and I thought that his parents might *want* to know. After all, if my children were doing likewise, I would have been furious if they hadn't told me. Then again, one risks a friendship by telling one's friends truths "for their own good." In most cases, it doesn't work, but this time I was lucky because the boy was very amenable to my suggestions that he think carefully about what he was doing.

164

• • •

Relationships with family, especially your children, have some of these same characteristics. Many widows and widowers whom I have spoken with over the years feel that they had received vital solace and help from their children as well as their extended families because they had worked hard to make the relationships more loving and more satisfying to everyone.

Some women I know had let relationships with family and friends slide before their widowhood, but when they rekindled them, they were a source of enormous help, pleasure, and strength. Many of my friends say they have even come to accept the behavior and values of some family members and friends that they previously eschewed, and found that once they were able to do so, they became even more involved in the lives of others. This, then, is all a part of widening one's horizons to keep loneliness at bay and to remain a part of the world you have grown accustomed to sharing.

One of the things I have found as a widow is that it can be tempting, in order to ease loneliness, to use our children as substitutes for our dead husbands, at least in terms of seeking emotional closeness and satisfaction. This almost never works out and creates resentment on both sides—on the grown children's part because unreasonable burdens are placed on them, and on the widow's part because her expectations and needs can never be satisfied.

If you have a good and healthy relationship with your children, these problems can be minimized and talked about. For instance, when you visit with your children, whether by letter, by phone, or in person, try to keep things pleasant and cheerful and keep your minor physical and emotional complaints to yourself. As a matter of fact, don't complain about anything at all—unless you've just had a serious heart attack! No one likes a whiner, and if one day you are in dire need of help, you will be much more likely to get it if you are known, by your family as well as your friends, as a strong and self-sufficient person who does not ask for help unless it is *really* needed.

Constant criticism, spoken or silent, erodes much of the natural love that children want to express to their parents. Therefore, as a widow with too much time on your hands and a big, gaping hole in your heart, you may be tempted to turn your need to express yourself toward someone you think will understand your need to "help" and to offer unwanted suggestions and advice.

Don't do it. Wait for the right time for confidences to come out, and try to learn to sense when your children need you and when they don't. One of the ways to avoid overcriticism is to turn your negative comments into positive ones. Find ways to praise your children often, and you will find that they will open up to you and ask your opinion, which then becomes the right time to express negative thoughts—although always in a nonhurtful way.

But if you absolutely cannot keep your mouth shut and find yourself criticizing, then apologize afterward. Say that you did it only because you love your child so much—which goes for your children's spouses as well.

My daughters are now in a period of maximum responsibility and I sympathize with them. They are caught in the middle between being responsible for their own children and for their mother and mother-in-law, each of whom is widowed.

I make an effort not to be an "old mom" waiting to be invited over, but sometimes I think I may be overdoing it. I have so tightly scheduled my time, in an effort to prevent my daughters from feeling guilty, that they don't invite me to their homes all the time, that often I'm busy when they *do* extend an invitation. My justification to myself is that someday I may really need them, and I don't want to impose on them before then.

When I was younger, I had fantasies, as do all mothers, about how life would be when my girls were grown and mothers themselves. I pictured us lunching out together, talking about their children and their own childhood. They would tell me stories of their social lives and their emotional ups and downs. We would laugh over who they were seeing and what they would be doing that evening. We would share recipes, I thought, and go through each other's closets and choose outfits to wear for the next social occasion.

Now I am alone with no husband to care for, and they are grown up and have busy lives. It hasn't worked out that way at all. I imagine the fantasy hasn't come true for the rest of you, either.

If we raise our children to be happy, productive adults, then they have full, active lives now and don't have time to sit around gossiping with their mothers over three-hour lunches, talking about clothes and hairdos like adolescent schoolgirls. Those of us alone would do well to strengthen our family ties whenever possible. Blood *is* thicker than water, and in a pinch, most of the time, it is a family member who rallies round in times of trouble or need.

• • •

Many of my clients tell me that divorced people are even lonelier than widows. Grief is terrible, but it's not failure and rejection—or at least the sense of failure and rejection common to most divorced women. As a widow whose marriage was happy, I dwell often on the joyous times that Sam and I shared, and that sustains me.

Although even divorced people can look back to happiness in their marriage and can take pleasure from the fact that it once existed, the fact of the divorce itself—and the failure that it represents—can blot out the pleasure with bitterness. Friends can help here, too. Find a divorced friend who you know has been through a bad time and "build her up" with kindness and a sympathetic ear.

• • •

Perhaps wanting and working toward friendship is a selfish exercise, but worth doing all the same. Kahlil Gibran said, "Your friend is your need answered," and I have found that sentiment to be borne out time and again.

When I look at the various friendships I've had over the years, I think of the laughter—and tears—we have shared and realize how many of my most basic needs were met through friendships. For instance, my wonderful "best roommate before Sam," a beautiful and accomplished mother of fine sons, who is now a retired lawyer, reminds me of the good times we shared when we lived on a shoestring in Washington. We used to say, "All we need to make us happy is a little sleep!"

Now, forty years later, we still laugh over our escapades, and we still know exactly what we mean when we talk about needing some sleep. We are the only two who understand the implications of those memories, and it and other memories form the basis of our deep friendship.

Another of my best friends was once my client. About twenty years ago, when we went to Mexico to arrange final details for the purchase of her house, our picture was taken descending the ramp of the airplane in the Mexico City airport. When Sam saw the picture, he said he had never seen two more determined and resolute women because we had been preparing to meet with the owner to do some hard bargaining about the terms of the purchase.

I still have the photo, and neither of us can look at it without bursting into gales of laughter. We look ridiculous to our friends who weren't there, but we still chuckle over how frustrating the experience was and how naïve we were in thinking that two young American women could make the Mexican system meet our demands. Now one of the best parts of the photograph is that the memories add to our present intimacy.

When I get together with old friends (and I travel endlessly to do so because they mean so much to me), we sometimes talk about what brought us together in the first place. These kinds of talks are an important part of friendship because they serve to rekindle the foundations of closeness and trust.

My friends and I pine for one another when we're apart, and we shall continue to care about each other until we are permanently parted by death.

And speaking of loss of friends through death, I believe it is important as we grow older to develop friendships with people of all ages, mainly because it is silly to reject a potential friend because he or she is younger or older than oneself. The older we become, the more friends we lose to death; thus, it is doubly important to make a few good new friends every few years to replace those lost. You need to maintain contact with people who will always be strong forces in your life.

However, younger people will not be interested in you unless you are interested in them and unless you are an interesting person (not an older person, just a person) who is knowledgeable but not a "know-it-all" and concerned about the issues of the day. Therefore, you must make it a top priority to read the news, editorials, and journals so that you can contribute ideas and opinions to just about any group of people.

• • •

You also need to look for friends in a variety of places. Your golfing and bridge club friends may be quite separate from the friends you make through charity work or through your job. Not everyone will become a "bosom buddy" and not all close acquaintances will become true and lasting friends, but you *can* expand your circle of friendships by looking all over for them.

I consider myself blessed with many friends and someone once said to me, "You can't have real friendships with all the people you call 'friends.' You'd be extending your already extended psyche too far— spreading yourself too thin."

I don't think this is true, and perhaps that man and I define friendship very differently. But I believe we need all kinds of friends, and I feel that my life is much happier for each and every one of these relationships—whatever you choose to call them.

Perhaps the reason this person sees my relationships differently is because he is a man. For the most part, women find it much easier than men do to share feelings and to develop close, lasting relationships. But that can get to be too much of a good thing, too. Susan Jacoby, in a *New York Times* article of about a decade ago, said, "Sharing of feelings has become the debased currency in the therapeutic society of which I am a card-carrying member. Enough with the feelings. Bring me some matzoh-ball soup."

She has a point, and I now divide the people in my life into two categories: those who stuck by me when I was sick, recently widowed, *and* feeling down, and the fair-weather friends. Tolerance of my self-centeredness during a recent illness—which, given the intensity of my pain, I could not control—was the greatest gift my friends gave me, and it was interesting to note that the men to whom I was closest tended to react either with open irritation or with cheerful reassurance about how good I looked (when I knew I looked terrible).

Good and close friendship means not needing to look perfect all the time and not needing to explain everything (although love does *not* mean never having to say you're sorry; apologizing to those you love is one of the most important things you must do to maintain a friend-

169

ship). It means inviting people to your house even if the Sunday papers are still all over the floor on Wednesday evening and there's a fine coat of dust on everything—and it means not noticing the dust on anyone else's furniture!

We don't have to pretend with our friends. With casual acquaintances, we have to respond, "Fine, thank you," to queries about our well-being. But we can tell true friends how we're really feeling, although we cannot use them as sounding boards for constant whining, either.

Our good friends know us so well that we think they're mind readers, but they are not judges. They may be critical, but they may not be unkind. Good friends may make enormous impositions on each other, but they also need to congratulate each other and provide a shoulder to cry on. Communication should be as total as is possible with another human being—spoken and unspoken—that represents an unbreakable bond.

Lately I've been noticing a phenomenon that may have been going on for quite a while when I wasn't paying attention: women who are so involved in their careers that they have no time for friendship, who are so busy chasing after professional success that they have given loving friends low priority in their lives.

Men have known for years that time is the scarcest item on life's balance sheet, but they have also recognized that if they went "all out" for a career, they needed an understanding and patient wife who made few demands on their time and emotional resources. But most of these men had no real friends except professional colleagues and co-workers, and perhaps it was only years later, when they had achieved success (and perhaps the "little woman" had gotten tired of playing the patient waiting game), that they realized the lack of close attachments with other men.

Are "new age" women now following this male role model to the extent of forsaking that which is *really* important? If so, I believe they are making a terrible error that they will regret for the rest of their lives.

If a friendship is worth keeping, it is worth taking the time and trouble to nourish. Here are some things that I think can make you a better friend—and can earn you new ones.

• Keep up the contacts that you value. A Christmas card every year is not enough for the people who really count, although it is better than nothing. Close friendships require time and effort. Call often, even if it's long distance (the rates are cheaper in the evening and on weekends, so do it then if money is a problem).

Christmas cards with long notes on them (I've just sunk to a post-Christmas one-page typed letter with special personal messages at the bottom) are a very good way, but for people who really count with you (friends and relatives), an interim communiqué is great. A lot of people you care about no longer have anyone to send them a Valentine, so *you* should. It's an expression of your caring for them and the value of their friendship.

• Make arrangements to see your friends. Even the busiest people admit that they make time to do the things that they want to do, the things that are most important to them. So if your friends are important, make time to see them.

• Give things to your friends. I don't mean showering people with presents that they can't afford to reciprocate. But a small gift every now and then for no reason is a welcome surprise and shows that you have been thinking about the other person.

One woman I know was seeing a man who gave her expensive gifts on all the appropriate occasions, but he also used to cut articles out of the newspaper and magazines and mail them to her. "Those were the things that really touched my heart," she said. "It showed that he cared about what I was interested in and really listened to what I had to say—and thought about it afterward."

• Do things for your friends, especially those that they can't do for themselves. If someone you know has arthritis, put your old clothes on and go over and rake her yard in the autumn. Drive someone to the doctor for the first checkup after surgery. Go to the supermarket for a friend who's home in bed with the flu. Surprise someone at the end of a vacation or business trip by picking him or her up at the airport when he expects to have to take a taxi home alone.

• Don't gossip—or at least, if you must, do it in the least hurtful way possible. Everyone gossips just a little; it's an irresistible pastime and makes for delicious lunch and dinner conversation. But don't be malicious, don't tell lies, and don't derive pleasure from someone else's misfortune, no matter how much you dislike the subject of the gossip.

Creative gossip makes for a sought-after dinner guest, especially if his or her tidbits are about public figures. But it's easy to go too far. One dinner party wit said to me, after one of his nonstop soliloquies, "You know, Phil, it's difficult to pick a cut-off moment. Gossip is like eating peanuts, but I always try to stop short of hurting anyone."

I have a personal rule that you might think about adopting: I never allow anyone to say rude things in my presence about a friend of mine.

• Encourage confidence and trust by giving it. If you promise to keep something secret, then do. Never, never break a promise and never, never betray a confidence. If you follow these two simple rules, people will see you as a true friend because you will *be* a true friend.

When you become a widow, you may have to face a painful situation about friendship: many lifelong friends that you had as a couple will no longer be your friends. It's not that they've stopped liking you; it's that your situation has changed. Either they don't feel comfortable having an extra woman around, or the friendship was based mainly on the husband's business relationship or contacts.

I have friends whose husbands have been crippled or otherwise disabled, blind, or very deaf to the point that social intercourse is almost impossible. This is very difficult for a comparatively healthy spouse. I find husbands of wives with hopeless Parkinson's or Alzheimer's disease tend to be invited out by their mutual friends. Wives similarly situated don't find many dinner invitations in their mailboxes. I guess their friends assume that they prefer to loyally stay home with their ailing loved one.

This hurts. If they were friends and now drop you because you're alone, then perhaps they weren't really friends after all. Most people do not cast aside friendships because certain circumstances have changed. It's a little like their dropping you because you lost all your money or suddenly developed an illness with unpleasant manifestations. Nevertheless, the pain of loss is real—almost like a small death.

172

If the friendship evaporates because it was more business than social (which is increasingly common these days when so many "social" activities are really business functions in disguise), then what you are feeling is loneliness rather than true grief as a result of a loss of something valuable.

I am not trivializing the lack of social outlets, because they are so important; rather, I'm trying to get you to distinguish between what is really a friendship and what is a casual acquaintance.

However, when friends stay with you through the grief of loss, you are truly blessed. Rose Lewis had that kind of good fortune. Her husband went in an instant from being perfectly healthy ("He was never sick a day in his life") to being a helpless invalid. He had a massive stroke and lived for nine weeks, and during that time Rose's friends gathered round and offered love and support that she had never expected.

"During those nine weeks and for the first few months after Nate died, I was in a state of clinical depression," said Rose. "I couldn't eat, I couldn't sleep. I couldn't do anything. But my friends were wonderful. They always included me in the same activities we used to do when Nate was alive. I didn't spend a Saturday night alone for two years."

But Rose does not give full credit where credit is due—to herself. One of the reasons that her friends never deserted her is that she didn't *use* them to whine to or to carry on in a maudlin fashion about how sad she was, how devastated. Rose grieved privately with her immediate family and did not impose her grief on friends. "No one wants to hear your troubles," she said.

I believe she is correct. Contrary to all the pop philosophy that abounds today about "sharing" the minutest feelings with others, people remain wrapped up in their own affairs and do not have the time or inclination for your misery. It's not that they are not sympathetic, it's that life is lived at such a hectic pace and people are so self-centered these days that they have little time for the unhappiness of others.

So accept people's condolences graciously, but pour out your heart to only very few trusted and closest friends (and to them not very often). To everyone else, say, "Fine, thank you, how are you?" to all queries about your emotional as well as physical health.

Divorced people have even more complex problems with friendships when they split up. Many of their friends might feel that they must make choices, between the divorcing husband and wife, about whom they remain loyal to, and this can create almost as much pain and anger as a child custody battle. In a divorce, you lose friends as well as a spouse. Although this is a difficult period for all concerned, it is also a good opportunity to make new friends who don't know you as part of a couple.

●   ●   ●

One thing that widows and divorcées have in common are the many sad surprises in store for them as a single woman in relation to married women or couples.

• Men who were your husband's business and golfing friends (many of whom are happily married) will make passes at you or say things they never would have dared when you were under your husband's protection.

• Married women whom you thought were friends will drop you because they are threatened by someone they perceive as being "after" their husbands—even though you aren't at all interested in them.

• Single women whom you thought were friends will drop you because they perceive you as a new addition to the general competition for eligible bachelors. Even when you are still in the first throes of grief and believe that another romance is absolutely out of the question, you may be seen as a threat.

• You may find that married couples you know have been invited to parties from which you are excluded (and that you know you would have been invited to when you were married).

This typical example has happened to me and many of my single women friends: You see a couple that you saw a good deal of when you were married. They have invited you to dinner and have been a guest at your home many times. Then you introduce them to a man you have been seeing. There's no romance, but they know you go out with him often.

Then you find out that they have had a number of dinner parties and have invited him (whom they met through you), but you were left out.

You tell yourself that people are free to invite whomever they wish to dinner, that it's none of your business. It's true, but it hurts. It would have been much nicer if the first time they invited your male friend, they would have invited you as well. After that, they could have left you out if they chose, without your resenting it. After all, it's a free country.

It's easy to start putting yourself down over all these situations and to believe that the only reason you were ever invited any place at all was because of your husband. Don't do it. Don't let yourself sink into self-pity that can lead to serious depression. It can happen easily if you give into the feelings that so often assail you in your recently lone status, feelings that you are unwanted—a rejected old woman.

I have felt this way so many times since Sam died, but I have learned to develop strategies to pull myself out of bouts of self-pity and depression, and made new friends in the process. Some of them might work for you.

• Make a list (yes, an actual list on paper) of the people who like you. Don't be shy and succumb to false modesty. You know who these people are. Write down their names and watch the list grow.

• Look back over your engagement calendar for the past three or four months and list (yes, again in writing) the activities you participated in that had nothing to do with your once having been part of a couple. Include the parties you were invited to, meals with male and female friends, work for charitable organizations, classes taken, lectures attended—every part of your busy life.

• Reflect on things that you have been able to do for yourself since your husband died: contract with a plumber to get the leaky faucets fixed; arrange to have the car serviced; getting yourself to and from a formal dinner party alone (and having a good time there); giving a dinner party—anything and everything that demonstrates your worth as an independent woman.

• Initiate an activity yourself. Plan a dinner party that includes a mix of single men, single women (both widowed and divorced—and don't forget to vary the ages), and married couples. You'll be amazed at how smoothly the conversation flows, and perhaps you will be gratified to see a few friendly sparks fly.

• Keep your lines of communication open. Remember to be a giver, not a taker—regardless of how many people take things from you (including your single men for their dinner parties).

• Do volunteer work. This is one of the best ways to meet people who are potential friends. If I had had to rely on my professional relationships (most of whom had no time to nurture friendship) to help me through my first five years alone, I never would have made it. The friends I made in my volunteer life had the time and the inclination to invite me to dinner, to have long lunches with good conversation— and to introduce me to unattached men when I was feeling ready to meet them.

Although I will discuss in detail in Chapter 7 how to cope with men (and the absence of them) in your life, I should say a word here—in the chapter on friendship because it is so appropriate—about friendships with men.

I am *not* in search of a husband, although I have come to a point in my life when the thought of sharing the rest of it with someone other than Sam doesn't fill me with sadness and dread. But there's no getting around the fact that we women alone need male friends whom we can ask to escort us to certain places and just to provide masculine company and points of view to our life. However, the best of all possible worlds is to have the friendship of both men and women.

During our many years of marriage, I knew only two or three unattached men, but a lively and very intelligent divorced friend told me that she had made it her business to "collect" bachelors. I think I have tried to follow her example, and I now count among my "best" friends men as well as women.

I miss Sam's nightly discussions of his work and other activities, the amusing jokes he brought home from the office and from business functions. I miss hearing whom he saw, what they said, and what they were doing. This lack of sharing the male perspective on the world in an intimate and candid way is one of the most dreadful parts of being a widow, and I'm not alone in feeling this. In this age of women's liberation, many of my sex think it's "politically incorrect" to crave the companionship of men, but I think it's just as sexist to ignore the existence of men, especially if you were married as long as I was. The world is indeed made up of two sexes, so don't be ashamed if you feel a need to have male companionship in your life. Just don't make the mistake of believing that life is empty or meaningless without a *man* in it.

This doesn't mean that lunch or dinner with women doesn't interest me, because it does; I enjoy sharing confidences about our lives and our common interests, but I also want to spend time in the company of male friends or co-ed groups.

• • •

For widows as well as divorcées, holidays and other special occasions can pose problems. All my married life I cherished birthdays, holidays, and special days, but when Sam died I didn't think I could face those celebrations. It got easier after a while—but not for several years, and I still have particular trouble dealing with his birthday, our wedding anniversary, and the anniversary of his death. All widows do, no matter how long they have been alone, how healthy their adjustment to widowhood, and how much they protest to the contrary.

We all have to learn how to make it through the red-letter days, especially the ones in which our husbands played a major role. The day will never be the same. Accept that fact and put its realization behind you. Without his familiar face at the head of the table, it can still be special if we note his absence while experiencing the presence of his spirit and making an effort to find the real meaning of the occasion.

Holidays, especially Christmas and other occasions that are tradi-

177

tionally family oriented, are stressful for many people, even those who celebrate them in the bosom of a happy and intact family. So when the almost universal anxiety that accompanies special occasions (How will I ever get all that cooking done? Who's going to keep the fighting relatives apart? I need a new dress but can't afford it, etc.) is combined with the loneliness and depression of widowhood, you could end up with almost unbearable stress. But there are ways to prevent and relieve it.

The most important thing is to understand what is especially stressful and painful for *you* and do things that relieve that stress. For instance, for a reason she never was able to understand, the Fourth of July was particularly difficult for my friend Carolyn. Even when her husband was alive, she'd sometimes sink into depression. After he died, she dreaded the long weekend and often ruined the entire month of June worrying about it. One year she took three Valium on the morning of the Fourth and managed to escape the day by sleeping through it.

She knew her dread of that great American day was silly and irrational, but taking drugs to avoid it frightened her badly enough to think about what she was doing and to prevent something like that—or worse—from happening again.

So she decided to prevent the stress by planning ahead. Now she arranges far in advance to visit friends who have a beach house or she travels to another country where the day slips by unnoticed. One year, her plans fell through at the last minute, but instead of falling into a serious depression or taking drugs, she went to three movies in a row. "I had a terrible headache at the end of the day," she said with a rueful laugh, "but at least I got through it without wanting to die."

The first Christmas after Sam died was one of the worst times of my life. Right around the first of December I started thinking about our happy times together, buying and decorating the tree, choosing gifts for our daughters and each other, and planning parties.

I forced myself to buy a small tree that year, but when I took out the box of ornaments, I was overwhelmed by memories. Most of the tree decorations we had bought together or had received as gifts throughout forty years. The "worst" were the ones made by our children when they were little girls in Sunday school. Each bauble triggered fresh sadness and tears, and an evening's worth of work to decorate the tree ended up taking three days because there were times when I just couldn't go on. But I finished the job and am glad I did because the next year I cried a little less. I don't cry at all now—despite the sizable lump in my throat when I take the box of ornaments from the top shelf of the closet.

I have recently discovered Sunday lunch at the Christmas season. There are two Sundays before the big day by which time you can have your home decorated, and the most sought-after couples *and* singles are likely to be free, especially when you invite them far ahead of time. You can have a goody (perhaps one big sinful praline or brownie gaily wrapped) for each guest to take home, and it makes everyone, especially you, feel better about the season. And having company helps get you through those times when you are alone.

One of the most important things that widows can do to ease the loneliness of holidays is to plan *as far in advance as possible* to make certain you're not alone. Much more important than not being alone is making sure that you are with people you really like on those special days. Even if this means giving a birthday party for yourself, by all means do it. If you're still wearing summer clothes but you're worried about what you'll do on Thanksgiving, start planning now. It's never too early. Drop broad hints that you'd like to be invited to someone else's home before their guest list is complete, and don't be ashamed to say that you'd like to be included in their plans.

One woman whose husband had been dead for three years confided in a friend at lunch one day. "I'm terrified that I won't have any place to go for the Passover Seder this year," she said.

Her friend was astonished. "But you have dozens of friends! The only reason I've never invited you to our house is that I thought you'd be dated up long ago. Please come to us."

The woman did, and not only did she have a marvelous time, she met two other widows there who confessed to having the same feelings. Motto: Don't be shy about expressing your fears to and meeting your needs with those you count as friends.

Another friend of mine planned for her sixtieth birthday for almost two years. She joked about it a lot, but the idea of turning sixty alone terrified her. "When I wake up that morning, I want someone there to help me get through the day, and I don't want to be left alone for a single minute."

She said this over and over in a bantering way, but her friends took her seriously, and several of them let themselves into her apartment very quietly before she was awake. They put the coffeepot on, sneaked into her bedroom, and serenaded her awake with a chorus of "Happy Birthday." That evening they took her out to dinner—to a surprise party of about fifty people. "It was the best day I'd had since way before Ted got cancer," she said.

Sam and I always made a big fuss over each other's birthdays. Some people don't do that, and perhaps they're luckier in widowhood than I am, who feels the loss so acutely on my birthday—and his.

I usually have something to do in the evening, but birthdays start when you wake up in the morning, so I begin celebrating first thing. I make a special breakfast and eat it off my best china, and then I go out and buy myself a nice birthday present. It doesn't have to be expensive, but it does have to be something I want but don't *need*— usually an article of clothing. One year I spent the day at the Georgette Klinger salon getting a massage, manicure, pedicure, and hairstyling. It made me feel beautiful—and several years younger.

Some holidays are harder than others to endure. Valentine's Day is particularly difficult because it seems as though everyone in the world is happily paired with someone else. Even though you *know* that's not true, it doesn't matter. *You're* alone—that's what matters. However, there are several things you can do to take the edge off the loneliness.

- Give a party for single people only—don't let anyone bring an escort—and see what happens.
- Have dinner with one or two close women friends.
- Rent two or three good movies (preferably not romances that end happily) and stay home by yourself with a bowl of popcorn.
- Read a good book that will keep you engrossed for the evening.
- Ignore it—or think of the high divorce rate!

New Year's Eve is another tough one. If you're invited to a party, go. Although having an escort is always nice, don't refuse the invitation because you have to go alone. Once you get there, there will be plenty of people to talk with, and if you don't like the idea of driving home in the wee hours of the morning (perhaps with drunk drivers on the road), ask the hostess—in advance, of course—if you can spend the night on her couch. An alternative is to ask the hostess if any of the guests live near you and would be willing to give you a lift home.

The first time I forced myself to go to a New Year's Eve party alone, I worried about the silliest thing: Whom would I kiss at the stroke of midnight? When Sam and I went together to such gatherings, we would always seek each other out at about ten minutes before the hour so we could see in the new year with a hug and kiss.

But my fears were groundless. When the clock struck midnight, I happened to be in a small group of four or five people, and the conversation was so interesting and animated that we barely noticed when the host announced the new year. We all took a sip of the drinks we were holding, gave each other good wishes—and went back to the stimulating discussion. The dread moment was not only painless—it turned out to be pleasant!

Some women, particularly those of "a certain age," feel that they should not be expected to attend parties alone, that the host or hostess should provide an escort for them. That may have been the case forty years ago, but times have changed, and women alone (regardless of how they came to be in that situation) are expected to be independent enough to manage by themselves. If you happen to be going out, even occasionally, with a man who is not invited to the party, and if you know the hostess well (and are pretty certain that an extra person will not upset her arrangements), ask if you may bring him along.

· · ·

Religious holidays are also hard. Even now that eight years have passed since Sam died, I find myself welling up with tears at the beautiful choir voices and soloists that made Sam himself cry during holiday church services. Although each religious season has a spiritual significance and is celebrated at least in part in church or synagogue, there is always a strong family component to them. But that is no reason for you to feel left out. You *have* a family. Your husband may be dead, and of course he was your closest and most significant family member, but you have children, brothers, sisters, in-laws, and perhaps a slew of cousins. Spend the holiday with them. For a day or so before the event, cook something special—to serve at home or to bring with you. Every religious holiday features food and its meticulous preparation as the central secular theme, and even if you don't like to cook, shop for a particularly delectable holiday assortment of food as a gift for your family.

If your family, especially your children and grandchildren, lives out of town, this may be one of the few times each year you get to see them, so take advantage of it. If you have children, spend some time alone with your grandchildren, getting to know them. You'll enjoy it, and your children will be grateful to have the baby-sitting services for a while. Also, don't forget to sit quietly with your children and help them remember their father. After all, they have suffered the loss of a central figure in their lives too, and providing a soft shoulder for their expressions of grief will do you both good. If you don't have children, then, again, plan ahead to be with one or two close friends.

Religious holidays also provide food for the soul, and these, in addition to Thanksgiving, are appropriate occasions to go outside your own unhappiness and loneliness to give to others. For instance, why not work in a shelter for the homeless on Christmas or Thanksgiving? You'll spend all day preparing and serving the food, and you'll be surprised how good the exhaustion feels, and how grateful you are for your own blessings, when you finally sit down to eat with the other volunteers.

Religious occasions also offer the opportunity to take stock of your life, to think about what you have been lucky enough to have and the goals you have not yet fulfilled. For the introspective, the chance to look inside the soul can be a truly meaningful experience and a respite from the hurly-burly of everyday life.

Another thing you can do to ease the loneliness of holidays is to start traditions to replace the ones in which your husband played a central role.

- Have a cook-out with all the trimmings in your backyard every year on Labor Day.
- If you are Jewish, invite a dozen of your closest friends to break the fast with you on Yom Kippur.

- Volunteer to read traditional stories and tell poems at a settlement house for children in a poor neighborhood on St. Patrick's Day.
- Give a brunch on New Year's Day.
- Cook and serve dinner at a shelter for the homeless on Thanksgiving or Christmas.
- Take a drive in the country on Columbus Day with a friend, admire the foliage, buy apples, and have dinner at a country inn.

Many widows find that their anger with their dead husbands ("Why did you have to go off and leave me to cope alone? You're dead, I'm not, but perhaps I'd like to be.") returns on holidays, even after years of widowhood and when they thought they had gotten all that out of their system. It's natural and nothing to be ashamed or afraid of, even though many women feel guilty about feeling angry with their dead husband.

Give in to the anger—but only for a few minutes. Denying it isn't going to help, and feeling guilty about it will only depress you further. So curse him out once or twice, and then get out and enjoy the day.

Christmas Eve is sometimes more difficult to bear than Christmas Day itself. I have started a tradition, which by now has become a regular practice. Ever since Sam died, I invite my eight grandchildren (luckily, they live nearby) to lunch on Christmas Eve.

I feed them at home most of the time because taking them to a restaurant is too expensive, and then we form a phalanx, with the oldest one helping me keep a semblance of order, and take a trip to see the Christmas tree at a museum or the planetarium. Once or twice we have gone to an appropriate movie.

This past year I felt that we had seen every major museum and Christmas attraction that the city had to offer (after all, my oldest grandchild is applying to law school!), and I thought a movie rated for family viewing was just the trick. The nice girl won out, romance and goodness prevailed, and so we went. The movie was a pleasant experience, which was a great help, and we went early and came back to my apartment to have spaghetti and pizza. Now that they are older, we were able to discuss the movie and talk about the best and worst moments of their year or what they thought the new president's biggest problems will be. This has turned out, for me, to be a very enjoyable Christmas tradition.

If you don't have young relatives nearby to share Christmas Eve, adopt some of your young friends. You'll enjoy it, make new friends, and perhaps start a tradition of your own.

11

THE IMPORTANCE OF PASSIONS

*I*t's important to be passionate about *something.* I'm not speaking about sexual love (although I certainly don't knock that!); rather, I see passion as a fervent interest, espousal of a cause that's important to you, enthusiasm for a variety of activities, academic study—or anything that this great and varied life has to offer.

You can develop or indulge in a passion for any activity on earth, and if you do, you will soon find that because you are sharing it with like-minded people, you will be less lonely. You will also find that the pursuit of passion requires energy that you might otherwise have devoted to feeling depressed and sorry for yourself.

For people who have been recently widowed or divorced, plunging into a passion can help begin life alone. My own first step was to join a neighborhood church. I first tried the one closest to my apartment building but found it frighteningly forbidding. My first Sunday there, I went to the coffee hour after the service, and no one gave me the slightest welcome. I never went back and in fact didn't go to church for a few months. Then someone recommended another church of a similar denomination about a dozen blocks south, and at that coffee hour several people made a point of coming over to me, saying how glad they were to see me and expressing a hope that I would return and worship with them again soon.

The Importance of Passions

That church has been my spiritual home ever since, and I miss it when I am out of town on Sundays. I look forward to the church suppers, the annual fair, adult Bible classes, and all the other activities I take part in.

One of the many reasons why my church is so special and why it brings me so much fulfillment is the people I meet there. Our oldest congregant is ninety-four years old and recently married a charming lady of eighty-three. He says he is the oldest acolyte in the United States (and quite possibly he is!) and assists at chapel services, offers his own grace at church suppers, and occasionally delivers a toast or speech that has people laughing and lost in thought at the same time.

But finding a passion is one thing, being "sappy" and falsely enthusiastic about it is quite another, and nothing turns people off more than forced cheeriness and a fake smile—except perhaps the unrelenting insistence that others share your own passions.

Widows are free to do anything they want, given only the restrictions of money and health. Here are some of the things my friends and I have found to be passionate about:

• Helping others. It may sound trite, but it is nevertheless true that helping those who are less fortunate increases your own measure of yourself and provides satisfaction in all the right places. Volunteer for something and commit yourself to it on a regular basis.

• Games. Bingo, cards, backgammon, it doesn't matter what game you choose because the major advantage of all of them is that you can't play them alone. Sociability is an important asset. In addition, they require regular practice and are thus effective ways to fill blocks of time, especially in the evening. There are also tours organized around games so that you can travel to meet others interested in your game.

• Books. Books engage the mind like nothing else. They are an escape, a trip into different worlds, sources of information, and comfort. They are truly friends. They can also lead you to "real" friends if you join a reading group (that meets once a month to discuss a book all have read), volunteer at the library, join the literary friends, or teach illiterates to read.

186

• Art. Almost all towns of any size have a museum nearby as well as an art gallery or two (the difference between the two is that in the latter the works of art are for sale). These institutions can provide food for the soul, time spent away from home, and many educational opportunities in the form of classes, lectures, docent-led tours, and seminars. You might also follow your urge to pick up a paintbrush or a lump of clay yourself.

• Music. Go to concerts, recitals (many of which are free), lectures, and symposia. Join the choir at church or a community chorus. Take music lessons.

• Religion. Although you probably don't want to turn into a religious fanatic, you might find solace (especially while you are still in the first throes of grief) in renewing your spiritual faith—and there are groups of widows or single people your age at many churches and synagogues.

• Food and cooking. Are you a gourmet cook? Then look for some of the many clubs that abound in major metropolitan areas, or organize one of your own. Gourmet clubs operate in a variety of ways (some members take turns hosting the dinner, and some do progressive dinners: each course at a different home), but all share an interest in food and wine, well prepared and enjoyed in a convivial atmosphere. What could be more conducive to increasing your social life—and pleasing your palate at the same time!

• Exercise and sports. You don't have to turn into a "jock," but a regular exercise program (see Chapter 9 for a short discussion of good exercises for older women) will make you feel better, it may introduce you to other people who are out walking in your neighborhood or who belong to the same health club, and it will take up a chunk of time each week.

• Gardening. Those of you who are already passionate about gardening don't need a pep talk from me, and those of you who live in a city apartment will have to restrict yourself to pots (but I have seen some marvelous greenhouse windows that have transformed an ordinary room into a tropical paradise). But for the rest of you, consider the joy of digging in the dirt, nourishing green things, and making them respond to your care. Gardening is a passion that, once developed, intensifies and gives added pleasure each year.

• Other hobbies that used to interest you but have fallen by the wayside in the press of keeping other aspects of your life in order. Did you take art classes in college and then have dreams of your own north-lighted studio? Then buy a set of paints and go to it! Do you play the piano occasionally and bemoan the fact that there's never time to practice? Sign up for lessons and be serious about it. Turn on your phone machine while you practice, and eventually give a small recital for your friends.

VOLUNTEERING

Let's talk about other people first because that is, after all, the primary reason we live—to be of service to others. Lest you think I'm being a "goody two-shoes" about this, I am not. I enjoy pleasure as much as the next person, and I've already admitted that I have a terrible weakness for pretty clothes and other things (and there was that gift of a fur coat that I was unable to resist!), but it is in the service to others that most people find their greatest fulfillment.

You don't have to turn into Joan of Arc, and no one is asking you to don a hair shirt and give up all your luxuries. But if you contribute something to society on a regular basis, *you* will be a richer person.

To be a "do-gooder" or volunteer is not as sneered at as it was a few years ago, when all women wanted their efforts to be rewarded with money, regardless of whether they had any real market value—and regardless of whether they needed the money or not. I think more people now feel a satisfaction and sense of dignity in helping others without personal gain and without public recognition. The pendulum is starting to swing back, even among adolescents who, in my opinion, were starting to turn into a gang of monsters interested only in buying whatever they saw advertised on television.

Volunteering means coming to terms with who you are, learning what gives you satisfaction and what makes you content with your own values, and developing more mature, other-directed values.

Ninety million Americans have already discovered the fulfillment that volunteerism can bring, and there is even some documented evidence that volunteering can enhance self-esteem, foster a sense of accomplishment and worthiness, and can be an antidote to depression. In fact, some psychologists believe that people who volunteer tend to be healthier and happier and live longer than those who do not. For example, a ten-year study of 2,700 people in Tecumseh, Michigan, revealed that the people who did no volunteer work were two and a half times more likely to die during the period of the study than those who volunteered. True, there are dozens of other variables operating here, but the psychological importance of giving of oneself to others is well documented.

Volunteerism is particularly important for older people and those who are alone. Donating time and energy to others can take you out of yourself and your own unhappiness for a while—and the effects have been known to turn "real," that is, to become internalized so that the gratification you provide to others ends up making *you* happy.

One of the most popular and rewarding activities for older people is foster grandparenting, a program in which older people are teamed with youngsters who are emotionally or physically handicapped or have been abused and/or neglected. Some children have been in trouble with the law, but all have a variety of serious problems. Volunteer grandparents visit with them regularly and involve them in a series of activities designed to return them to the normal and productive mainstream of life.

In a program called Senior Companions, people run errands for and transport to doctor appointments those who are housebound. Meals on Wheels is an organization that recruits and organizes volunteers to help deliver hot meals to those who cannot get out, and every community of every size has a senior citizens' center that always needs volunteers.

Volunteers age fifty and over are welcomed into VISTA and the Peace Corps, and SCORE (Service Core of Retired Executives) needs volunteers to advise young entrepreneurs.

There are dozens of other activities you can do, such as

- visiting children in hospitals and/or foster care homes;
- working in a nursing home;
- mobilizing disaster relief efforts for someone in your community who has been devastated by circumstances;
- working in a shelter for battered or homeless women;
- planning and building a community park or garden;
- taking care of children with AIDS whose parents have abandoned them;
- working with schoolchildren by helping with homework and teaching them to read and write;
- working in the thrift shop of a hospital or religious organization;
- leading a Girl Scout troop;
- serving as tour leader or docent of a municipal park or museum; and
- volunteering in a hospital in a variety of capacities.

Contact the following national organizations for their activities in your area:

- Action, the national volunteer agency that is an umbrella organization for programs like Foster Grandparents. Call (202) 634-9406, or write Action, Washington, DC 20525.
- Retired Senior Volunteer Programs (RSVP), 806 Connecticut Avenue, NW, Washington, DC 20525; (202) 634-9353.
- Contact Literacy Center, which offers volunteers the opportunity to teach adults to read. Call (800) 228-6935.
- The Peace Corps and VISTA (Volunteers in Service to America). Call (800) 424-8580.
- Habitat for Humanity. Write to Habitat and Church streets, Americus, GA 31709; (912) 924-6935.
- Volunteer Vacations, which conducts outdoor projects. Write to American Hiking Society/Volunteer Vacations, Box 86, North Scituate, MA 02060; or the American Hiking Society, 1015 31st Street, NW, Washington, DC 20007.
- National Mental Health Consumer Self-Help Clearinghouse. Write 311 South Juniper St., Room 902, Philadelphia, PA 19107; (215) 735-2465.

- Public Education Association, 39 West 32 Street, New York, NY; (212) 868-1640, to find out about tutorial positions in public schools.
- Girl Scouts of the U.S.A., 830 Third Avenue, New York, NY; (212) 940-7500.
- Girls Clubs of America, 205 Lexington Avenue, New York, NY; (212) 689-3700.
- The Legal Aid Society. Look up your local chapter in the white pages, or in the yellow pages under "Lawyers."

GAMES

Many people have found mental stimulation, social contacts, and even friendship in playing games regularly. Some games, like bingo, are not particularly intellectually challenging and might be classed more as time-killers than arousers of passion, but do not underrate them as a pleasant way to spend an evening, especially if they help support the efforts of your church, labor union, or other charitable organization.

Other games, however, such as bridge, backgammon, and chess, require thought-provoking effort. Then there are games that make you get off your duff and work up a sweat, like golf and tennis. They involve mental concentration too, require regular practice to achieve some expertise, and cannot be played alone, so they provide social interaction. And perhaps, most important, they get you out of the house and take some doing to arrange.

Another advantage of a passion for games is that there are fascinating tours organized around them, and they always involve groups of other players with whom you can travel, sightsee, have meals, and socialize.

I have never wanted to take such a trip because I'm afraid that I'd be in the middle of an exciting game when my ship passed through the Panama Canal or docked at some exotic port and I'd miss the whole thing. But my friends who go on these tours always return with glorious reports of exciting times and new friendships formed. Two people I know even found spouses on these voyages!

Bridge seems to be very popular with people my age, particularly for those with physical limitations. If you don't play well enough to be part of a regular group, or want to improve your skills before you join one, take lessons. Most YWCAs have inexpensive bridge classes, as do many local community colleges.

BOOKS

Eleanor Roosevelt used to give a party each year at the White House for all the professional women working in the federal government, and although I was at the bottom of the category of federal workers who received invitations, I managed to squeak through, and one year I was lucky enough to be in the group of women that Mrs. Roosevelt herself escorted through the family quarters.

As a greenhorn lawyer from the sticks, I was absolutely in awe of the First Lady, who was so natural and unaffected and made each guest feel that she had been waiting all day just to talk to her.

There was a round table in the sitting room stacked with several books, and as we passed it, she said, "Oh, those books! I meant to put them away before this afternoon. Books are like rabbits—they multiply so fast that no sooner do you put one down, than four more appear alongside it!"

It was easy to see what one of Mrs. Roosevelt's passions was. A brilliant young lawyer to whom I was briefly engaged was of the opposite view. "Phil," he said, "stop spending all your money on books and go to the beauty shop."

I was hurt—because I thought I looked fine. But I got his message. My passion for buying books that I wanted to read, or felt that I couldn't live without owning, had overtaken my capacity for getting around to reading them. But I knew why he was criticizing me, and even though that young man's remarks stung at the time, I didn't believe he was justified in his criticism.

As an only child for eight years, I consider books my salvation—as they have been since my widowhood. As a child, I took out three books a day from the local library during the summer beach holidays. This was not just an escape. My childhood was a happy one; I just loved to read.

My mother and father were avid readers and both read aloud to me since I had been a baby, and one of the many aspects of my daughters' mothering that I admire most is that they read aloud long and often to their children who, as a result, have a passion for reading.

A good friend of mine remembers the day she got her first library card. "My mother treated it as a special—and very grown-up—privilege, and impressed on me that library books were to be treasured and treated with the utmost care. She bought me a bookmark and warned me against dog-earing the pages, and I remember to this day the hell she raised when I inadvertently left a library book out in the rain. She made me pay for it out of my allowance!"

That library was a significant rite of passage for my friend, who turned out to be a wonderful writer as well as a great reader.

Reading books set in the geographical area where you were raised is especially pleasurable, as are novels about your own ethnic or cultural group that bring back memories of your experiences.

Many people find particular joy in sharing reading pleasure with others and have formed reading groups for this purpose. The group meets once a month and each member reads the same book. Everyone then discusses it over wine and cheese or other light refreshment. Sharing insights that the book stimulated and hearing how others reacted to what you have just read creates an added pleasure.

One friend of mine has had such a group in her life ever since her first child was born. She said that she feared that her mind would turn to cotton candy without something intelligent and grown-up to do while she dealt in bottles of formula and baby talk all day. She also wanted to have something outside of their own lives to discuss with her husband in the evening. Her group had a committee that drew up the year's list of books, but other groups function quite well on a consensus basis, deciding from month to month what to read for the next meeting.

If you have stopped reading for pleasure because so many other activities have taken precedence, I recommend going back to it. It doesn't require much money (none, if you always use the library), and one good reading binge will almost always lead to another. And it's so much more rewarding than television!

A few months ago I read a book that I found intensely compelling,

The Silence of the Lambs by Thomas Harris, and lent it to a friend who I know enjoys psychological thrillers. She said, "Not only didn't I prepare the speech I was planning to write on Sunday afternoon, I took it with me to the office on Monday, locked the door, and finished it!"

I loved it that she played hooky from work to "sneak-read" a book that I had recommended. It made me love the book even more. Now that's a true passion for books.

ART

During the last year of my undergraduate education, a young red-headed economic geography professor used to invite a few of us to his home on Saturday afternoons to listen to the Metropolitan Opera on the radio. As we listened and sipped sherry, he gave us his Metropolitan Museum of Art books to pore over, and the combination of listening to that sublime music and looking at the reproductions of some of the most beautiful paintings in the world is one of my happiest memories of college. I think my passion for viewing and collecting art began then.

Looking at sculpture, pictures, quilts, and other art forms can easily turn into an obsession. I have just returned from a pilgrimage that indulged this obsession to its fullest extent: I went from Paris to Spain feasting my eyes and other senses, and felt as though I had drunk an intoxicating nectar after having seen so many beautiful things.

These were tenth- to sixteenth-century art objects made for the Romanesque churches that were built to give the pilgrims of the Middle Ages physical and spiritual shelter and strength. Some of the same moral urgencies that existed then are with us today, and sharing those early expressions of them helps one to know how much we have always had in common with one another.

One does not have to be an artist or a collector to become an art *aficionado.* But if you strive for any sort of collection, it is essential to learn as much as you can.

I once complained bitterly to a museum director who had given over an entire wall to what I considered just a glob of paint on a huge white background. "Do you understand T. S. Eliot's poem, *Sweeney Agonistes?*" he asked.

I admitted that I did not, "unless it is explained with all its symbolism and mythological references."

"Then," he countered, "how can you expect to understand why we have given this picture such an important place? Eliot's poem is in a medium you use and understand—written language—and you need it explained. This piece of art is in a medium you have neither used nor studied—oil paint on canvas."

He proceeded to justify his choice and its placement. I had to bow to his superior knowledge and of course to his authority as director of the museum, but I didn't have to like the painting or consider it worthy.

You don't have to be passionate about all art. Choose one or several periods that interest you, or one special artist or group of artists, such as the American Hudson River School, Dutch landscapists, Italian primitives, Rodin, or Rubens—whatever pleases you.

Then read about the artists or period and learn as much as you can. Rent or buy slides to show at a party, and give a charming little lecture as you do.

My own countless hours in Holland, spent alone while my husband worked, put me totally under the spell of the old Dutch Masters. Sometimes I had traveling companions then, and I often do now, and they have taught me so much about looking at art and seeing more deeply into painting than I ever had before.

I also go to lectures, almost always free at museums, with friends or alone. The study and enjoyment of art can open up a whole new life style for you. If you have never had an interest in it, it can make you a more knowledgeable and interesting person.

If you have been thinking about reawakening a long-buried passion for art, what are you waiting for?

MUSIC

Most people, unless they are completely tone deaf or tremendously culturally deprived, enjoy listening to music. In fact, it's almost impossible to get through a day without being surrounded by music—much of it intrusive (like that played from "ghetto blasters" on the street or emanating from supposedly muffled earphones on the subway) and some of it so boring as to be intolerable—like what's played in elevators, on the telephone when you're on hold, and even on airplanes as passengers are squeezing themselves and their luggage into spaces meant for midgets.

Some of the very young—and some who ought to know better—like rock music played so loud that it damages their hearing. (And by the way, there is incontrovertible proof that this happens in a very short time.) Many people like overarranged "easy listening" music that is played on so many radio stations and does nothing to challenge the emotions or intellect.

But as our taste and sophistication develop, and as we are trained to appreciate the finer things in life, we learn to succumb to the glories of opera, symphonies, chamber music, and other forms of intellectual and emotional stimulation brought to us on waves of sound. A solo appearance of a superb interpreter of music such as Itzhak Perlman or Isaac Stern on the violin, or André Watts at the piano can be unforgettable. And a full orchestra with chorus and soloists singing Mozart's Requiem Mass or Beethoven's Ninth Symphony is one of the sublime moments in human experience.

There is something about music that distinguishes it from all other art forms. The critic Bernard Levin says, "Music sets out to conquer the heart of man by combining a variety of sounds. How does an art that denies itself all acknowledged forms of communication nonetheless communicate its meaning with such power?"

One of the things that has always amazed me about the power of music is that it is so ephemeral, so capable of differences of nuance each time it is played. In painting, sculpture, and literature, the words or pictorial representations are always the same; they have been permanently inscribed by the artist, and the only differences in the way they are perceived lie in the person of the beholder. But with music (and to some extent with dance), the notes exist, but they must be played anew each time in order for the art to come alive. And therein lies music's infinite variety and enduring magic: No two musicians play the same notes exactly the same way, and no single musician plays them the same way each time he or she takes up the instrument.

A love of fine music either exists in your soul or it doesn't, but if it does, the passion can be increased by reading about the lives of composers and musicians and the theory of music. When you go to concerts, read the program notes, which are always written by knowledgeable people, and do the same when you buy a recording.

Listening to and learning about music can be enjoyed alone or with another person, and it can be turned into a lovely social activity. For example, why not organize a Saturday afternoon get-together around the radio broadcasts of the Metropolitan Opera—and extend the pleasure off-season with opera recordings? Invite a few friends over (insist they show up on time), participate in the intermission opera quiz, and then serve light refreshments when the opera is over. You might even coordinate the refreshments with the opera: paella after *Carmen* (but no cigarettes of course!); humus, tahini, and pita for dipping during the intermissions of *Aïda;* French fare after *La Bohème;* and sushi during *Madama Butterfly.*

One friend of mine buys two tickets to the Philharmonic season and invites a different person to each concert. She provides the music and the other person provides the dinner beforehand or a light supper afterward.

Many museums have free concerts and lectures or classes on music appreciation. One of the best such programs, if you happen to be lucky enough to live nearby, is provided by the Smithsonian Institution Resident Associates Program in Washington, D.C. The Frick Museum in New York City and the Isabella Stewart Gardner Museum in Boston are other examples of concert-going surrounded by magnificent art. Call your local museum to find out what musical events are planned.

Churches and synagogues are also wellsprings of fine music. Some of the most beautiful and passionate music ever composed is liturgical in nature, and don't forget that much of what we pay to hear in concert halls was written to the glory of God and was intended to be performed in houses of worship.

COOKING

A passion for cooking does not necessarily have to be bad for your waistline or your heart. In fact, cooking healthful foods that are delicious is probably even more challenging than just loading everything with cream, butter, and cheese.

One of the most delightful ways to indulge your passion for food is to join or form a gourmet club that meets periodically to sample the culinary creations of the members. The meetings are usually once a month and can be arranged in one of two ways.

• Have everyone contribute to the meal by bringing an assigned course, with the host making the dish that is the least portable.

• The members of the club can rotate and one person can do all the menu planning and preparation for the evening.

But whatever way you choose to organize your gourmet club, people who enjoy good food, fine wine, and intelligent conversation spend a convivial evening in the pursuit of these hedonistic pleasures.

With the latest craze of controlling cholesterol, why not have an oat-bran-tasting lunch or supper, with each of your friends who like to cook bringing their own special version of a dish made of oat bran? Each dish is identified by number, and then all the guests vote on which is the most delicious. Not only can you learn to make delicious, healthful things, but it's an excuse for an inexpensive social evening.

If you have a passion for cooking, you might think about turning it into a money-making proposition. I know a woman who makes what all her friends tell her is the world's greatest cheesecake. Whenever she served it, there would never be a crumb left over, no matter how full people were from the "real" meal she had just prepared. Everyone said she ought to sell it. "Oh, no," she replied. "There are other cakes that are just as good, and besides, who would pay all that money that the ingredients cost, not to mention the time it takes?"

One day a mutual friend brought a restaurateur over to taste the cheesecake, and he immediately asked Bess to make two for his restaurant dessert menu. She did, and he paid her full price on delivery. His customers went wild, and the rest is history. She now employs two full-time bakers and has branched out into chocolate and other flavors and is thinking of making things other than cheesecake.

Bess doesn't really need the money and gives most of it away to shelters for the homeless, but she says, "You know, running my own little business is one of the most satisfying things I've ever done. It has given me a wonderful sense of my own ability. I like feeling productive, and I like being able to help feed people who might otherwise go hungry with the money I earn on making food for those who can afford to buy very expensive cake. It satisfied my sense of contributing to justice in the world."

12

HEALTH AND FITNESS

$\mathcal{A}$lthough health and fitness concerns are not specific to widows, and this chapter will certainly not be a compendium of what you have to do to stay healthy—and above all, it will not offer medical advice—there are some health concerns that widows need to pay special attention to: those that particularly affect middle-age and older women, and those that you can do something about before you are hit with the full effect of major medical bills.

STRESS

The death of a spouse is one of the most stressful of life's events, and the effects last forever. True, the stress levels tend to decrease over time, and the intensity waxes and wanes at various times, depending on what else is going on in your life, but the stress of having to develop an entirely new life style is permanent.

I have found that the only effective way of coping with stress is to acknowledge that it exists and to tackle it as I would any other problem, that is, to determine the ways in which it affects me and then to look for methods to lessen the stress, or at least ameliorate its effect.

The ancient Greek adage "Know thyself" is true for all areas of life, but most especially when it comes to realizing what is stressful for *you*. The best "advice" I can give along these lines is not advice at all, but rather a series of rules that I have devised for myself about how to cope with stress:

• I schedule the most difficult and unpleasant tasks for the times that I feel at my physical, mental, and emotional peak—for that particular task. For instance, I always do laundry in the evenings and write thank-you notes during the wee hours of the morning when I can't sleep. Neither of these jobs is intellectually challenging or stimulating; I call them "busy work" that requires a certain low level of attention.

If I need to do something that requires my full mental capability, I do it first thing in the morning, and I know that by Friday afternoon and evening I'm not capable of much more than reading a good novel or going to a movie with a friend. The point is that I *never* schedule an important business meeting for those times because I know from past experience that the stress of fatigue would increase the general stress associated with such an important task.

• I have devised a number of stress-reduction techniques that work for me: long walks and long soaks in a hot tub. Some people find that meditation works, and others find that doing strenuous exercise and/ or deep breathing reduces stress. Try a number of things and settle on a few that work for you.

A friend tells a story about how her stress level increased (and her self-concept plummeted) when she tried to do meditation as a stress-reduction technique. "Everyone said it worked like a charm," she told me, "but when I lay quietly and tried to clear my mind and do all that sequential deep-muscle relaxation, all I could think about was how much time I was wasting and how much work I still had to do. It just increased my stress, and besides, I felt guilty because I couldn't medi-tate like everyone else!"

My friend got her stress under control only when she stopped trying so hard.

• I have found that frequent, short vacations are better for me than a long annual holiday. I've made a lot of mistakes in this regard and have taken fascinating long trips, only to come back to two months' worth of unopened mail, which almost destroyed the therapeutic change that the trips provided in the first place. Besides, I like the idea of being able to look forward to getting away several times a year; even the anticipation is a stress reducer.

■ When I was younger, I used to thrive on a lot of deadline pressure. Life always seemed so boring and unchallenging without a lot of pressure, and I considered it positive stress. That is still true for some people, but as I have grown older I realize that much of the pressure and deadlines were artificial and meaningless; therefore the stress turned negative. I have now learned to look at the things in my life that have been done and try to sort them into an order of what is really important and has a "real" deadline, and what can be put off.

■ Although I have never fallen into the habit of using drugs (alcohol, tranquilizers and sleeping pills, and the like) to relieve stress, I know that many people do. We live in a society that emphasizes a quick pharmaceutical remedy for all types of ailments, and stress has become a "fashionable" ailment of late. Instead of turning to a pill or Scotch bottle if you are so inclined to take something to reduce stress, take a hot bath, make an appointment to have a massage or a facial, or brew a cup of herbal tea.

■ If you are having physiologic symptoms of stress (some people call them anxiety attacks) such as heart palpitations, stomach pains, frequent headaches, or severe insomnia, see your doctor. Although these are indeed symptoms of stress, they may also indicate a true physical illness that you need to have checked.

SLEEP

The complaints of so many middle-aged and older women are that they do not get enough "restorative" sleep. But, strangely enough, this dilemma rarely affects men of the same ages.

Practically all of my friends say that they are *not* content with their sleep patterns, and recent reports more than confirms their beliefs. An estimated 30 million adults in the U.S. suffer from sleep deprivation, if not classic insomnia.

Each of us are so varied in our physical and psychological makeup that generalities here are worthless. The medical fraternity is just now beginning to come to grips with sleep problems, yet, everyone I know has asked that I expand my findings on "sleep" — or the lack of.

But there is really no "Scoop on Sleep," as the title of a recent published article suggests, although the lack of it is suffered by a large part of the adult population. To say "let sleep come to me" will not result in your falling into the arms of Morpheus.

While one third of the nation is tossing through the night, the male population is more often snoring his way through, to bounce out of bed the next morning refreshed. Not so with their spouses, and even less with their widows or the women they have divorced.

Worse still, "worrying about the lack of sleep results in even less sleep," says Peter Hauri, Ph.D, Director of the Mayo Clinic Insomnia program. People are, in fact, sleeping about an hour and a half less than they did at the turn of the century.

So many people today work indoors so they have less exposure to true darkness as well as normal bright natural light. Sleep centers which are beginning to exist in diagnostic clinics in the great metropolitan hospitals insist that their patients stop taking sleep-inducing medication. Many harried souls who enroll in these programs not only do so as a last resort and are, under a doctor's prescription, already addicted to barbiturates such as Halcion or Ambien, or Melatonin (a sleeping medicine which can be bought over the counter). Researchers are still looking for a safer and more effective sleeping medicine.

Many researchers believe that REM (rapid eye movement) sleep (deep) bestows benefits, allowing learning and memory to gel. Rats deprived of REM died in five weeks.

"When you're asleep, the brain organizes information accumulated while you were awake," says Dr. Bruce McNaughton, Pd.D. from the University of Arizona sleep project. "The brain is like a cluttered desktop at day's end, and sleep provides the opportunity to file away the clutter."

GREAT! Most of us could just sink into that kind of surcease. We try very hard to do everything we have heard, or that has been recommended by friends. We only feel that we have had two or three hours of "deep" sleep and fitful spurts of restless sleep after that. We awaken with fuzzy thinking and memory gaps — along with a bad disposition. Doctors knowing what they do about REM can now bring about "a miracle of restoration" to many insomniacs, according to

Verlyn Klinkewborn in a *New York Times* magazine article in January 1997.

It's important to remember that divorce, deaths, births, job pressures, and current personal anxieties can trigger and even escalate your sleeplessness.

A good doctor will analyze your own personal problems, experiment with non-addictive medicines, prescribe a variety of ways to reduce the stress or grief factors which have caused your disturbed sleep patterns, and, more than likely, be of some help.

Also, place a lot of emphasis on exercise — preferably the outdoor variety — such as long walks. Also stay away from wine, other forms of alcohol, and heavy dinner meals. These can act as immediate sleep inducers, but stimulates only two or three hours of sleep, after which one is wakeful. Several confidants reveal that over a long stressful professional crisis, they have almost become addicted to sleeping medication just to continue their output.

But they are inaccurate witnesses of how long or how well they have slept. How can any of us judge how long in a night we have been unconscious?

People who have found sound medical advice report that they were told that it could take months to discover the exact formula for their particular needs. But they find it worth the try and now, for the most part, sleep better and more restoratively.

Still, though, friends who feel they have survived and learned to live with the abandonment of a divorce, the death of a spouse or a child, or an extreme personal crisis, say they *still* cannot get enough sleep. They get up after an hour or two of tossing about and write thank you letters, iron laundry, clean up their files or personal rolodex, or do any of those tedious tasks which always awaits one.

Sleep patterns vary from infancy to old age. As we age, some of our ability to produce deep sleep begins to deteriorate in the late 30s. In some rare cases, sleep deficit results in geriatric depression, which is why it is so important to find treatment. All of us will continue to try to get enough sleep to restore our body and soul and it is worth the effort to try any and everything. We must remember that a *night* of quiet wakefulness is different from the same period of quiet wakefulness in the *daytime*. A pragmatic solution is to take two aspirin at one or two o'clock in the morning when one awakes from the first deep sleep. Turn on the History Channel on Cable TV, relish the refresher course in history it provides, and a great majority of the time you will have fallen asleep within 20 minutes and missed the climax of the story. But, you can always catch the re-run on George III or Evita later in the week.

Try it!

YOUR PHYSICAL APPEARANCE

Good grooming is one of the most important things you can do for yourself and for your overall health. Even if you are feeling terrible, if your hair is styled becomingly, your shoes are repaired and well polished, and your nails are buffed and filed neatly, you will give the appearance of being in top form — and that's half the battle.

After age forty a woman's hair should be shorter rather than longer, and unless you have the time and money to spend at the hairdresser's every other day, you ought to have a simple hairstyle that you can arrange yourself. Only the most beautiful and statuesque older women look good with long hair or with ribbons or bows as adornments. Most of us look best with something simple and short, even for evening.

But very short "tomboy" hair isn't good, either. It's as difficult to wear becomingly as long hair and is rarely flattering to a woman whose skin is not as perfect as it once was.

I have resisted getting rid of my gray hair (but happily, so did Barbara Bush after becoming the First Lady), even though I know it makes me look older. And I think that artificially colored hair on a woman of a certain age looks ludicrous — and sad.

Men don't seem to worry about gray hair as much as women. In fact, when they are young, they seem to take steps, such as growing a mustache, to make themselves appear older, perhaps to inspire confidence, or to look more mature.

When I was a young lawyer, I had the idea that graying hair made me look older and wiser, and therefore more professional, and even as I aged, I never worried about the increasing number of white hairs because I always felt that I looked younger than I was, especially since Sam was eleven years my senior.

And speaking of hair, do take care of your facial hair. Tweeze those strays that appear on your chin and neck, bleach or use a depilatory cream on your upper-lip hair if it is dark or overly abundant. If the problem is serious, you might want to consider electrolysis, but before you consider treatment, investigate the person carefully—as carefully as you would a doctor or other professional.

I suppose I'm showing my age, but I still get a jolt when I see coiffures that look as though they have been slept on or haven't been combed for several days and realize that this effect is deliberate. How could anyone want to look like that?

Once when I mentioned to my thirteen-year-old granddaughter that she needed to comb her hair, she replied, "But, Goggi, I just did!"

My reaction is the same when I see untied shoe laces, sloppy huge jackets that people buy in thrift shops, and undershorts deliberately hanging beneath the hem of tennis skirts. It makes me feel ancient because, to my mind, it looks ridiculous. But I've decided not to fight it because it's probably a generational thing, and these kids grow out of it—I hope!

•   •   •

Several years after Sam died, I decided to have the wrinkles taken away from around my eyes and under my chin. It's plastic surgery but not of an especially complex nature (still, you must seek out a competent board-certified plastic surgeon who comes highly recommended), and it has made me look and *feel* so much better.

It's not that I look especially younger; rather, I look rested and alert without all that extra skin hanging on where it doesn't belong.

If you decide to do plastic surgery, consider doing it earlier rather than waiting until you are so wrinkled that not only will the results not be as effective, but you will look too different. And try a little at a time to see what it can do for you.

One friend of mine just had her entire face done and she looks awful—too stretched around her eyes that now seem to stare out at you in the most distressing way. She reminds me of a middle-aged Barbie doll, so artificial is the look.

•   •   •

Pay close attention to your makeup, and if you don't feel confident doing your face yourself, invest in a lesson or two at Georgette Klinger or Elizabeth Arden or another salon. Many department stores have free makeup consultants in their cosmetics departments.

Too much makeup is as big a mistake as too little or the wrong kind, and you have to learn by trial and error what is the right look for you. Practice alone in front of the bathroom mirror, just the way you did when you were a child!

You might well wonder why I'm talking about hair and plastic surgery and makeup to readers who have been taking good care of themselves for their entire lives. "If I don't know how to get myself together by now," you're probably saying to yourself, perhaps a little testily, "I'll never know!"

That's not what I'm saying. Of course, you know how to get dressed and have your hair done and are probably perfectly groomed. But I know, because I went through it myself, that you're most likely not *feeling* all that attractive. You're lonely and suddenly single in what can feel like a frighteningly hostile world, and you may feel as grubby and dumpy as I did, even though to outsiders you look fine—like your old self.

And that's the trouble. In many ways, you are no longer your old self. You are no longer married, and the man who knew and loved you exactly as you were is gone. Thus your greatest source of support and confidence is gone, and you may feel unsure of yourself and of the way you look.

Perhaps you haven't changed your hairstyle in a decade because your husband liked the way you wore it, and maybe your clothes are just a little old-fashioned because you and he didn't entertain or go out much and you didn't feel the need to be right on the edge of new fashions.

But now you need to start a new life alone, and a new "look" might be just the lift you need. So look in the mirror, go through your closets, and throw out all your old eye shadow and buy some new, flattering colors.

TAKING A TRIP TO THE HOSPITAL: SURVIVAL TECHNIQUES

Throughout my entire life I have never had to have a trip to the hospital alone. I have always been lucky enough to have parents, and then my husband, Sam, to smooth things out for me and see me through the experience. Even when our third daughter was delivered and Sam was in Brazil, my sister moved in for a while and saw me through the ordeal.

I still have my sister, and I know that my daughters would be attentive to my needs if I were to be hospitalized again (and as we grow older, the likelihood of that increases), but it is still a good idea to be able to get through the experience alone and to learn a little about the political and social systems that make a hospital operate.

Probably the most frustrating thing about being a patient in a hospital is the powerlessness that comes from not understanding what is happening. For the most part, hospital personnel are not good at explaining the reasons for the things they do, and hospitals, like all institutions, have a great many rules, regulations, and procedures that are often murky in origin and rationale.

But there are two things operating in your favor: The first is economic and the second is legal. First, the vast majority of hospitals are now operated either for profit or as nonprofit corporations. Either way, hospital administrators are faced with intense and increasing competition for patients and are therefore running their institutions more like a business than a social/health-care institution. This means that you as a patient are viewed as a paying customer, which you are, and hospital personnel are more likely to be nice to you in order to win your business the next time—and to increase the chances of your saying positive things to your friends.

Second, everyone in hospitals is scared to death of being sued—for good reason. The number of medical malpractice suits has increased dramatically over the past decade and the size of jury awards and out-of-court settlements have also increased. This makes hospital personnel jumpy and more likely to be careful of the way they treat you.

Even so, there are a few things you ought to keep in mind when you enter a hospital.

• Before you even leave the house, plan carefully for your return. Even if a friend or family member will stay with you for a few days after your discharge, make sure you clean the house (especially the bathroom), put fresh sheets on the bed, and stock the refrigerator (or freezer, if your stay will be more than a few days) with things that you will be tempted to eat on your return. Remember that you probably will not feel very well when you get home, and your strength and energy level will be at an all-time low.

• When you check into the hospital, make certain you have your health insurance card with you, and be certain to leave *all* valuables at home: Don't take more than five dollars in cash and wear no jewelry. Bring toilet articles with you, especially a light cologne and body lotion, and one or two nightgowns, but not your very best ones. Also bring a bathrobe that buttons down the front, slippers, and a bedjacket if you have one. Take some *light* reading material, preferably something humorous, and a small inexpensive portable radio. You might also want to take a small pillow from home for extra comfort.

• Be certain you understand exactly what is going to be done to you and the reasons for your operation (or other procedure). You should have discussed all this with your physician beforehand, but if you still have questions or if some come to mind after you have entered the hospital, write them down and ask your doctor before the procedure. If you are being hospitalized for an operation, you will see or speak with the surgeon the night before or the morning of the operation, so do take the time to ask questions. You might also ask the resident physician, who may or may not be able to give you satisfactory answers.

• Many people will advise you to hire private duty nurses for two or three days immediately following surgery. This is not necessarily to your advantage for a variety of reasons: Depending on the hospital, routine postoperative care is usually very well done and is done so often by the nurses employed by the hospital that there is little likelihood of mistakes; nurses employed by a hospital are under more supervision and control than self-employed nurses; and if your physician does not think private duty nursing care is medically necessary, he will not order it in writing and your insurance company probably will not pay for it. However, if you and your doctor believe that private duty nurses are necessary, hire them *before* you go into the hospital, and check out the nurses' agency as carefully as you would any other professional association.

• During the course of your hospitalization, ask questions. Ask as many as you need to, and do *not* feel that you are making a nuisance of yourself. Think of yourself as a paying customer (with the average total charge for a day in the hospital in a major metropolitan area closing in at one thousand dollars, you *are* paying—through the nose!), and demand the service you are supposed to receive.

• Do not let anyone do anything to you that you don't understand and have not given consent for. Do not let anyone examine you unless you know who he or she is, and always remember that you have the right to refuse *any and all* treatments or procedures. Even if you change your mind about your operation after you have been strapped to the table and are staring at that huge operating room light, you can say, "Hold it! I want to go home."

• Hospital food can be pretty awful, but, unless you are on a restricted diet, you don't have to eat it. When your friends call before they visit and ask if there's anything you need, order food. Have visitors bring in your favorite tidbits and at least give yourself some pleasure at mealtime.

• When you are ready to be discharged, find out what your limitations will be, what you can do and what you should avoid, what you can eat, how long until you can climb stairs, lift bags of groceries, drive a car, etc. Given the fact that patients are being discharged earlier and earlier (sometimes several days before they feel ready to face the world), it might be a good idea to engage a part-time helper in the house or even a visiting nurse. This is especially important if you live alone, and the hospital's social work department can arrange it for you.

If something goes wrong with the care you are receiving (medical, nursing, housekeeping, or any other care provided by the hospital), seek a remedy right away. Do not suffer in silence, because whatever is wrong can usually be easily corrected. If the hospital does not have an ombudsman or other patient representative, call the administrator's office and complain.

You also should know your rights as a hospital patient. The American Hospital Association publishes a list of patient rights, which many institutions display prominently in patient rooms. If you want to look at it, a copy will be available in the administrator's office. As a general summary, these include but are not limited to the right to

- informed participation in all treatment decisions;
- privacy and confidentiality, regardless of the source of payment for care;
- a clear, concise explanation, in lay terms, of all procedures, including all known risks involved;
- know the identity and professional status of all individuals providing care;
- all information contained in your medical record;
- visitors and access to the outside by telephone;
- leave the hospital or other health care facility at any time regardless of medical condition and regardless of medical advice;
- receive a detailed copy of the bill, regardless of source of payment, including all charges incurred.

SLEEP—OR THE LACK OF IT

A good night's deep sleep can be one of the most refreshing things known to humankind, but the lack of sleep must surely be one of life's greatest frustrations.

Insomnia is a serious problem of widowhood, although this is generally not known or talked about much. Part of the problem stems from depression and is a self-limiting phenomenon; that is, once the first throes of grief have passed, you will begin to sleep better. Part of it arises from the anxiety of having to start a new life and having to worry about things you always took for granted before or never had to think about. And part of the insomnia of widowhood just goes with the generally high level of stress you are experiencing now. Rarely, there are physiological causes.

But whatever the cause, take some comfort in the fact that you are not alone. About 35 percent of the American population has trouble sleeping from time to time. Insomnia is a symptom rather than a disease, and identifying the reason for your sleeplessness is the first and most important thing you can do to solve the problem. Insomnia falls into three general patterns:

- difficulty falling asleep—for sometimes as much as three hours of wakefulness after turning out the light;
- early morning awakening and inability to fall back asleep; and
- frequent awakening during the night.

Whatever the cause and pattern of your insomnia, one thing is certain: Habitual use of prescription or over-the-counter sleeping pills is *not* the answer. In fact, sleeping pills (called hypnotics) make the problem worse in the long run because they carry the risk of "rebound effect," a sleep disturbance that begins when you stop taking the drug, and your sleep may be even more disturbed than it was when you started taking the hypnotics. And getting "hooked" on sleeping pills is far too easy.

Neither is alcohol the way to "treat" insomnia. A small glass of wine once in a while at bedtime may help relax you, but stronger drink disturbs the quality of sleep, leaving you unrefreshed in the morning. Moreover, the temptation to increase alcohol intake to "put oneself to sleep" is dangerous and should be avoided.

If you do take sleeping pills, they should be on the advice of your physician, and you should let him or her know how you are doing with them. But before you even go to the doctor with an insomnia problem, try these self-help measures first.

- If you lead a busy life and are always "on the go," try to unwind for an hour or so before bedtime: read for a while or listen to some soothing music or watch a television program that doesn't require much intellect (my favorite is Ted Koppel's "Nightline");

• establish a regular sleep schedule and stick to it—even on weekends;

• don't concentrate on falling asleep—let it happen naturally because it will not happen if you force it;

• avoid beverages with caffeine in late afternoon or evening;

• avoid strenuous exercise in the evening;

• take a warm bath before getting into bed—a bath can relax tense muscles, as can a warm shower (although some people find the latter too invigorating);

• make your sleep environment as pleasant and comfortable as possible, with clean sheets, a feminine nightgown that makes you feel pampered, a dot of your favorite cologne, comfortable mattress and pillows, a cool room under warm blankets, no light, and absolute quiet (you might also consider eyeshades, a water bed, earplugs, and an electric blanket);

• sex at bedtime can be wonderfully relaxing, but if it leaves you frustrated and unsatisfied, it's worse than no sex at all, so either find a good lover or don't spend the night with him;

• avoid taking afternoon and evening naps; and

• try a glass of warm milk and a *light* carbohydrate snack, but don't eat a heavy meal right before bedtime; neither should you go to sleep hungry.

EXERCISE

My physical fitness program consists of regular golf games, dancing, membership in an exercise class in our church basement, and walking, which is probably one of the best forms of exercise—particularly for older women—if it is done on a regular schedule and in a certain manner.

I am not going to describe the various types of exercises you should engage in, first because I don't know anything about your needs, your situation, and your limitations, and second because there are dozens of perfectly fine exercise books on the shelves of your local bookstore and library. In addition, whatever exercise program you choose should be tailored to your own particular needs.

However, you *should* embark on regular exercise, either on your own or through a course at a spa, local gym, or YMCA or YWCA. Exercise tones up your body, gives you stamina, improves your general energy and endurance level, and makes you feel good about yourself. Don't forget about the exercise classes on television. Most of them are early in the morning, so check your TV listings, watch them all and decide which best suits your needs. Many people think that exercise has psychological effects as well, such as reducing anxiety and stress, and increasing the sense of self-worth. And don't forget that it burns up calories!

Although there is no definitive empirical evidence, most medical researchers believe that people who exercise, especially aerobically, have fewer heart attacks and other types of cardiovascular diseases than those who do not. And those heart attacks that do occur, happen later in life and are less severe than in sedentary people.

Flexibility exercises—those in which you bend, stretch, and twist your muscles—contribute to increased stamina and ease of movement, and keep your muscles and joints in better condition so you can remain active longer.

Exercising regularly (not necessarily every day) is important because bouts of inactivity interspersed with frenetic overexertion has the opposite effect than the one you desire: It saps energy and can do damage to muscles and ligaments. And exercising too much or too strenuously is just as bad as not doing it at all. You must accept the fact that you are older than you used to be, and even though you feel wonderful, your muscles, bones, and connective tissue are not as elastic and strong as they were. You also may tire more easily and will have to learn to recognize your body's signals that it is time to stop exercising.

Before you embark on any exercise plan, you should do the following:

- be certain that it will not aggravate any physical condition, such as arthritis, tendonitis, or other bone or muscle disease (check with your doctor first);

- choose a series of exercises that use physical skills different from those you use every day at work or around the house;
- consider choosing an activity that you already do or enjoy, and simply increase the time and energy level devoted to it (walking, swimming, bicycling, for example);
- begin any exercise program gradually and work up slowly to your desired level of fitness;
- use exercise equipment that is the right size or weight for your physical size and level of physical skill (if you are going to join a spa, make certain it is a reputable one with highly trained instructors who are willing to devote time to your special needs);
- begin each exercise time with a gradual warm-up period of at least five minutes and end with a cool-down period that gradually brings your body back to rest;
- use common sense when you exercise and pay attention to your body's signals (pain, overexhaustion, and serious shortness of breath) that tell you to stop; and
- never exercise after a heavy meal or after drinking alcohol—and if you feel sick or dizzy, stop immediately.

Also, make certain that you exercise safely by following these rules:

- after exercising, drink plenty of fluids (cool—not ice cold—water is best) to avoid dehydration;
- in summer, or if you live in a warm climate, exercise indoors or outdoors only in early morning, late afternoon, or early evening to avoid the heat of the day;
- in winter, or if you live in a cold climate, protect yourself against frostbite, wear a loosely knit scarf over your nose and mouth to warm the air before inhaling it (to prevent lung damage), wear a hat, and cool down very gradually after working up a sweat; and
- when the humidity is over 80 percent, do not exercise at all outdoors, or do so very cautiously.

NUTRITION

Don't worry, I'm not going to tell you to go on a diet! Unless you are very thin, or the perfect weight (which so few people are), you hear that enough from your doctor and friends who have no business minding your business!

Also, I'm not going to give you nutritional advice because that is up to your physician or a registered nutritionist, and again, there are enough books on diet and nutrition to fill a small library. You might also want to contact the following for more information on nutrition:

- Community Nutrition Institute, 1146 19th St., NW, Washington, DC 20036
- The American Dietetic Association, 430 N. Michigan Ave., Chicago, IL 60611
- Department of Foods and Nutrition, American Medical Association, 535 N. Dearborn St., Chicago, IL 60610

You already know that you need to eat an appropriate proportion of protein, carbohydrate, vitamins, fats, minerals, and fiber (the best free resource guide is *Nutritive Value of Foods,* Home and Garden Bulletin #27 from the U.S. Department of Agriculture, available from the U.S. Government Printing Office, Washington, DC 20402), but you may not be aware of some of the special nutritional needs of older women and some of the problems that widowhood creates regarding the preparation and consumption of food.

As you age, your metabolism slows, so although you need the same type of nutrients, your calorie intake should diminish. In addition:

- Osteoporosis (the lowered density of bone, leading to increased risk of fracture) becomes a problem; therefore you need an increased amount of dietary calcium, found in milk products and some vegetables.

- Increased amounts of dietary fiber, found in cereal products and certain fruits and vegetables, can help prevent certain intestinal problems (including constipation) that tend to appear with age.

- Certain chronic conditions (heart disease, high blood pressure, diabetes, etc.) require special diets that should be more carefully and frequently monitored by your physician as you age.

COMMON SENSE TIPS FOR A
HEALTHIER AND HAPPIER LIFE

Of all the premature deaths in the United States — that is, those that occur earlier than the national average — only 20 percent are due to hereditary factors. This means, obviously, that 80 percent could be avoided through health maintenance and prevention techniques, accident prevention, and careful medical care.

You may or may not have been living the type of life that tends to court disaster (eating high-cholesterol diet, for example, or not getting enough exercise), but that does not mean that you cannot modify your lifestyle now. Disease and illness are *not* natural consequences of aging, and there are things that you can do at almost any age that will make you live a healthier, perhaps longer life.

Although it is impractical to expect yourself to change the entire way you live, it is not too much to ask that you read over the following common-sense tips and try to incorporate as many of them as possible into your life.

■ Quit smoking— *now!* Surely you realize that smoking places you in serious jeopardy of cardiovascular and respiratory disease, to name the two most common health problems related to smoking, and you know that no good can possibly come of you continuing to puff away.

■ If you are saying to yourself right now, "I've been smoking all my life and nothing has happened yet. Don't kid yourself. You are a heart and lung disaster waiting to happen. So get yourself to a smoking cessation clinic. Or call your local health department or look up the telephone numbers of the American Cancer Society, American Heart Association, or the American Lung Association. They will be happy to give you the names of several smoking cessation programs in your area.

■ Get help, if you have to, and learn how to throw away those cigarettes!

And remember, most HMOs and health insurance plans either offer or support these cessation programs by covering them under the group insurance policy. Also, don't discount the various "patches" that are on the market. However, one should always check with a physician before jumping on this bandwagon.

• Eat a balanced diet and maintain your optimum weight. Diet is strongly related to heart disease, certain types of cancer, diabetes, and stroke, which are among the leading causes of death in the United States. So don't compound your chances of dying of one of these health problems by eating all the foods you shouldn't and by being more than twenty pounds overweight.

• Exercise regularly.

• Have regular health checkups and see a physician when you have a problem. There is a good deal of controversy about the advisability of having an annual physical examination. Some health professionals say it does nothing to detect the most common causes of serious illness and death, but others believe that it serves the purpose of general monitoring of health, and it keeps you at the attention of a physician. Surely some blood tests are advisable on a periodic basis, such as blood cholesterol and blood sugar, especially if you have a family history of heart disease or diabetes.

You also need to see your dentist regularly, usually every six months for a professional cleaning and examination, and you should have your eyes examined every two or three years.

• Drink alcoholic beverages only in moderation, and do not drive after you have been drinking. As you age, your tolerance for alcohol decreases significantly, and even a glass of wine at dinner, especially if you are tired, can impair your function seriously enough to make you a dangerous driver.

• Wear your seat belt at all times. According to the U.S. Department of Transportation, within the next ten years you are likely to be in a motor vehicle accident that is serious enough to kill or seriously injure you. Therefore, since the statistical odds are against you, increase your chances of staying alive and relatively unharmed by *always* wearing a seat belt. Older drivers have a higher accident rate than younger ones and are more likely to be seriously injured in an accident because of the fragility of their bones. And the most effective way to prevent injury in a motor vehicle accident is to wear a seat belt.

• Avoid exposure to the sun and to extreme heat or cold. As the body ages, it becomes more susceptible to damage from the elements.

Overexposure to the sun causes skin cancer, and heat and humidity can result in heat stroke, which can be fatal and is surely exacerbated by heart or circulatory problems and diabetes. Cold weather can also be fatal due to hypothermia. So dress sensibly and do not pit yourself against the elements. Mother Nature is more adaptable and changeable than you are—and she has been around longer!

• Prevent accidents in your home. Hold the railing when you go up and down stairs, put antiskid mats or stickers in your bathtub and install a handrail. Keep a fire extinguisher in the kitchen, and make certain your smoke detectors are working (the kind that are wired right into the electricity are better than battery-operated ones). Keep a list of emergency numbers taped to every phone in your house, and make certain that you have an escape route planned ahead of time in the event of fire. Always keep a phone by your bed, and practice dialing the operator with your eyes closed so you can do it in the dark in an emergency.

YOUR GYNECOLOGIC HEALTH

Although you should pay attention to all aspects of your physical self, most women are most concerned with the gynecologic aspects of health, and middle-age women are the most concerned of all—with good reason. Middle age is when things start to change. In fact, the average age of menopause is fifty, and that is when the incidence of cancer of various parts of the reproductive system, as well as the breast, begins to increase.

You should not worry constantly about getting cancer, and certainly menopause is not a "big deal" to most modern women, especially now that estrogen replacement therapy to control the most unpleasant aspects of menopause has become a safe and accepted way of dealing with menopause.

But on the other hand, caution is in order, and you should not neglect your annual visit to the gynecologist, nor should you stop doing breast self-examination just because you are growing older and are having an annual mammogram (you *are* having this highly specialized X ray, aren't you?).

Therefore, I urge you to think about the following things and discuss them with your physician if it is appropriate.

• Estrogen replacement therapy (ERT) during menopause. Although ERT has gotten somewhat of a "bad rap" in recent years because, until replacement estrogens were given with progestogen (another important female hormone), there was a higher incidence of endometrial cancer in women taking replacement estrogens. But now the treatment is remarkably safe (although it is imperative that you be followed closely by your physician) and it is the single best way to prevent osteoporosis after menopause. There is also evidence that ERT prevents the increased incidence of cardiovascular disease that seems to plague postmenopausal women, and it certainly eases the negative symptoms of menopause, most notably hot flashes.

But not everyone wants to take ERT, so discuss the matter with your physician, read up on it, talk with your women friends, and then decide for yourself.

• The physical details of your sex life will change, but there is no reason why women in their sixties, seventies, and even eighties cannot enjoy pleasurable sex. There are indeed physiologic and hormonal changes that make the sexual response different from what it was in younger years, but that doesn't mean that the sexual urges and responses die. Mostly they slow down, become less sharp and intense, and take longer to get going again. The most noticeable difference is the amount of vaginal lubrication during arousal. This can be corrected by a variety of means (water soluble lubricants and estrogen cream, for example).

But probably the worst sexual problem that older women encounter is the lack of available men. Many have to learn to live with sexual loneliness, and masturbation can help ease physical tension and gratify short-term needs. Indeed, some women say that orgasm during masturbation is more intense and more pleasurable than it is during sex with a partner. But sexuality is more than the quest for an orgasm, and masturbation is only partially satisfying. It does not fulfill the need for closeness, intimacy, and the physical presence of another person.

• Learn to understand the emotional realities—and the myths—of middle age and menopause, and make certain that you can distinguish between them. For instance, menopause does not *cause* depression, but it is sometimes accompanied by feelings of sadness and loss. This is an important distinction. If a menopausal woman feels depressed, it is not necessarily because she is menopausal; it is probably the result of other things going on in her life—widowhood, for instance.

This is an area where you will probably find more help and support from your women friends than from your physician. Doctors tend to look at all bodily and spiritual phenomena as physical problems that can be fixed or cured—or not—while in reality most of the things that are happening to you are caused by your life situation and create problems that can usually be solved.

Anxiety may be a real factor in your life from time to time, but it is mostly misdiagnosed in menopausal and postmenopausal women. What many physicians interpret as anxiety may really be misunderstood, poorly expressed, or poorly articulated fear. There are *real* fears out there, especially now that you are alone, but most of them can be conquered with understanding, with learning to face them, and with planning to prevent them.

• Visit your gynecologist at least once a year, and more often if you have a problem. Most women go through menopause and middle age with no problems, but they do exist, and ignoring trouble signs is one of the most dangerous things you can do.

The most common single sign of trouble is unusual or abnormal vaginal bleeding. However, it is not so easy to distinguish between bleeding that is the result of normal changes in the menstrual pattern and the unusual bleeding that may indicate a real problem. The only appropriate thing to do is make an appointment with your doctor and report as accurately as you can the nature of the bleeding.

OSTEOPOROSIS

It's called "dowager's hump" and the "little old lady's syndrome." It's more prevalent in women than men, but sooner or later it happens to almost everyone who grows old—sooner to women than to men. It can cause a hip or wrist fracture from a simple fall, and it decreases life expectancy because hip fracture is the leading cause of accidental death in people aged forty-five to seventy-four.

The name of the disease is osteoporosis, and its definition is "a decreased amount of bone." It's almost that simple: less bone.

As the skeleton ages, the character of bone changes, and each bone contains less bone tissue, which becomes softer and spongier. Thus the skeletal structure, on which muscles, tendons, and all the other tissues and organs of the body depend for support, weakens. The chemical composition of the bones remains unchanged, so osteoporosis is not like a car rusting away with age. Instead, bone tissue is destroyed faster than it can be replaced by the formation of new, whole bone. It's rather like a frame house that looks fine from the outside but is being eaten away by termites from within. Even that analogy is not altogether precise, because some people with advanced osteoporosis don't look fine from the outside. They grow shorter and frailer, almost as if they were caving in on themselves. They literally waste away with age.

Significant bone loss generally starts at menopause in women and somewhat later in men. It continues to the end of life at the rate of approximately 1 percent per year in women and one-half of 1 percent in men. Fifty percent of all women have osteoporosis by age seventy, and 100 percent of them have it by age ninety. About 50 percent of all men have osteoporosis by age eighty.

Each year approximately 200,000 women suffer fractures that are directly attributable to osteoporosis, and 40,000 of them die of fracture complications. In fact, 30 percent of all women and 17 percent of all men will suffer at least one hip fracture by age ninety, and hip fractures result in a 12 percent decrease in life expectancy. They are a significant cause of death. In addition, 24 percent of all women and 5 percent of all men will suffer a fractured wrist.

It is likely that a survivor of a hip fracture will never walk again. A full 50 percent of those who break a hip will never again be able to live independently, and a large portion will require permanent nursing home care. The economic burden of osteoporosis is enormous.

Certain people are more likely to get osteoporosis than others, to contract it earlier, and to have a more severe case. Following are some risk factors for osteoporosis, some of which you can do something about.

• Alcoholism is one of the strongest risk behaviors for osteoporosis. It is unclear why alcoholics should be at such high risk, but some scientists speculate that they have poor calcium absorption. If you are an alcoholic or have a serious drinking problem, get help immediately— for a wide variety of reasons, not just to protect your bones.

• Diabetes mellitus. If you have diabetes, there is not much you can do about it because diabetes is incurable. However, you can follow all of your physician's and nutritionist's advice about diet and do your best to keep your diabetes under control.

• Where you live. Osteoporosis is more prevalent in temperate zones than in the tropics. This may have something to do with the higher ultraviolet radiation in the tropics, which stimulates absorption of vitamin D, an important component in the absorption of calcium.

• Race. Osteoporosis occurs more among whites than nonwhites. Blacks have substantially greater bone density than whites, which may or may not be a genetic predisposition; it also may be the result of generations of living in more tropical climates than whites.

• Low body weight. Thin women with a light skeletal frame are at higher risk of osteoporosis than women who are bigger. This is no excuse to let yourself grow fat, but by the same token, whoever said, "You can't be too thin or too rich." was wrong about the first part of that phrase.

• A family history of osteoporosis

• Smaller than average muscle mass in proportion to bone, so get out there and start exercising

• Lack of exercise or a sedentary life style

• Low calcium intake, which I will discuss shortly

• Early menopause or oophorectomy (surgical removal of the ovaries)

• Cigarette smoking

• Greater than normal consumption of protein, fiber, and caffeine. Vegetarians seem to have a lower than average risk of osteoporosis.

• Low body fat. Obese women rarely develop osteoporosis because estrogen is stored in subcutaneous fat (fat stored beneath the skin) and continues to be released long after menopause. Moreover, androgen, a male hormone, is converted to estrogen by adipose (fatty) tissue after menopause.

• Childlessness. Estrogen production increases markedly during pregnancy, and although women are not permanently pregnant of course, some scientists believe that the temporary increase in estrogen production has a permanent positive effect on bone by stimulating the production of certain substances and activating vitamin D. However, no one knows exactly why bearing children lowers the risk of osteoporosis.

• Taking drugs such as corticosteroids (commonly called steroids), phenobarbital (a central nervous system depressant, or "downer"), aluminum-containing antacids (such as Gelusil and Maalox), some diuretics (drugs that rid the body of excess fluid), and thyroxin (a thyroid hormone)

• Drinking nonfluoridated water

• Having taken oral contraceptives seems to have an inhibitory effect on osteoporosis, although no one knows why. The estrogen in the pills may have the same kind of positive influence on bone that pregnancy does.

I hope I have not thoroughly frightened you about osteoporosis, but it *is* a serious and debilitating disease that you will almost surely fall victim to. However, you can minimize its effects and stave off the inevitable for a longer time if you take certain preventive measures, which will help but will not totally prevent the eventual onset of osteoporosis.

• Increase your total *dietary* calcium intake, especially before menopause, to about 1,500 milligrams (mg) a day. There are plenty of nutrition books available to describe how to increase calcium, but just as an example, I have included a few representative foods here.

Food	Amount	Mg Calcium
Whole milk	1 cup	290
Skim milk	1 cup	302
Buttermilk	1 cup	285
Plain low-fat yogurt	1 cup	245
Vanilla ice cream	1 cup	176
Cheddar cheese	1 oz	204
Swiss cheese	1 oz	272
Skim-milk ricotta	1 cup	669
Grated Parmesan	1 cup	1,376
Egg	1	28
Salmon	3 oz	225
Oysters	1 cup	343
Oil-packed tuna	3 oz	199
Lean roast beef	3 oz	158
Broccoli	1 cup	176
Spinach	1 cup	196

• Take calcium supplements that are available in any drugstore or supermarket (be sure to read the label to find out how much pure calcium is in the tablet; brands differ widely), although there is a good deal of controversy about the effectiveness of calcium supplements as opposed to that obtained naturally through food.

• The role of fluoride supplements in treating osteoporosis, or preventing its onset, is unclear. There is some evidence that it stimulates the production of new bone, but the safety of high doses of fluoride has yet to be established. Your best bet is to find out if your municipal water supply is fluoridated (most places are).

• Make certain that you have a sufficient intake of vitamin D (400 units is the recommended daily allowance), although if you drink enough milk or take a daily multivitamin, you will be in the clear. Vitamin D deficiency is a problem only for women with a lactose intolerance and who do not take a vitamin pill every morning. By the way, megadoses of vitamin D (some people take as much as 5,000 to 50,000 units a day) will not stimulate new bone formation or prevent fractures, even when taken in combination with calcium. There is also evidence that too much vitamin D will cause headaches, nausea, dizziness, blurred vision, and a host of other dangerous and unpleasant symptoms.

• Moderate physical activity, especially weight-bearing exercise such as walking or running, is both desirable and practical for building bone mass, but heavy exertion is not only impractical for older people, it will not do much good in terms of augmenting bone mass or preventing fractures.

• Begin a course of estrogen replacement therapy at menopause, *but always in conjunction with and on the advice of your physician.* Research has shown that estrogens, taken with a cyclical course of progestogen, is the best preventive factor for osteoporosis, as well as decreasing the risk of heart attacks in postmenopausal women.

13

YOU AND THE SOCIAL SCENE

If you're like most people, many of your "friends" are business acquaintances and professional associates rather than true friends. There's nothing wrong with that, but you may find that many of these relationships came into your life through your husband's business, and now that he's dead, they will disappear. If you had not seen them for what they were originally, it will be disappointing when the guys from the office and their wives don't call after they've made the obligatory postfuneral condolence call, and you'll find the number of dinner invitations slipping drastically.

At first you'll tell yourself that you don't feel like dining out anyway, but after a while you'll notice the holes in your once-busy social life. It hurts, but it happens to everyone, and your job is to accept it as part of married-then-not-married life and to get on with restructuring your life so your friends are really friends.

Get out your yellow pad again, put it next to your social engagement book for the past year, and make a list of all the people you spent time with. Next to each name, write a few comments about that person, whether he or she is a real friend or a business acquaintance, how much you liked being in that person's company, what interests you have in common—those kinds of things. Then go over the list again and write down all the people whom you *enjoyed* being with, regardless of how you came to know them. That will form the core of your real friendships, and from there you can expand into new ones.

Although I don't mean to be flippant, there may be one positive side to widowhood: You never again will have to spend long, boring evenings with your husband's business buddies with whom you have nothing in common. For the rest of your life you'll have the luxury of being with only people you really want to be with. And you can do things you've always wanted to do but didn't because your husband didn't enjoy them or you didn't have time or you thought he wouldn't want you to do them without him. You're your own person now, and although you would not have chosen independence in this sad way, you're free to do the things *you* want to do.

• • •

And that brings us to getting back into the social swim. The most important part of any social life is variety. Alternate big parties with small dinners (ones you give yourself or ones to which you are invited) and evenings with one special friend. Go away to a country inn or on a day trip the weekend after you've given an elegant dinner. Try new restaurants; go for a drive in the country without a road map and follow your impulses. Make an overture of friendship to someone who doesn't seem your type—and see what happens.

When you're invited to a party or other gathering, go alone. If the host insists that you bring someone, don't feel obligated to unless you *want* to. Assume that you have been invited for your own good company and anticipate an evening of making new acquaintances—and don't forget to give your calling card to those you'd like to see again. You'll find people to talk to, and you don't *need* someone to take you home. You arrived under your own power and can leave the same way.

Even if you're the only woman alone in the entire party, you can still have a delightful time. I've never yet been to a gathering where the guests are glued together two-by-two and speak in unison. After all, you've been invited to a party, not a cruise aboard Noah's ark, and people are as individual there (and are as interesting or as dull) as they are anywhere else.

There are a variety of ways to rekindle your social life.

• With couples. There's no reason why you still can't be friends with couples, even though you're single now. It's a myth that married women believe that single, divorced, or widowed women are predatory creatures out to get their husbands (and the reverse for single men). If friendships between individuals are based on mutual trust and respect, then friendship between a single person and a couple should have the same foundation. If it doesn't, it's not much of a friendship.

• With one spouse and not the other. This is more difficult to work out because most couples operate as a unit, but it can be done. Both married and single people find themselves disliking one half of a couple, and although the logistics are sometimes complicated, friendship is most certainly possible.

• With men when romance is not involved. I discuss this fully in Chapter 10 but these relationships can be most rewarding and long-lasting because they contain the spiciness of difference without the complications of sex and romance. A man friend can come in handy when you're invited to a function that absolutely requires a partner for the evening (although these are surprisingly rare nowadays), such as a formal dance.

• With women. These can be the most pleasant and relaxed of all social occasions. There's nothing like a potluck supper with "the girls" to refresh the spirit and provide jollity, intimacy, and just plain fun.

• Children. Don't forget their company—if you like them. Most parents are delighted to "lend" their children for an afternoon, or even an entire weekend at the zoo, the museum, or an amusement park. A day with a child can do wonders for putting things into perspective, for seeing the world through fresh eyes, or for having an excuse to do something childish that *you* want to do.

Entertaining

I had always enjoyed, and been good at, giving dinner parties, but when Sam died, I thought I'd never cook another meal for guests. I was too tired and too depressed to think about cooking for myself, let alone inviting people over. The thought of doing the whole thing myself seemed like too much effort.

But you must. Start by inviting one close woman friend to a very informal supper and then gradually work your way up the ladder of formality and numbers, perhaps with a Fourth of July picnic in your backyard or an in-front-of-the-TV pickup supper for the last game of the World Series. Snacks for an organizational meeting at your house and an informal Sunday brunch all count as entertaining and are not as rigorous and nerve-wracking as a big dinner party. Although most women over age fifty or so believe as I do that the table has to be balanced, younger people don't have that requirement. If you can bring yourself to relax your "boy-girl-boy-girl" strictures, you'll have an easier time at a sit-down dinner.

But there are other ways to entertain, as you well know, many of which may be easier and more suitable. The only important ingredients of a successful gathering are the congeniality of the guests and delectability of the food. If the food and conversation are boring, the party will flop, regardless of the host's and guests' marital status. You must invite an interesting mix of people chosen for their conversational ability, wit, and interests, rather than the current state of their romantic lives/marriages.

If one of your guests asks if he or she can bring a "date," do as you wish. You are not obligated to assent to strangers at your parties, but if you know the person well and trust that the guest's guest will be congenial, say yes. Some people are not as confident as others about going to parties alone, and you want your guests to be comfortable and happy. In addition, you may make a new friend and get invited to that person's home in reciprocation.

When you do decide to give your first big party alone without your husband as co-host, ask one or two close friends to help with small tasks. For instance, request that one keep an eye on the ice bucket and refill it as necessary. If the meal is a buffet, ask another friend to be first in line when dinner is announced so other guests won't mill around reluctantly, hesitant to be first in line.

I remember the first dinner party I gave as a widow, about three months after Sam died. I finally got up the energy to invite twelve people to supper, and I was a nervous wreck because I had to do everything myself.

I made an enormous effort (and everything seemed to take twice the energy it used to)—shopping for and preparing the food, setting the table, arranging the flowers, selecting the wine. For the first time, there was no one to send out on a last-minute errand, to chat with while I was getting dressed, to set up the bar and make sure there would be enough liquor and ice. I had to remember all the little details I had never bothered with before. And I would have to greet the guests alone and see that everyone was properly introduced, a task that Sam had always done so well.

My hair was still up in curlers, my face unmade, when the doorbell rang. There stood Fred, one of Sam's oldest friends, himself recently widowed. "You're half an hour early," I cried with dismay. He had never seen me looking so un-put-together and I was embarrassed.

"I know it, Phil," he said. "I just thought you might need a bartender."

I was touched to tears by his thoughtfulness. "Go fix yourself a drink and one for me," I told him, "then come into the bedroom and we'll talk while I brush out my hair."

The strangeness and embarrassment evaporated when he walked into the room and handed me my drink. "You know, Phil," he said with a smile and a wink, "this must be some kind of record for the shortest time it's ever taken me to get into a woman's bedroom!"

We both broke into laughter. His caring dissolved my anxiety and tension, and the evening was a huge success.

THE LOGISTICS OF LIVING ALONE

Keeping Your Abode Together

One of the most annoying things about living alone, especially if you're out all or most of the day, is scheduling repairmen, accepting package deliveries and special delivery mail, and other logistical problems. The best solution is to make arrangements with a neighbor. A person living alone *must* have a support network of people who live close by. It is not simply a matter of friendliness and convenience, although that surely is important: Your safety and perhaps your very life may depend on people being able to get to you quickly.

One or two neighbors ought to have your house key so they can rescue you if you fall ill and can't get to the door or if there is a fire or gas leak when you're not home. That key will also come in handy if you lock yourself out.

And, by the way, when you're out, *never* leave a note on the door to that effect (some people even include the time they expect to be back, thus telling would-be burglars exactly how much time they have to clean out the place!); it's an open invitation to uninvited guests.

One of the major problems of older women living alone is that the multitude of physical chores involved in just keeping the house together soon becomes onerous, especially if your husband did most of the outside physical work like mowing the lawn, cleaning the gutters, raking leaves, and doing other yard work. Just taking the garbage cans to the curb once or twice a week or hauling the laundry down to the machines in the basement may be too much.

If you can't or don't want to do the work, either pay someone else to do it (which is expensive and often unreliable) or move to a maintenance-free home like a multi-unit building or a retirement community. In southern Florida and other parts of the country where many older people live, it's possible to buy home-maintenance insurance policies. They work much like health insurance: You pay a fixed premium, and when something goes wrong, the service company does the repairs. These contracts vary as widely as health insurance policies, so read the fine print before signing up.

Going It Alone

No matter how many friends we have or how great an effort we make to reestablish social communications, the day inevitably comes when we must go it alone—to dinner, to another city, to the hospital, to the car mechanic. Don't panic. You can cope with these situations by

- inviting a friend along;
- finding out in advance as much as you can about what you'll find when you arrive;
- arranging to go alone but be escorted home (as to a dinner party);
- throwing your shoulders back, lifting your head, and toughing it out by yourself (the pride of accomplishment is often better than the experience itself!).

Your Car

I've been driving since I was thirteen years old (in Florida in the 1930s you didn't need a driver's license and I had skipped some grades in school, so no one knew I was too young to learn to drive!); I've always considered myself a "car idiot," however.

I'm a good driver and I know enough to put gas in and have the oil checked now and again; but beyond that, I have no idea how a car works. Sam and I always chose our cars together, but he took complete charge of the repairs and maintenance. Once in a while it occurred to me to take a consumers' course in auto mechanics, but as soon as the courses were announced at my club or the YWCA, they were oversubscribed and I never cared enough to put myself on the waiting list. Also, I was afraid of not being able to understand it, which is silly because I'm an intelligent woman who understands the complexities of the law. Perhaps fear of auto mechanics in women is similar to fear of math: It's something we endure as children and never seem to be able to overcome.

I'm not sure that Sam knew anything more about cars than I do, but he always seemed to be able to handle the jargon with the various mechanics and that's all you really need.

A friend of mine from Philadelphia took a course given free—and open to women only—at a Cadillac dealership, which she says helped her immensely. "I have no intention of *doing* any of the stuff I learned," she says, "but at least now when someone says 'universal joint' or 'piston' I know what they're talking about."

She understands the basic principles on which her car works and knows which parts are supposed to do what to make the car go and what's likely to be wrong when it won't go. She also has a clear idea of what routine maintenance is mandatory and why she shouldn't neglect it. Her car is nine years old, runs like a top, and she says it's the most dependable thing in her life!

I'm not suggesting you turn yourself into a car mechanic, but there are a few things you ought to do if you're going to own a car and don't want to spend more than you have to on it—in money and in wear and tear on your nerves.

• Read the owner's manual that comes with every new car, and keep it in the glove compartment (not in the bottom drawer of your desk at home) where it will always be handy. If your car is old and you've lost the manual, go to a dealership and ask them to photocopy one for your make and model.

233

• Buy an emergency car-tool kit (including flares and a good flashlight) and keep it in your trunk. Learn what all the tools are for, how to use them—either for yourself or in the event a good Samaritan comes along when you break down.

• Join the American Automobile Association. Not only are they essential in an emergency, they're a good source of free road maps, tour guides, passport photos, and other travel services.

• Take a course in auto mechanics at an adult education center or a local car dealership. The AAA sometimes offers courses, and they always know where to find one.

• Get a good, honest mechanic and never leave him. You are more likely to find honest, reputable service at an independent garage than a car dealership, but this isn't always true, so shop around and ask your friends. Ask to have *everything* explained and always ask for the old parts when one needs to be replaced. Even if you throw it on the trash heap when you get home, make the mechanic give it to you. He doesn't know what you're going to do with it, and if you have been cheated or sold an unnecessary replacement part, it will be your only proof.

• Be faithful about required maintenance. The most important thing you can do for your car is have the oil and filter changed regularly, but do pay attention to the recommended requirements listed in your owner's manual. Have your tire tread and brake fluid checked periodically also.

Your Personal Safety

Although we are grown-up women and are fully aware of the dangers of living in the world, many of us are used to going out at night in the company of our husbands and therefore feel alone and more vulnerable now. And in a sense we are.

This doesn't mean we should lock ourselves in when the sun goes down (a useless precaution because there are almost as many daytime muggings as nighttime ones) or refuse to go out unless we are escorted by a man (I recently had my purse snatched by a gang of young adolescents—in the company of a man—in front of my apartment house on one of the "safest" streets in New York), but there are certain precautions one should take.

• When you're alone in the car, don't keep your purse on the seat beside you; put it on the floor so it can't be grabbed through an open window.

• When pumping your own gas, don't leave your purse in the car with the door open. Either lock the car or take your purse with you when you pump and pay the attendant.

• When going to a mall, avoid indoor multilevel parking garages and park in an outdoor lot as close to a light as possible. If you must park in a garage, take a space close to the elevator. If it's crowded, you might consider waiting in your car until you see another person walking to the elevator and ask if you can walk together. When going back to your car, try walking with another person as far as you can.

• If you must leave your car with a garage attendant, leave only the ignition key and don't keep personal identification tags on your car key.

• Keep your major credit cards separate from your wallet. That way, if your wallet is stolen, you won't lose everything.

• Don't ever put your purse down on a counter in a store or a public rest room. And while you're in a public toilet stall, don't hang your purse on a hook on the door or put it on the floor. Either hang it on a side hook if there is one or keep it in your lap—inconvenient and uncomfortable as that is!

• When walking alone at night (or during the day, for that matter), don't *look* like a victim and there's less of a chance you will become one. Walk quickly and purposefully (and wear shoes that will let you run if you have to), keep your head up, and look around you from time to time as if scanning your immediate vicinity for potential danger. Put the straps of your purse over your shoulder, or sling it across your chest bandolier style if the strap is long enough, and then tuck it under your arm with the clasp inward. If you think someone is following you, cross the street and see if he does the same. If he does, go into a store, restaurant, or building where you know there will be people. If no shelter is readily available, scream—run and keep screaming until the man either leaves you alone or goes the other way.

• Have your car or house keys ready in your hand as you approach, but don't walk down the street with them dangling from your fingers. They can be easily snatched. If you carry a whistle, keep it instantly available. One woman I know keeps one between her teeth when she's walking alone at night.

• Take a self-defense course if you're physically fit enough. You may never use the techniques, but it will give you the confidence that you *can* take care of yourself. However, some self-defense measures can land you in jail, so beware of using sophisticated and dangerous maneuvers unless you know what you're doing and unless your life is clearly in jeopardy. For instance, suppose a man steps out of the shadows, but before he has a chance to ask for the correct time you assume he's up to no good and give him a karate chop. He falls over, seriously injured or dead. If you used reasonable force under a reasonably assumed danger, you would not be liable. But unless you can prove impending jeopardy (there are probably no witnesses to help you), the man or his family can sue you for his injuries or death.

• Never open your door to anyone you don't know. If you don't have a window or peephole in your front and back doors, have one installed. Never give your house keys to workmen. If you're having work done in your house, stay home or arrange to have someone there you trust.

Hiring People to Do What You Can't

Although Chapter 5 will go into detail about signing contracts, making wills, and hiring lawyers, there are a few general things you should know about hiring people to do what you can't or don't want to do for yourself. And that includes your doctor, dentist, stockbroker, car mechanic, accountant, and the boy down the street who cuts the grass and cleans out your gutters in the spring and fall.

Not all workmen and professionals are equally competent, even if they are licensed to practice their trade. Neither are all those who *are* competent right for a particular job. To some people, the workman's personality and attitude are as important as his or her credentials, and some don't care if the person is brusque or friendly as long as he or she gets the job done.

However, there are certain things you should evaluate.

• Competence to practice. Find out if the workman/professional is licensed to practice and, if appropriate, certified as a specialist. In the case of a doctor, for instance, you should know what certification means, and why it is important.

• Willingness to discuss fees and make arrangements for long-term payment of expensive work

• The way the office is run and the competence of support staff

• Keeping appointments on time and meeting deadlines except in the case of a genuine emergency. For instance, if you're having your kitchen remodeled, get a time and money estimate in writing with built-in rewards and penalties for finishing early or late.

• Ability to explain the job, diagnosis, or procedure in understandable language and then to lay out the various courses of action and the consequences of each. You should know why your plumbing (your body's or your house's) needs attention and what will happen if you don't take care of whatever is wrong.

• Willingness to answer all questions thoroughly and with good grace

• Availability after hours for an emergency

• Willingness to call in a specialist, suggest a second opinion, or hire a subcontractor.

14

TRAVEL

$\mathcal{G}$o wherever you please, and as often as you please and can afford. If you choose to travel with someone, fine, but know also that you can have a fine time alone.

First, you need to find an experienced travel agent who understands the pleasures and occasional problems of traveling alone; describe the kind of trip you would like, how much you can afford to spend, and be honest about what makes you nervous. You'll be surprised at how much good advice you get and how often you can avoid potential problems.

Following are some of the services you can and should expect from a travel agent.

- The best price available on plane and train fares, as well as hotel rooms and package plans
- Recommendations for tour operators to suit your wishes and special needs. Travel agents get a lot of free trips, and this experience provides them with firsthand knowledge of what the tours they recommend are really like. (If they choose small hotels or private transport, be prepared to pay the cable or long distance phone bills necessary to make the arrangements.)
- Travel insurance (Do not buy extra health insurance unless you are

238

positive that your own policy does not cover you away from home, which is *very* rare.)
- Help with making claims if a provider of travel services (a common carrier, hotel, privately hired cars, and the like) fail to deliver the service you arranged and possibly paid for in advance
- Help with obtaining all the required documentation, such as tickets, hotel reservation confirmations, visas, etc.

Go where you like, but keep in mind that some places are more problematic than others for women traveling alone. For instance, a friend of mine took a month-long trip to the British Isles in winter. She is a college professor, had the time then, and wanted to avoid the crowds and higher prices of summer.

The first ten days she stayed at a bed-and-breakfast in London near the British Museum (better than a large hotel for a single person because they are small and intimate—everyone eats breakfast together—and conducive to meeting people, and they are usually much less expensive).

Then a friend drove her to Oxford, where she picked up a rental car and spent a few days touring the west of England and driving north through Wales to Liverpool. There she left the car and took the train to Edinburgh. She toured Edinburgh on foot for a few days and took another train to Glasgow and back for a day trip. From Scotland she flew to Dublin, where she stayed a few days and then rented another car for a leisurely drive across Ireland to Shannon for the flight home.

"The best things about the trip," she said, "were the absolute freedom of going where I pleased, with no timetable and no appointment except the flight home. I also enjoyed talking to strangers and meeting interesting people with whom I shared museum trips, meals, and evenings at the theater. Also, I didn't feel rushed and obligated to be where I didn't feel like being. The utter freedom and relaxation were wonderful."

But there were a few less-than-pleasant things. One was the problem of lonely evenings in small towns. London, Dublin, and Edinburgh were after-dark delights with a wide choice of things to do, but places where the sheep outnumbered the human inhabitants posed a problem. "Pubs offered the only social life as far as I could tell," said

Bonnie, "but my limit was about an hour or two a week in those smoke-filled dens, so I stopped in every bookstore I passed and got a lot more reading done on this trip than I had anticipated!"

Also, she said she stayed too long. A month was about a week too much, and she was thoroughly sick of traveling and living out of a suitcase by the time she boarded the Aer Lingus jet in Shannon.

The other occasional problem was that as she drove around the countryside alone and exclaimed over the beauty of the landscape or the charming nuisance of stopping to allow a thousand sheep to cross the road, there was no one to share it with. Sometimes, she said, she would have liked to talk about what she had seen, although the absence of a companion didn't make the experience any less pleasurable.

"Oddly enough," Bonnie mused, "two years after that, I took a trip alone to Southern California and Arizona. I had always wanted to go to the San Diego Zoo and spent the whole day there, and then I got into my rented car and drove around the desert and mountains—including the Grand Canyon, which is almost beyond believing what you are actually seeing—for a week, and never felt lonely once."

In fact, she said she relished the solitude and took a certain amount of pleasure in the fact that no one in the entire world knew where she was. "Even I didn't know where I'd be that afternoon or the next day! I kept waiting for a black cloud of loneliness to settle over me in those vast reaches of desert and towering mountains, but it never did, and that trip turned out to be one of the most pleasant and relaxing vacations I've ever taken."

On Bonnie's trip to Britain, dinner alone was never a problem because she thought of a way to prevent it. Each evening she went to a restaurant with a paperback book in her purse—just in case. When she arrived, she told the headwaiter that she was alone and would be happy to share a table. Sometimes it didn't work out, but more often than not, she had a pleasant dinner companion or two, and the headwaiter was delighted to comply because he gained an extra table.

• • •

After you have dealt with the mechanical details of setting up your life as a widow, travel can be very therapeutic. I think that frequent short vacations are much more desirable than one long annual holiday.

I have learned this the hard way by taking fascinating but long trips, only to come back to six or seven weeks of unopened mail, which almost destroyed the pleasure that the trips provided in the first place. Since Sam died, I have been blessed with extraordinary luck in having trips available that were related to my law work: two to China, one of which was sponsored by my local bar association. Even in hindsight, I wouldn't have missed the opportunity to go to that great and mysterious country, but I still believe that many short vacations are to be recommended if you can afford them.

Don't think (unless you are in poor health) that you are too old to embark on a long journey. There are some organized tours that insist that if you are over age seventy-five you must be accompanied by a spouse or companion, but that doesn't seem reasonable to me (and the courts might consider it age discrimination if a tour company were sued on that basis). People of all ages jog, fly planes, ride bicycles, play hard tennis, and go on archeological digs all over the world, so there is no reason why they cannot travel where they please.

PLANNING AND PREPARATION

One of the most important aspects of travel is planning—unless you deliberately set out to take a completely unstructured vacation, and even then you need to reserve a seat on an airplane and perhaps a rental car.

Two wise women (one an aunt who died just this year and who had lived alone for more than thirty years) taught me a great deal about traveling alone, without a friend or the framework of a group tour. One insisted that even in small hotels and inns, many couples and other travelers will invite you to join their table or even join their tour the next day. Some invited her for an after-dinner walk, and she believes that if you have a traveling companion, these offers are never made.

Two of the best sources of vacation planning are your local library (or travel bookstore) and the American Automobile Association (AAA). The AAA has maps from all over the world, travel books, and itineraries, as well as competent travel agents to help you plan and answer questions. Of course, you must be an AAA member, but I have always found that membership in that organization was one of the best thirty-five dollars a year I ever spent.

If you decide to take an organized tour, book it through a travel agent for all the reasons I discussed above. But remember that you will encounter all sorts of people on the tour and you will be stuck with them for the duration. So if you have a low tolerance for being in close proximity with strangers for a few weeks, think carefully before you plunk down money to be in such a situation.

Organized tours are almost indispensable if you are not an experienced traveler or if you wish to go to countries where the language is not written in the Roman alphabet so that no dictionary can help you, such as countries of the Far East, the Middle East, Russia, and some Warsaw Pact countries. (In Western Europe and South and Central America, many people speak English and you are not apt to feel lost there.)

But if you decide to go on a tour, remember to be a cheerful and uncomplaining travel companion. Keep a smile pasted to your face, no matter how difficult other people are, and no matter how disorganized the travel arrangements and how late the flights.

Groups sponsored by an alumni association or other academic organization are the best kinds of tours I know. University-sponsored trips have several advantages, the most important of which is that the people will be well educated and are probably interested in learning some of the same things you are about your destination. Thus you have a built-in guarantee of good conversation.

• • •

When it comes to packing, the first thing you want to avoid is duplication of effort. For example, a permanently packed toiletries kit is a must. Why pack and repack the same items for every trip? Moisturizer, toothbrush, toothpaste, hairbrush, and aspirin are just a few of the items you will want to include. To pack lightly and inexpensively, buy economy-size products and several small plastic bottles. Transfer the products into the small containers, and at the end of each trip refill the little bottles.

Stock up on other small, lightweight items that also can remain permanently packed, for example, a battery-operated travel alarm clock, shower cap, wash-up towelettes, collapsible skirt hanger, lint brush, stain remover, sewing kit, and medicines. (However, be sure that the latter are fresh, especially if you don't travel often.)

Your basic packing checklist (including all the things I mentioned above) can be used over and over, although there will be variations on the clothing you will want to take. The list will also serve as a reminder for easily forgotten items, such as your address book, belts, sunglasses, hair dryer, and the like.

Invest in a good piece of light, carry-on luggage that is not too heavy to carry for several blocks so you don't have to check your bags for short trips. If you travel for longer periods of time, select a suitcase with wheels so you can drag it around yourself in airports and train stations. You might also invest in a collapsible cart like the ones that cabin attendants use. You can put not only luggage on it but a rolled-up coat and shopping bags full of purchases.

In hotels and motels in the United States and many good hotels abroad, you can ask to borrow some items that you have forgotten, and of course almost all American hotels and motels now provide little bottles of shampoo, lotion, and other goodies. I have even gotten toothbrushes that way!

When traveling from colder to warmer weather, consider wearing several layers of clothes on the plane. Then, when you reach your destination, peel off what you don't need, and you'll be dressed appropriately for the new climate. You will also not have so much to carry!

And always take a raincoat. There are plenty of attractive light-weight ones that take in stride the punishment of being wrinkled for hours and not cleaned for weeks. If you choose a black one of some shiny material, you can also use it for an evening wrap.

One piece of advice that holds true whether you are traveling with a tour or on your own is to put all necessary tickets, passports, travelers checks, money, medicine, cosmetics, and everything else that you need for the day together at your bedside or very visible on your bureau so you can get to them first thing in the morning and don't have to waste valuable time gathering the day's necessities. You'll sleep better and will avoid a last-minute panic if you know where everything important is before retiring.

If you are going to be away for a week or more, there are a number of things you need to take care of before you leave.

• Make a list of household and other chores that have to be done before your departure.

• Go through your engagement book and reschedule appointments for after your return.

• Give a copy of your itinerary to a relative or close friend so that you can be reached in an emergency. If you cannot be reached because you don't know where you are going to be, arrange for someone to expect periodic check-in calls from you from time to time.

• Either have your mail held at the post office or arrange for someone to pick it up for you at your home. If you are expecting an important document, ask someone to watch out for it and let you know when it arrives. I once accepted a friend's offer to do this because she and her husband were going to live in our apartment while we were away for a month. She put an important legal document, which had to be answered within five days, in with the junk mail. If she had opened it and showed it to her husband, the person to whom I delegated my legal work would have filed the required response, and I would have been saved a great deal of trouble.

• Stop delivery on your newspapers and magazines, or have someone collect your mail.

• Get someone to water your plants and feed your cat.

• Make a reservation at the kennel for your dog.

• Lock all doors and windows, but leave the radio playing and make certain you have timers on some of your lamps.

• Adjust the thermostat and check to see that the gas is shut off and all electrical appliances are unplugged.

• • •

HOTELS AND INNS

In Europe and many other countries abroad, hotels are rated by a system of stars, by Michelin and Gault-Millaut, according to beauty, food, existence of a swimming pool and other sports facilities, general amenities, and of course, price.

In the United States, the AAA and Mobil have hotel rating systems that are similar to the European style and include proximity to interstate highways and airports. There are also other companies that publish hotel guides, some geared specifically for business travelers.

However, the best information about hotels and inns usually comes from friends and acquaintances who have been there recently and who share your taste and needs.

Most people have similar requirements for a hotel: cleanliness, comfortable beds, a television (nowadays many hotels offer rental videos to be played on the VCR attached to the TV or there is a movie service that can be turned on through the TV system itself), and proximity to the town you are visiting.

If you are going to be staying for a few days or more, then you might need a pool, tennis courts, a gym, and other facilities. You might also want a hotel that is near a grocery store or supermarket, a laundromat, and a movie theater so you can save money by not using the hotel facilities for everything.

Most large hotels all over the world have several restaurants, and even small motels just off interstate highways have at least a coffee shop where you can get an adequate breakfast. Some more expensive hotels have mini-bars in the guest rooms, but remember you will pay premium prices for the drinks, chocolate bars, and pretzels.

If you want a room on a high floor (or a low floor if you are afraid of fires), a nonsmoking room, a room with a view, or a particularly quiet location, ask your travel agent to specify this when making the reservation, or do it yourself if you are making your own arrangements. Get a confirmation in writing of these special arrangements in advance, but do not be surprised if they don't pan out. Hotels are notorious for renting out the rooms *they* want rather than the ones *you* want.

One friend of mine booked a hotel for two nights in San Diego recently. She wanted a view of the marina and was willing to pay the extra ten dollars that the hotel charged. When she arrived, the desk clerk said that no such rooms were available, and she had no choice but to take an ordinary room, but she insisted on paying ten dollars less. When she got to her room, she found that the door chain had been removed. She requested another room, which the clerk gave her grudgingly. The second room also had no chain, and with teeth gritted, she went to the desk to complain—this time to the manager. That worked because she ended up on the top floor with a magnificent view of the marina, a small balcony—and a door chain that worked.

Neither did she have to pay the extra ten dollars. "I felt they owed it to me by that time," she said. "They lied about the availability of the room (I wonder who they were saving it for!) and treated me badly—probably because I am an older woman traveling alone."

The moral of the story is, I think, stick to your guns and get what you want if at all possible.

In any event, always get a confirmation when you make a hotel reservation because hotels, like airlines, overbook. If you reserve with a credit card, your room will be held all night, but remember, many hotels will charge you for a day's stay if you do not cancel the reservation. And don't forget that if you are over sixty-five, you will receive a senior citizens' discount at most major hotels.

Allow yourself plenty of time when you check out, so you can go over the bill carefully. I have been charged for calls I didn't make, days I wasn't there, meals I didn't eat, and a variety of other "phantom" charges.

Some people like the comfort of large chain hotels that have practically any amenity you can think of, including toll-free reservation service. But I prefer off-the-beaten-path small hotels and inns that are cheery and more apt to have congenial fellow travelers in the lobby or bar if you wish company.

Most cities have bed-and-breakfast accommodation directories, and bookstores and your local AAA office are filled with national and regional directories of inns and small hotels. Many people prefer to stay at a bed-and-breakfast because the proprietors are usually friendly, outgoing people who will tell you lots about the local area. They can add immeasurably to the pleasure of your trip.

You should, however, find out the following about a bed-and-breakfast:

- What are the bathroom accommodations? How many people will you have to share it with and how far is it from your bedroom?
- What type of breakfast do you get (a full meal or a continental breakfast)?
- How many beds are in the room and what size are they?
- Is there a television (if that is important to you)?
- Will you have access to a telephone?
- Are there stairs or other physical impediments that may pose a problem?
- Do the owners have animals to which you may be allergic?
- How close is the house to the center of town or to where you want to be? Is parking accessible; is it reasonably priced; and is there public transportation nearby?
- Are there restaurants nearby where you can have dinner?

Whatever the size or type of hotel, always ask to see the room before you register, and inspect everything carefully before you unpack.

One problem that women alone seem to have in hotels is the matter of tipping: the doorman, the bellman (if you can find one—most hotels these days seem to expect you to carry your own bags), the room service waiter, and the bartender. Everyone expects something, and I hesitate to recommend a particular amount, but as a general rule in the United States, when you are paying for a service that costs money (a restaurant meal, a drink, etc.) the tip should be 15 percent of the bill. Abroad, tipping customs vary so widely that it's best to ask fellow travelers or your travel agent what to do.

There are, however, certain people that I don't feel it necessary to tip *unless* he or she goes way out of the way to be of *special* service—or if you are staying at the hotel for a long time. These people include room maids (except on cruise ships, where tipping seems to be customary) and doormen who get taxis. Hall porters and concierges generally do not expect a tip, but maître d's in restaurants do. I refuse to tip the latter simply for showing me to a table, but I understand that some people like to give monetary gifts to maître d's at restaurants they frequent often.

Women have a reputation of being bad tippers, possibly because the mania for tipping in the Western world drives most of us to distraction. Most of us would probably prefer a standard 15 percent added to each bill to avoid the glares of taxi drivers, beauticians, doormen, or waiters when they feel they haven't been given a large enough tip.

GETTING THERE

Cars

Traveling by car is usually the cheapest way to go, and you can be almost infinitely flexible. You can also carry much more baggage in the trunk of your car than would be practical to take on an airplane.

But when you are comparing costs, remember to take into consideration the gas, oil, tolls, extra meals, and hotel rooms (and perhaps an additional charge for the hotel garage) you will have to pay for. Add up all those things and then compare the total with today's discount air fares to make certain that you are indeed saving money by taking your car.

Driving is also tiring, even when you share the burden with a traveling companion, but the pleasure of seeing the American countryside at your leisure through the windows of your own or a rented car may be worth the extra hassle and expense.

Do, however, keep some of these tips in mind before you start out.

• Join the AAA—the trouble and expense of having just one flat tire changed and fixed is worth the price of membership.

• Try to do almost all your driving in daylight unless you are very familiar with the area. If your destination is a major city, plan your arrival either before or after the evening rush hour.

• Keep an extra set of car keys that are not attached to the original—and don't keep them in the car!

• Never leave anything more valuable than a road map in the passenger compartment of the car, even if you lock it. My sister and her husband had all their luggage, which contained everything they needed for a three-day wedding celebration, stolen from a *locked* car parked for three hours in front of my New York City apartment. Put everything in the trunk and keep that locked.

Taking Care of a Car

I had a great deal of frustration when I had to take care of the family car, especially after Sam died. I have been driving since I was thirteen years old because in Florida, where I grew up, one didn't need a driver's license then. A classmate who was sixteen (I had skipped three grades) taught me how to drive and parallel park, so no one knew that I was far too young. I have been driving with confidence ever since.

My husband and I always chose the cars we bought, but he took complete charge of the repairs and maintenance. Some people are knowledgeable about what goes on under the hood of a car, and others know little and seem to care even less. I am one of the latter. I was, and still am, a car idiot. I never took one of those courses for amateurs because I was afraid that I wouldn't be able to understand the basics—which is ridiculous for someone with a law degree!

Actually, I'm not sure that Sam knew anything more about car engines than he did about the mysterious working of the radio or television. But he *seemed* to be able to handle the mechanics and to use their jargon, and that's what you have to learn. The easiest way is to take a course (there are usually several available at community colleges or in community education centers), but the next best thing is to read the owner's manual that came with your car. Spend some time familiarizing yourself with the main parts and functions of an internal combustion engine, and then find yourself a qualified, reliable, and honest mechanic and put yourself at his mercy—but not *too* helplessly.

As a widow, I suddenly found myself with two cars. My own Chevrolet station wagon, air-conditioned and a gas guzzler, was only a year old and I loved it. Sam's pride and joy (up on blocks and taken off the insurance policy during the six winter months when it rested comfortably in the Westhampton Beach garage) was a 1966 Mercedes sedan, without air-conditioning. I had no use for two cars, and the gas shortage, which was at its peak in the spring of 1979, exasperated me when I had to wait in long lines.

I offered to sell the station wagon to each of my two married daughters, who were about to return from three years of living abroad, but they were not interested in a car that drank that much gas. So I sold it for almost nothing because I needed the money. Now both couples realize what a mistake they made. The cost of the difference between the cars they bought and the $1,500 I sold the Chevrolet for could have paid for the additional gas for twenty years.

But then I became the custodian of Sam's almost vintage "playtoy" of a car. It is difficult for anyone who hasn't had the experience to realize how stupid I was. During those first six months, I drove the Mercedes around as though I were in a trance. Everyone assumed that I was competent and capable, so I must have given off some semblance of that kind of an aura. But I was behaving foolishly. I should have immediately found a reputable Mercedes mechanic and let him check the car over periodically. And after paying the bill, I should have looked him squarely in the eye and said, "Now, sir, go over in detail with me just what this bill reflects and tell me what I must do regularly and what things I must watch for in the future of this fifteen-year-old car."

Instead, I simply got in, drove around with the oil leaking and goodness knows what else that needed work. My neglect and ignorance in operating that machine cost a lot of unnecessary and expensive repairs. In view of the damage that I did to that Mercedes by neglecting it for so long, I offer the following suggestions to help avoid what I had to go through.

• Watch out for sounds and sights of trouble. These include metallic scraping, moans and groans from any part of your car, rattles and clanks, and anything else that doesn't sound right. If your gas and oil gauges are not telling you when your fuel and lubricant are low, have these indicators checked. If, when you turn on the ignition, there is no quick lighting of these gauges, then they are not operating properly.

• If the oil light goes on while you are driving, pull into a gas station as soon as you can and have your oil level checked. Never drive a car that is low on oil; it's the quickest way to ruin an engine.

• If the temperature gauge goes into the danger zone, pull into a gas station immediately if there is one within a mile. Have the attendant check your radiator, but be sure to warn him that your car is overheating. If there is no gas station immediately available, here's "first aid" for an overheating motor: Turn *both* the heat and fan on to their highest settings and let the hot air blow off the engine and into the passenger compartment. You'll probably fry your toes, but you will notice the temperature gauge begin to drop into the normal zone immediately.

• If you smell something unusual (gas fumes or burning, for instance), take the car to your mechanic.

• Make certain that you have a well-stocked first-aid kit and a working flashlight in the car and that the supplies are fresh.

• Make certain that your spare tire is in good condition and that you have a jack—and *do* learn how to change a tire. It's easy and it's one of the survival skills that any woman alone should have.

• Check your car for drips every now and then. When you pull out of a parking spot, look back to see if there is fresh oil or any other liquid on the pavement.

• Put yourself in the hands of a reliable mechanic (find one on your own or through a friend who owns the same make of car) and keep going back to the same shop. If you use a variety of workmen for your car, each can blame the other for some failure, but a solo mechanic can't wiggle out of a mistake if he is the only one who touched that automobile.

For many reasons, some of them sentimental, I am still driving Sam's old car. Various people offer to buy it, saying, "They don't make them like that anymore!" Maybe in a year, when it is twenty-five years old and a true vintage car, the sentimental satisfaction of touching the same steering wheel and sitting in Sam's driver's seat will have worn off and I will be able to sell it without remorse. But then again, maybe I won't!

Airplanes

Getting there on an airplane is no fun. Airports are like zoos where the animals are getting restless, the planes are crowded, the food is practically inedible, airlines overbook, and departures are almost never on time.

But having said that, I must describe the exceptions. It is much easier to fly long distances than short hops, and some airlines, especially foreign carriers, do their best to make an uncomfortable situation as agreeable as possible. You can see a movie, have a drink and a meal, read, listen to a wide variety of music, and, if there is an empty seat next to yours, stretch out for a nap.

Actually, I am writing this shortly after an exhausting round-the-world trip that included several fifteen-hour flights in narrow seats. A physician friend of mine who travels abroad a good deal says that he always stands up frequently during a long flight and remarked that airplanes are triumphs of uncomfortable architecture!

Remember that it doesn't cost any more to make your reservation through a travel agent, and he or she will have all available flight and fare information on computer. Nevertheless, when you have your ticket in hand be sure to check that all the information is correct. Also, it's a good idea to keep a serial number of the ticket, which is printed at the bottom, in a separate place in case you lose the ticket or have to correspond with the airline. I have only just learned to do this after fifty years of international travel.

Losing your ticket is a major disaster, especially in the United States. In foreign countries, you must show a valid passport in order to travel by air, but here no such proof of identity is necessary. If you do lose your ticket, inform the airline immediately, and they will check to see if you have paid for it and will then issue a new one. Some airlines charge a fee for this replacement service.

A few years ago, I checked into an airport hotel in Hawaii after an eleven-hour flight. My connecting plane didn't depart for another six hours, so I hoped to have a bath, take an aspirin, redo my makeup, and get a few hours of sleep before crossing the rest of the Pacific Ocean and the continental United States.

The hotel operator woke me at the appointed time, and I dressed and went to the airport. But when I arrived at the check-in counter, I couldn't find my ticket. Panic! After five frantic searches of my purse and luggage, it still didn't turn up and I had to buy another one. I had not yet learned to write the serial number of my ticket on a separate piece of paper. Luckily I had a credit card and enough credit available to buy another ticket.

What had I done with the first ticket? Just before falling asleep, I had efficiently checked my flight departure time with the airline, but what I had done *inefficiently* was to leave the ticket on top of the covers, which I flung back when I awoke, thus hiding the ticket.

Before take-off, I called the hotel and asked them to check the room while I stayed on the line. Sure enough, they had found the ticket in the blankets and mailed it to me so that I could get a full refund. But that experience taught me an important lesson: Be absolutely certain, before checking out of a hotel (or leaving a friend's home, for that matter) that you have searched the room, and the bathroom as well, to make sure you have left nothing behind. Then check your purse to make sure that your money, travelers checks, tickets, and passport are all where they should be.

Here are some helpful hints about making your trip by air more pleasant—or at least not quite so hideous.

• Get a seat assignment when you make your reservation, not right before you are ready to board. This has two advantages: If you book early, you'll get your pick of seats; and you won't have to stand in line at the gate (in the area that I like to call the "holding pen" because I always feel like an animal about to go to slaughter!).

• Avoid the middle seat, but the choice of an aisle or window seat is up to you.

• When you get on the plane, take a blanket and pillow before take-off because you might not get one later—there are rarely enough to go around.

• If you anticipate a long flight and the plane is not full, notice where the empty seats are and move there immediately after take-off so you can stretch out.

• Know that you can order special meals: kosher, vegetarian, low-salt, diabetic, or the like. (These meals are often much better than the regular ones.)

• If you want to carry your baggage with you on the plane, be sure it will fit under your seat. Airlines are now very strict about what they consider carry-on bags and how many pieces they will allow.

• If you check your luggage, examine the tag that the agent affixes to each piece; make certain that the flight number and destination are correct, and don't lose your baggage stubs or you may have trouble getting out of the airport.

• Get your bags from the carousel before doing anything else, such as lining up a cab, making a hotel reservation, calling friends, etc. If you let your bags spin around and around on the carousel, there is more chance of their being stolen.

• Make your luggage easily identifiable with bright, colorful tags or straps.

• If you check your luggage, take with you on the plane a change of clothes and fresh underwear (along with medicines, jewelry, and other valuables) so you'll have something to wear if your luggage is lost.

DINING OUT

It used to be that restaurants and shops in big-city hotels were more expensive than those outside, but this is not true anymore in most parts of the world. In your hotel's immediate neighborhood, you might indeed find less expensive and more interesting places to eat and shop, but there are places where this may not be a good idea. For instance, having just returned from India, I can say the hotel dining rooms were excellent, and the cleanest in the country.

But everything is relative. Don't forget that water and uncooked vegetables and peeled fruits are taboo in most third-world countries.

If you are driving your own car, try not to eat in the hotel—you will find much more desirable and cheaper restaurants elsewhere. You can also economize on breakfast and lunch and then splurge on dinner after you've had a bath to wash off the grime of the day's travel. If you are too exhausted to go out, you can order from room service. Although the food is no cheaper, and the menu is usually less extensive (and you don't get the waiter to recite the list of the day's specials), you can have the luxury of eating in your robe and watching television or listening to the music *you* like.

The thing that most women traveling alone fear the most is going alone to a fine restaurant. I admit that it can be intimidating at first, but make a reservation (almost essential everywhere these days) in an authoritative, but not bossy, tone of voice. Try to make it for forty-five minutes before you think most of the clientele will arrive, or you stand a good chance of being put behind a pillar, next to the kitchen door, or someplace equally undesirable.

When you arrive, the head waiter or maître d' will inevitably look around for your companion. Just smile sweetly and say, "My name is Ms. So-and-so and I have a reservation." If you don't like the table you have been assigned, and assuming there are empty ones available, ask politely for another. If you see one you'd like, ask for it. Say, "I'd like that table over there by window," and start walking toward it.

Most Americans who travel abroad arrive in a half-empty restaurant because they are accustomed to eating much earlier than most Europeans or South Americans, who often don't get started with dinner until nine or ten in the evening.

If you are worried about what other diners will think about your eating alone, don't. First of all, most people don't care what you do and never give it a thought; and second, more and more women travel and eat alone these days, for business and just for fun. Long before I was widowed, when I traveled on business, I would order dinner in my room so that I wouldn't feel awkward. This was particularly true in Japan and in Spanish-speaking countries where the "macho" image prevailed, and still does to a large extent, and women out alone at night were not well tolerated.

While I was in Mexico City on business one December, I discovered that my hotel had a recently redecorated roof garden restaurant that overlooked a beautiful park. Huge papier-mâché Magi figures and beautiful Christmas trees had been installed, and I decided beforehand not to be relegated to the miserable little room without a view. (I had asked for the cheapest single bedroom in order to save my client money for my expenses.) So, armed with resolve and a small leaflet about the city's weekly offerings, I entered, had the type of encounter with the maître d' that I've described, and got the table I wanted. I enjoyed that meal tremendously because I ate slowly (a good way not to overeat) and hope I looked as though I dined alone every evening.

Some women think that a legal folder or some other evidence of business pursuits gives them confidence, and some bring a book or crossword puzzle. Even browsing through the weekly section of what's going on in that city might be sufficient reading material and will provide you with something to do other than studying the view or other diners, although I happen to find the latter almost endlessly fascinating.

If by chance a man asks if he can join you, let him, if he seems acceptable. He'd rather not eat alone either, but always pay for your own meal, and do *not* tell him your hotel room number or give out any other personal information that could place you in jeopardy.

Unless you plan to eat breakfast in the downstairs coffee shop, place your order with room service the night before in order to save time in the morning. Plan the timing so that breakfast doesn't arrive when you are in the shower or not yet sufficiently dressed.

DRIVING AND SHOPPING ALONE

During the summer and on weekends I live two hours from Manhattan, on eastern Long Island. If no one else is in the car with me, I am inclined to daydream. I know this worries my friends and children, but I am making an enormous effort to concentrate on the task at hand. In addition to driving alone, I shop alone, as most women do. A few cautionary words might be welcome here about driving and shopping alone.

• Never drive with your pocketbook beside you on the car seat, especially in spring or summer when the windows are open. Put it on the floor next to you to prevent it from being snatched through an open window or unlocked door.

• Keep your doors locked at all times when you are in the car.

• When you pump your own gas, be sure to take your purse with you and sling it over your arm when you are at the gas pump, or if you must leave it in your car, lock it and hold the keys in your hand.

• Carry your money in one place, your credit cards in another, and your key ring separately from everything else.

• Don't put your purse down on a shelf in a public rest room, and when you are sitting in a toilet stall, do not hang your purse on a high hook on the stall door. Use a side hook if one is provided, the fold-down shelf, or hold your purse on your lap. This is especially important in busy rest rooms in high-transient areas like airports and train stations.

Many women, especially those living in the suburbs, shop in malls, and crime there has grown alarmingly. Victims are now suing the stores and adjacent banks for lack of reasonable security. Recently a lawyer won a $2 million award on behalf of a woman who was abducted from a small parking lot and shot. The lawyer, in preparing the case, found that forty-three serious crimes had occurred at the same site. "Bad guys know that this is where to find women with money—vulnerable and alone," he said.

Car theft from suburban malls is also increasing, so in order to avoid being a victim of any type of shopping mall crime, park as close as you can to the elevators in a multilevel parking garage, and ask other shoppers getting off the elevator at your level if one (preferably a woman) would walk with you to your car. In an attended garage, leave only your ignition key. Be alert to loiterers, don't wear a lot of jewelry (even costume jewelry) when you are out shopping, and *never* flash a wad of money.

•   •   •

A male friend, a tall, strong fellow, and I were traveling together and arrived in Barcelona, Spain, just before midday. I had never been to Barcelona before, but he knew the city well and insisted that we check into our hotel quickly and go to the cathedral about six blocks away to see the dancers who perform at noon on Saturdays in the plaza in front of the church.

We did what he suggested, and a block away from our destination, a man tried to wrest my purse from me. *Everything* of value that I had with me was in that purse, and I wasn't going to let him get away with it. I struggled, kicked him in the groin, and yelled (difficult to do in a time of such stress and fear). He finally fled, leaving me with a broken finger, a ripped purse handle, and completely shaken.

Needless to say, the day was ruined and I was in shock. I reproached my friend: "Where in the world were *you* when I was struggling for my life and my belongings?"

His reply: "Well, it all happened so fast, and you asked for it—you walk around Europe looking chic with a Louis Vuitton purse and naturally you're a likely prey!"

I replied that it was only a fake Vuitton that I had bought for a song in Florence from a street vendor, but he pointed out—rightly and logically—that the thief had no way of knowing that.

The lesson I learned from that experience is that one must avoid looking too prosperous when on city streets: in the United States or abroad. It's a shame. I am from a generation that dressed in a nice traveling suit to get on a train or airplane, but if you have been to a terminal lately, you know that people wear slacks, sweaters, flat shoes, and all manner of casual attire for travel. To avoid problems, I guess one has to do likewise.

SELF-DEFENSE

Unfortunately, bad things happen in this world, and you can take all the precautions any reasonable person could be expected to think of and still find yourself in a dangerous situation. This is where the art of self-defense can get you out of a jam—but only if you are experienced and know how to use it properly.

Women of all ages take karate and similar forms of self-defense that were developed in the ancient Far East when travelers were assailed by bandits and needed an effective system of unarmed protection. The days of the Old West are long gone—except perhaps in New York City's subways—and modern society does not permit you to take the law into your own hands. You must rely on the police, but they are often not around when you need them most.

Therefore, you are on your own a good deal of the time, and you ought to know that there are self-defense measures that you can legally and properly take, and there are others that might land you in jail.

Many people who get about alone, especially older women living in apartment houses, are mugged. The most dangerous areas are un-lighted corners or parts of blocks where you live. According to Professor Arthur Miller of Harvard Law School, these kinds of perilous areas abound. In most states, laws regarding self-defense allow you to use "reasonable" force, or the same amount of force that your assailant uses, in order to repel an attack. There are, however, some states that have a "duty to retreat" law, which requires you to back off or escape the attack if you can do so safely.

Regarding an attack in your own home, most states' laws allow you more latitude in the matter of self-protection, although there are limitations even here.

Professor Miller suggests that you find out what the laws are in your state and also suggests that you take—and complete—a self-defense course so you will be prepared to use your skills against an attacker.

But there are pitfalls: Suppose, asks Miller, someone approaches you to ask for the correct time. You are alone on the street and feeling skittish, and assume that he is a threat to your life when he comes toward you from the shadows behind the bus stop sign. So you use your newly acquired karate skills and give him a chop. He falls to the pavement and dies.

You used reasonable force under a reasonably assumed danger, but you might or might not be held criminally liable. Because the man died, you might be accused of manslaughter. But unless you can supply credible reasons for your act, you could be sued by this man's family (or if he had not died, by him directly).

What if you are attacked by a potential rapist? The Safety and

Fitness Exchange, Inc. (SAFE) in New York has published an extremely helpful pamphlet, *Don't Stick Your Head in the Sand.* According to SAFE, statistics show that most rapes are planned in advance, and a woman's initial response will often determine the results. Here are some tips that will make you appear more assertive and less an available victim.

• Look confident, walk quickly, don't make eye contact with male strangers, and don't show your fear.

• Don't let threats and comments intimidate you.

• Trust your intuition; *run* if you suspect danger.

• Carry a whistle in your hand, or even between your teeth. Some people suggest carrying something that can be used as a weapon, such as an umbrella, keys, or a screwdriver.

• Don't be afraid to scream, make a scene, or appear rude. Practice screaming into a pillow because, contrary to popular belief, screaming does not come naturally to most women.

• Stay alert on the street, and wear clothing and shoes that let you move easily.

If you find yourself in a dangerous situation, breathe deeply and assess your options. Can you see people nearby, or is there an open store or building? If there are no avenues of escape, and if you are attacked, fight back with all your might. A half-hearted attempt only increases your danger because your attacker will sense your fear and lack of prowess. Even if you are untrained in self-defense, you can try any or all of the following:

• tense your fingers, bend them slightly, and jab them into your attacker's eye;
• grab one of his pinky fingers and try to break it;
• aim a kick to the groin if you can manage it, or the kneecap; and
• poke him in the hollow of his throat with your fingers, keys, umbrella, or anything else handy.

If you kill a really dangerous attacker or rapist, there are many good defenses open to you. Men who attack women are usually physically stronger, which is a good defense, especially if the attacker has a police record. However, the difficulty here is proving the reasonableness of the fear that caused you to stab—or shoot. (And this brings up the subject of guns. Do *not* carry a gun or keep one in your home. They invariably cause more trouble than they prevent, and the worst part is that they can be easily wrested from your grasp and used against you. Stay away from guns.)

Even if you are acquitted of criminal charges, you have killed or permanently injured someone, and it will cost you time and money— not to mention personal agony.

Most common law assumes that physical altercations take place between men and other men, and some states hold that women's weaker physical status requires a double standard if they respond too quickly. I don't dare predict how long this advantage might hold.

I was always terrified of those strong girls in my high school basketball class who tried to block me while I, in a tremble, tried to shoot a basket. One of my friends enjoys telling of going to the high school football field to watch one of her sons play, and deciding that although he was equipped with a large, strong body, he had the courage of Peter Cottontail. Both sexes have strong and weak members, but generally a man can overpower a woman.

One day, perhaps, physical power may be more equal. One day too, our justice system may become more just, and a convicted criminal will receive the appropriate punishment. But for now, we must learn to protect ourselves while at the same time being as cautious as possible.

CONCLUSION

When I found myself suddenly alone—that is, without a husband—I felt a need to strengthen the connections to friends and family that I already had. Sam had taken so much of my time that I knew I needed to fill that void. Friendships had never been so important, and the relationship with my three girls and their husbands and children took on new meaning. My years as a full-time wife and mother taught me so much and gave me such joy that I cannot help but believe that I could pass that love on to others, especially other widows.

But it wasn't as easy as I have just made it sound in one paragraph. First, I had to convince myself that I *could* become a grown-up, self-sufficient woman who was able to enjoy a life alone. Not a solitary life—no one should be required to do that—but a life not dependent on others for happiness. I had to learn to do that, and it was a difficult task.

But I did it because I *wanted* to do it. I made myself happy because I wanted to be happy. I consciously set out to learn what gave me pleasure, and I filled my life with those things. I taught myself what is really important—human relationships, giving of oneself to others, and making oneself generally useful in society—and devoted my life to the pursuit of the things that would enhance those aspects of my existence.

And I have made a good life for myself. I like myself most of the time, and I am extremely proud of what I have been able to accomplish.

So what keeps us going if our friends have retired to gentler, far-away climates and our children have spread their wings (didn't we tell them to?), and both are long-distance calls away? None of them are around to relieve the lonely Saturday afternoons and Sundays. My own survival amounted to Herculean attempts to keep *connected* with family and friends.

One's family really wants to hear "She is doing just fine, so many interests and activities and things going for her." Perhaps it's true, it's surely the image you want to create. But, come on! We've been brave and self-reliant because we know that is what we want ourselves to be. If being older does anything, it's supposed to make us wiser, and wisdom says that interdependence is what it's all about. Whatever role reversals are in store for me, I'll accept like a welcoming hug. If you don't have a network behind you, create one, because you'll need it when times and days are discouraging. The physical disintegration needs coping with, for example, and a network helps delay that. Just make your own network and clasp your dear ones to your bosom and think how blessed you really are, compared to just about everyone else.

If I had to give some good general advice for widows, it would be this: Don't whine; don't complain; don't let anyone but your very closest friends know how unhappy you are (and even with them, don't dwell on it often); and don't think of yourself as a poor, unlucky person who has suffered the greatest tragedy in the world.

Widowhood *is* tragic. I have no desire to minimize your pain because I remember mine so clearly, and even now, it sometimes returns in a burst that is shocking in its sharpness and suddenness.

But you must rise above the pain, and you will have to do it yourself. Of course, there will be people you can call on for help from time to time, but basically you are on your own, and you have to develop an inner source of strength and self-reliance that you may not feel. But if you pretend long enough, you *will* become strong and self-reliant.

You *will* be able to manage on your own. You *will* find happiness without having to depend on another person.

If you sow seeds of satisfaction and pleasure by giving to others and cultivate the garden of your soul, there will be flowers in your heart. And I guarantee it.

Women entering their 60s, 70s or 80s find their marriage unraveling, a spouse dying, and their up-to-now rewarding life becoming stressful and inadequate. Even moving from one town to another is not the answer in most instances, even though often a switch in house or apartment does indeed give one "a new lease on life." Changing the pattern of one's daily routine, such as sleeping later or having a weekly supper at home with old and new friends, often helps.

You may have already offered your services as a volunteer in an area where you once worked and have some experience. If you have done the latter and outperformed those in that organization who are getting paid for it, you may find yourself with a new paying post and a big boost to your self esteem.

Some women deal with these "mid-life crises" through therapy, religion, cosmetic surgery, updating a wardrobe, or dipping into capital to take a dreamed-of trip.

Seeking help in alcohol, which too often happens, only leads to disaster and overweight.

The best solution is simply telling yourself, "I'm of age, and I'm going to try and live as happily as I can. I'm going to do everything possible to enjoy living alone."

Happiness is not necessarily achieved by marching two-by-two through life. Those of us who are alone can acquire contentment all by ourselves. We can discover how special we are down deep inside those layers of what we have already done well through life — being a wife, mother, daughter, sister and/or friend.

Remember, there are worse things than sleeping in the middle of the bed and not worrying about whether YOU snore, or worrying about how to get back to sleep while HE snores. Having to live without sex is not going to add any wrinkles or make your hair any grayer. Anyway, the latter can be fixed by any neighborhood beautician.

It has been proven that middle- and old-age can be the best times in one's life to make new friends. Work in church with friends . . . go on a trip or a hike with friends . . . purchase season theater tickets with friends . . . attend museum lectures with friends . . . or just talk to friends — now that you have lost your life's best friend.

INDEX

Index

267